Defenders of their Faith:

Power and Party in the Diocese of Sydney, 1909-1938

STEPHEN JUDD

Defenders Of Their Faith:
Power and Party in the Diocese of Sydney, 1909-1938

This edition published in 2021 by Mountain Street Media, NSW, Australia

https://mountainstreet.media/

Internal design by Impressum
www.impressum.com.au

ISBN:
978-0-6452650-1-9 (print)
978-0-9925595-1-9 (ebook)

NATIONAL LIBRARY OF AUSTRALIA

A catalogue record for this work is available from the National Library of Australia

TABLE OF CONTENTS

ACKNOWLEDGEMENTS

This dissertation has its roots in my chance reading as an undergraduate of an essay written by a friend, Andrew Newmarch. The essay was concerned with the structure of the Anglican Diocese of Sydney and power within that institutional framework. The essay fascinated me: I had not previously related power and politics to the internal workings of ecclesiastical institutions. It prompted me to follow a course of research which has led to this dissertation.

Associate Professor Ken Cable has supervised my Ph.D research. He gave appreciated advice and astute hypotheses, many of which were borne out by later research. In addition, the biographical data which Professor and Mrs. Cable and Noel Pollard have gathered on Australian Anglican clergymen were made available to me, and were of very great assistance.

Bishop David Garnsey generously made available, in his own home, an important and comprehensive collection of letters written to him by his father, Canon A.H. Garnsey.

In Sydney Mr. Kim Robinson, the Librarian at Moore Theological College, Canon Boyce Horsley, the Diocesan Archivist, and Miss Margaret Haig, the Deputy Registrar, were always very helpful. Miss Melanie Barber, the Deputy Archivist and Librarian at Lambeth Palace Library, Mr. Nigel Higson, the Archivist at the University of Hull, and the Rev.

Noel Pollard, the Librarian at St. John's, Nottingham, greatly assisted my research in England.

Robert Abbey generously gave me access to his personal computer which greatly expedited the re-drafting and editing of the work.

Dr. Peter Jensen and Archbishop Donald Robinson critically reviewed the second draft and saved me from many treacherous, invariably theological, shoals. Anne Robinson gave most incisive and constructive criticism throughout the various drafting stages, and I am especially grateful for her unfailing help in foot-noting and formatting the final draft.

ABBREVIATIONS

A.C. - *Australian Churchman* (Sydney).

A.C.L. - Anglican Church League.

A.C.R. - *The Australian Church Record* (Sydney)

A.E.G.M. - The Anglican Evangelical Group Movement.

A.H.G. to D.A.G. - Letters of Arthur Garnsey to his son, David Garnsey in the Garnsey Papers.

B.C.M.S. - Bible Churchman's Missionary Society.

B.L. - British Library.

C.C. - *Church Commonwealth* (Sydney)

C.M.S. - Church Missionary Society

C.S. - *Church Standard* (Sydney)

C.U.L. - Cambridge University Library.

D.T. - *Daily Telegraph*

Fisher. - Fisher Library, the University of Sydney.

I.C.M. - Irish Church Missions, Dublin

L.P.L. - Lambeth Palace Library.

J.R.H. - Journal of Religious History.

M.C.L. - Moore College Library

M.L. - Mitchell Library (Sydney)

P.C.E.U. - Protestant Church of England Union.

R.A.H.S.J. - *Royal Australian Historical Society Journal*

S.D.A. - Sydney Diocesan Archives.

S.D.M. - Sydney Diocesan Magazine.

S.M.H. - Sydney Morning Herald.

S.P.C.K. - Society for the Promotion of Christian Knowledge.

U.S.P.G. - United Society for the Propagation of the Gospel.

INTRODUCTION

During the 1960s the study of Australian religious history became increasingly professionalised. The clerical amateurs who had previously dominated the field were joined by lay professionals, whose presence in this area of historical research dramatically altered its orientation and focus. Whereas Australian religious history was once written by clergymen whose pious sense of duty compelled them into print with publications which were invariably denominational and biographical, they were increasingly overshadowed by historians who recognised religious history as a neglected aspect of the larger order of Australian social and cultural history.[1] The strong propensity towards triumphalism and hagiography which had long made Australian religious history suspect and second class was challenged by closer, more critical studies of an integral part of Australian culture.[2]

With this movement came the conviction that the simple study of a denomination was too cloistered and esoteric. No self-respecting historian would touch it. What was needed, it was believed, were historical studies which would drag religious history by the scruff of the neck into the mainstream of social history, by relating religious institutions to the society in which they existed. Only then would its research be respectable and relevant.[3] The result was a series of "church-society" studies: J.D. Bollen's *Protestantism and Social Reform in New South Wales 1890-1910*,

Richard Broome's *Treasure in Earthen Vessels; Protestant Christianity in New South Wales 1900-1914*, Michael McKernan's *Australian Churches at War: Attitudes and Activities of the Major Churches 1914-1918*, and Walter Phillips' *Defending "A Christian Country"; Churchmen and Society in New South Wales in the 1880s and after* appeared as major contributions to Australia's religious history.[4] These works brought valued insights into the relationship between the churches and their social environment and, in addition, served to legitimate the study of religious history in the critical eyes of secular social historians.

Yet there were intrinsic deficiencies with such "church-society" studies which resulted from the inadequate information on the denominational institutions which the authors were studying. That limitation inevitably blurred the authors' perceptions of the distinctiveness of denominations. Phillips' study was unusual in its sensitivity to the importance of denominational distinctions: most "church-society" studies embraced the similarities and ignored the differences and treated them as exceptional rather than intrinsic for the sake of a theoretical coherence.[5] A case in point is Richard Broome's examination of the Protestant responses to the perceived loss of religious influence in the community in early twentieth century New South Wales. Broome does not define Protestantism, but leaves the reader to assume that it must be 'something non-Roman Catholic'.[6] While Broome's use of "Protestantism" may be an acceptable analytical tool for an examination of non-episcopal churches, its usefulness must be seriously questioned when it includes the Anglican church, especially when no conclusive proof is presented of the existence of a community of thought between Anglicans and non-episcopals.[7] On several occasions in Broome's book Anglicans are portrayed as schismatically aloof and distanced from other Protestants. Yet this was because they did not readily identify with Protestant non-episcopals.[8] The all-embracing concept of "Protestantism" may be an attractive generality for relating churches to society, but given the intrinsic divisions between the denominations, any "schism" which is said to occur within it is essentially artificial and contrived.[9] Anglicans, Presbyterians, Methodists, Congregationalists and other Protestant churches do not constitute a monolithic entity which can be neatly packaged and labelled as "Protestant". There are significant differences between them and before we can confidently make further assessments on the relationships between the churches and the society in which they were placed, it will be necessary to understand the individual denominations themselves. This problem has been noted by other historians: David Hilliard has remarked that McKernan's treatment of Australian churches in the First World War demonstrated a failure to grasp the distinctive ethos of the different denominations upon which he passed judgment.[10]

Although the proper orientation for denominational research may vary from denomination to denomination, the logical orientation of research for Australian Anglicanism is the Diocese. The patterns of colonial settlement and the geographical isolation of those nineteenth century colonies meant that the diocesan polity rather than the national or provincial (state) ones developed as the primary unit.[11] A general history of Australian Anglicanism can only be properly written with diocesan histories as its building blocks. Similarly, diocesan rather than local or extra-parochial developments have been the major formative influences for the vast majority of ordinary parishes.

Australian diocesan histories have, to date, been focussed upon the administration of the bishops.[12] This was natural: whereas bishops in England were part of a system in which lay patronage supplied most parochial appointments and the Crown filled all important ecclesiastical positions, the colonial bishops alone had spiritual and temporal authority. Their personal influence was formative in the nineteenth century development of their dioceses.[13] This bishop-based structure of diocesan history was unduly biographical and chronological, and ignored important thematic developments. The focus on the bishop created a distorted picture in which nothing occurred in the diocese without the bidding of the bishop, and the other players only became animated when in relationship with him.[14]

This study departs from this traditional model of diocesan history. Instead, it is contended that there lies within Anglicanism an inherent tension which has often produced a powerful political dynamic. The examination of that dynamic is far more crucial to an understanding of the polity than the study of the policies and actions of its bishops: in fact, this political dynamic was independent of the bishops, although that episcopal hierarchy was rarely independent of it. It is further contended that the importance of that dynamic was heightened in the ecclesiastical context of Australia. The potential for party conflict was limited in England by the constraints of Establishment. In Australia, however, the absence of Establishment, together with other historical and environmental factors, was responsible for the emergence of a self-determining Anglicanism in which mere lobbying for influence was metamorphosed into an outright struggle for power.

This dissertation is, therefore, a study of power and party in Anglicanism in Sydney, rather than the history of the Anglican Diocese of Sydney. It traces the political rather than the biographical or chronological. There is no close examination of parochial life or the relationship between church and society: these are areas which can be more successfully treated after the issues of ecclesiastical power have been clarified. At the same time, it must be insisted that the development of political structures, disputes over millinery and the phenomenon of struggles for power in the church's decision-making councils are not divorced from the pew nor without social significance. No doubt the average parishioner and disinterested man in the street knew or cared little about these phenomena. But they nevertheless had a direct and profound bearing on the message which the pew and the society at large received. Social and economic conditions, ethnicity and other secondary factors did in part influence the form of that message and its reception, but it was the same sincere religious convictions which were at the heart of these disputes which were also the most formative and crucial factors in the developments and transmission of the message. Scholars who mistakenly attach pre-eminence to these secondary factors not only discount the importance and power of the sincerely-held beliefs of others but also project alien values onto their historical subjects.[15] The primary impulse in ecclesiastical polities is transcendent not immanent, and when that impulse is expressed in political terms it is essential for those political phenomena to be the focus of the historical research rather than social, biographical or other issues.

There are two reasons why the Diocese of Sydney is the subject of this dissertation. First, the predominantly Evangelical character of the Diocese sets it apart from the rest of the Anglican Communion. Whenever two or three people have been gathered together in the name of Australian religious history one question has always been raised: "why is the Diocese of Sydney so Evangelical?" While the great number of exclusively Anglo-Catholic dioceses have escaped the same critical enquiry the very singularity of Sydney, one of the most populous and powerful of Anglican dioceses, has been a matter of genuine puzzlement for observers of religious affairs.[16] That curiosity has been heightened by speculation that the differing developments and perceptions of Anglicanism in Sydney and Melbourne were a key to the comparative cultural styles of those two cities.[17] Second, the size of the Diocese of Sydney meant that there was far more scope for political tensions to develop and find expression in party organisation within the Diocese. These political dynamics were just as crucial to the character of a smaller diocese but were more difficult to identify because they were not usually institutionalised, but found expression in loose groupings of individuals.

There has been a dearth of historical research on the Diocese of Sydney which the handful of published biographical portraits of bishops and parochial clergymen fails to disguise.[18] The only attempt at a general history of the Diocese has been *Hewn From The Rock* , the published form of the 1976 Moorhouse Lectures on the origins and traditions of the Church in Sydney by Marcus Loane, Archbishop of Sydney from 1966 to 1982.[19] This work has become the most widely read and accepted work on the Church in Sydney. Yet it has grave limitations, which may be explained by its origin as a series of lectures. More than three-quarters of the book is concerned with the first 100 years and the author skates over the post-1882 period with the attractive but tenuous assertion that there was "a line of spiritual descent" between Bishop Barker (1853-1882) and Archbishop Mowll (1933-1958).[20] This romantic theme of lineal heritage provides comforting order and coherence to the Diocese's history by implying that any countervailing movements or ideals in the period 1882 to 1933 were mere aberrations from the irrepressible impulses which propelled the Diocese towards a Conservative Evangelical position. At the same time, it focusses the limelight on Barker and Mowll, two of Loane's personal heroes, while neatly avoiding detailed treatment of a period which previously appeared to be barren of source material.

The following examination of the period 1909 to 1938 sets aside that dubious thesis of spiritual descent. The formative influence of Bishop Barker is not disputed: indeed it was critical to the development of the Diocese. Nor is the weighty contribution of Archbishop Mowll to the Conservative Evangelicalism of the Diocese ignored, although much of Mowll's episcopate is outside the ambit of this dissertation. Yet it is asserted that the political developments which took place in the Diocese between 1909 and 1938 were primarily responsible for the ultimate character of Anglicanism in Sydney.

The lack of source material was a great hindrance to research in this period. Initially, there were few collections of papers of individual churchmen available. The surviving papers of Archbishops Smith, Wright and Mowll were inconsequential: with the exception of one memorandum book, the Smith papers were either returned to England with his sister and son, were distributed in Australia, or were destroyed; Wright was not one to keep written material; and Mowll's papers were destroyed after his death.[21] However, two privately-held and two previously unknown collections became available: the papers of Canon S.E. Langford Smith, while revealing little of the man, provided an unparalleled record of the movement towards a new Constitution of the Church in Australia; and the weekly letters of Arthur Garnsey to his son David in the 1930s gave a rare insight into Anglican affairs in Sydney at that time, particularly the Liberal Evangelical movement.[22] The papers of Hugh Corish, the Secretary of the Anglican Church League were crucial: they were a window into the engine-room of the A.C.L. party machine and complemented the Minute Books of the A.C.L.[23] Finally, the last chapter owes much of its material to the discovery of the original Memorial with relevant correspondence and documentation in the Sydney Diocesan Archives which complemented the Garnsey account of that time.[24]

The material gathered in England in 1981 filled many of the gaps in the Australian material. The papers of successive Archbishops of Canterbury were invaluable because Antipodean correspondents to Lambeth could not assume that the Archbishop was aware of the issues on which they were writing: they had to provide background information, outline the present situation and volunteer their opinion. This makes the Lambeth collections rich veins for the hungry Australian historian. The papers of the Anglican Evangelical Group Movement contained important evidence on the Evangelical school in which John Charles Wright moved before his departure for Australia, while J.W. Walmsley's unpublished Ph.D dissertation on the Evangelical Party in England from 1905 to 1928 provided an excellent account of Evangelicalism in England during the same period as this study and was a springboard to further research in an area which was basic to an understanding of Conservative Evangelicalism in Sydney in the 1930s.[25] Stephen Sykes' *The Integrity of Anglicanism and Authority in the Anglican Communion* provided some structural tools with which to tackle the theoretical issues of the comprehensiveness, authority and nature of Anglicanism.[26]

In the following pages there will be an examination of the underlying bases of the conflict within Anglicanism and how those factors were set in relief in the Australian ecclesiastical context where the exercise of power was conducive to and inseparable from the existence of party activity. A description of the development of the political structures and the emergence of party organisation in Sydney before 1909 will be then undertaken in order to provide the necessary background to the study of the developments in power and party between 1909 and 1938 which were determinative of the eventual character of the Diocese of Sydney.

NOTES - INTRODUCTION

1. J.D. Bollen et al. "Australian Religious History, 1960-1980" in *J.R.H.* 13,1,1980 p.17; Patrick O'Farrell, "Writing the General History of Australian History" in *J.R.H.*, 9,1, June 1976 pp. 67-68.
2. *ibid.*, pp. 17-18.
3. *ibid.*, pp. 27-28; O'Farrell, *op. cit.* , p.69.
4. Bollen — Melbourne University Press 1972, Broome — University of Queensland Press 1980, McKernan — Australian War Memorial Canberra 1980, Phillips — University of Queensland Press 1981.
5. Phillips, *op. cit.*, pp.6-12, 25-28; Broome, *op. cit.* , p. 94; McKernan, *op. cit.*, p.166.
6. e.g. Broome, *op. cit.*, p.75 ff.
7. *ibid* , p.80 ff.
8. *ibid*, p.61 for example.
9. *ibid.* Chapter Five.
10. David Hilliard, Review of Michael McKernan, *Australian Churches at War: Attitudes and Activities of the Major Churches 1914-1918* in *Flinders Journal of History and Politics*, vol. 7 1981 p.104. It is also interesting that Bollen spent much time on denominational history after his church-society study.
11. J.C. Wright to R.T. Davidson 20/12/1910 in "Australia" Davidson Papers.
12. e.g. A.P. Elkin, *The Diocese of Newcastle: A History* Australasian Medical Publishing Co. Sydney 1955; R.T. Wyatt, *The History of the Diocese of Goulburn*, Bragg and Sons Sydney 1937; Keith H. Aubrey,

"The Church of England in Northern New South Wales 1847-1867 and in the Dioceses of Grafton and Armidale 1867-1892", Unpublished M.A. Thesis University of New England 1964; Ruth Teale, "By Hook or By Crook: The Anglican Diocese of Bathurst 1870-1911", Unpublished M.A. Thesis University of Sydney 1967.

13. K.J. Cable, "Good Government in the Church". The Inaugural Bishop Perry Memorial Lecture April 1983. Transcript pp.5-6.

14. See e.g. Marcus L. Loane, *Hewn From the Rock* A.I.O. Sydney 1976 *passim*.

15. See Jill Roe, "A Tale of Religion in Two Cities", in Meanjin 1/81 pp. 48-55; D.E. Hansen, "The Churches and Society in N.S.W. 1919-1939" Ph.D Dissertation 1978. Macquarie University; J.D. Bollen, "Religion in Australian Society: An Historian's View", Leigh College Open Lectures. Leigh College 1973 pp.45-46; and Bollen, *op. cit.*; and Broome, *op. cit.*, pp.111, 116, 159 ff. For a scholar who ably marshals both the transcendent and non-transcendent, see George Marsden, *Fundamentalism and American Society: The Shaping of Twentieth Century Evangelicalism 1870-1925* Oxford Uni. Press New York 1980.

16. Roe, *op. cit.*, p.55; K.J. Cable, "Bishop Barker and his Clergy". First Moore College Library Lecture 17 April 1975. Transcript p.22.

17. Roe, *op. cit.*, p.55.

18. F.B. Boyce *Fourscore Years and Seven: The Memoirs of Archdeacon Boyce*, Angus and Robertson Sydney 1934; A.J.A. Fraser, *I Remember, I Remember* Dolphin Sydney 1977; B.G. Judd, *He That Doeth: The Life Story of Archdeacon R.B.S. Hammond*, Marshall, Morgan and Scott London 1951; M.L. Loane, *Archbishop Mowll*, Hodder and Stoughton London 1960; L.C. Rodd, *John Hope of Christ Church*, Alpha Books Sydney 1972; G.P. Shaw, *Patriarch and Patriot: W.G. Broughton* M.U.P. 1978 etcetera.

19. Archbishop M.L. Loane delivered the Moorhouse Lectures on the Origin and Traditions of the Church in Sydney in November 1976 and they were published in the same year.

20. Loane, *Hewn*, p.140.

21. See Loane, Mowll, p.9.
22. The papers of Canon Langford Smith were lent to me by the late Keith Langford Smith and after his death were returned to the family. The letters of A.H. Garnsey are in the possession of Bishop D.A. Garnsey, Canberra, who kindly made them available to me.
23. The papers of Hugh. A. Corish are to be found in the Australiana collection of Moore College Library.
24. The Original Memorial and related correspondence is to be found in Box 479, Sydney Diocesan Archives.
25. The papers of the Anglican Evangelical Group Movement is in the University Archives, The Brynmor Jones Library, The University of Hull, England. The 1978 unpublished dissertation by J.W. Walmsley, "The Evangelical Party in the Church of England 1905-1928", is also found in the Brynmor Jones Library, the University of Hull, England.
26. Stephen Sykes, *The Integrity of Anglicanism*, Mowbrays London 1978, and Stephen Sykes et al., *Authority in the Anglican Communion*. Four Papers prepared for the Anglican Primates Meeting Washington D.C. April 1981 Anglican Consultative Council London 1981.

CHAPTER ONE -

THE INHERENT TENSION

I

Anglicanism in the late nineteenth and early twentieth centuries encompassed a wide range of opinion and belief. There appeared to be no one Anglican faith but rather a shared Anglican attitude and atmosphere which was cultivated by the common strands of history, practice and formulary.[1] Anglican apologists later asserted that this comprehensiveness of thought was the very genius of the Anglican Church:

> it is only through a comprehensiveness which makes it possible
> to hold together in the Anglican Communion understandings of
> truth which are held in separation in other Churches, that the
> Anglican Communion is able to reach out in different directions
> and so to fulfil its special vocation....If at the present time one
> view were to prevail to the exclusion of all others, we should be
> delivered from our tensions, but only at the price of missing our
> opportunity and our vocation.[2]

There was, then, an ambivalence in Anglicanism: its ideal of a unifying comprehensiveness promoted unhappy tension and controversy.

While these tensions were clearly evident between all schools of thought, they were best exemplified in the uneasy co-existence within the one institutional fellowship of those churchmen who were at opposite ends of the spectrum: Conservative Evangelicals and Anglo-Catholics. It was the theological differences between these two schools of thought, ranging from different perceptions of the nature of the Church, the source of authority and the nature and relationship of Man and God, which were at the root of the inherent tension within Anglicanism.

Anglo-Catholics had a high conception of the historical and continuous tradition of faith and practice of the Catholic Church, and emphasised the ideal of a united visible Church. They had an inclusive concept of the Church. They believed that the Church was the whole company of the baptised, and because the baptised were identifiable the Church was visible, coinciding roughly with "the whole people." Its members may have been active, careless or even asleep, but all who had been baptised into the threefold Name were its members. The unity which the Body of Christ had in its Headship — "all one in Christ Jesus" — should have been reflected in the catholic unity of the earthly visible organisation. There was after all, Anglo-Catholics maintained, "one Lord, one faith, one baptism, one God and Father of all."[3]

Conservative Evangelicals were far more rigorous in their estimate of who comprised Christ's Church. Belief, not baptism, was the rule of membership. The Church as the body of Christ was the sum of all believers; the Church of England was merely the aggregate of a number of smaller congregations of believers, a human organisation whose purpose was to advance the aims and ideals of the Body's Head, Jesus Christ. They had, therefore, a high ideal of the Body, but a functional and pragmatic approach to the organisation.[4] It was a pragmatism which enabled Conservative Evangelicals to be forthright, direct and even ruthless in their inter-relationships within the denomination; churchmen who had a higher, transcendent ideal of the organisation did not have that freedom.

CHAPTER ONE - THE INHERENT TENSION

The two schools of thought had different perceptions of Man's relationship to God. The Conservative Evangelical believed that Man was an incorrigible sinner who could not save himself from eternal separation from God. He was saved by believing in Jesus Christ, who was the only One who had the authority to forgive. The authority for believing in salvation through personal faith in Jesus did not come from the church, but from Christ Himself. He was the sole authority, and his expression of that authority was to be found in the Bible, the word of God. The Bible determined faith and practice and it was the arbiter of Truth. The wretched sinfulness of Man, the redemptive work of Jesus Christ on the Cross (the Atonement), the need of a personal faith in Christ and his work, and the authoritative position of the Scriptures were the tenets of the Evangelical position.

The Anglo-Catholics perceived Man's relationship to God in different terms. While Conservative Evangelicals focussed upon Man's sinful nature, Anglo-Catholics stressed Man's filial relationship to the Father. This 'blood' relationship was indicated by faith, which was not so much the submission of contrary nature to the Father and a necessary pre-condition to salvation, but the inner consciousness that individuals were "of Another, whose mind and will alone make possible both the feeling that we feel, and also the capacity to feel it... an instinct of relationship based as an inner actual fact."[5] Christ, therefore, not only revealed God's glory to Man; He also showed the glory that was in Man, who was in God's image and whose nature had now been united with the divine. Natural man could be raised to holiness:

...the religion of the Incarnation has been a religion of humanity. The human body itself, which heathendom has so degraded, that noble minds could only view it as the enemy and prison of the soul, acquired a new meaning, exhibited new graces, shone with a new lustre in the light of the Word made Flesh; and thence, in widening circles, the family, society, the state, felt in their turn the impulse of Christian spirit, with its 'touches of things common, Till they rose to touch the sphere.'[6]

These two orientations were often contrasted in the juxtaposition of the doctrines of the Atonement (Man's reconciliation with God through the sacrificial death of Christ) and the Incarnation (the assumption of human form and nature by Jesus, the Son of God).[7] It was an unfortunate dichotomy because Anglo-Catholics were hardly uninterested in sin and personal reconciliation with God through the Cross, nor did Conservative Evangelicals ignore the significance of Christ's assumption of human form. But it was a juxtaposition which highlighted the respective emphases of the two schools of thought.

The most visible difference between the two schools of thought was on the question of worship. The Conservative Evangelicals' whole orientation towards the individual's personal reception or rejection of the Gospel found expression in worship services which exalted the rational and negated the symbolic, while the Anglo-Catholics' belief that the Church's vocation was to reconsecrate all of human society to God was reflected in acts of communal worship which emphasised the corporate experience.[8] Where the Conservative Evangelical relied upon a rational articulation of the Word to relate God's message to Man, the Anglo-Catholic relied upon the symbolic and ceremonial.

This dissonance was most clearly seen in the different perceptions of the sacramental principle. The Anglo-Catholic believed that these outward and visible signs of God's grace, such as the Eucharist and Baptism, were the vehicles of saving and sanctifying power. The sacraments were social and corporate rites of the Church in which Christ availed Himself of the principles of our physical nature and offered men, through the Church and its ministers, the redeeming power of His life. In each sacrament God Himself was actively present, bestowing grace by means of material things and, as God's work was always redemptive, the sacraments were always effectual.[9]

The Conservative Evangelicals believed that the sacraments were visible expressions of membership of the Society of those who received the Word and were assurances of the promises proclaimed in that word. The sacrament of Baptism was the covenant rite of initiation into that Society and the Lord's Supper the rite of continuation therein. Conservative Evangelicals did not deny that the sacraments were effectual signs of God's grace but stressed that they were only effectual vehicles of that grace if faithfully received. Indeed, where Anglo-Catholics stressed that the grace of God was the basis of the sacramental principle, Conservative Evangelicals declared that the principle of faith was the basis of that blessing and argued that God's grace was not limited to these sacramental vehicles alone, nor were these signs necessary to salvation.[10]

Each school of thought took exception to the other's perception of the sacraments. Anglo-Catholics argued that Conservative Evangelicals reduced the Eucharist to a mere fellowship and memorial meal and discounted the importance of a God-given means of grace, while Conservative Evangelicals charged that the Anglo-Catholics' concept of grace was mechanical and material, ignored the importance of personal faith, and by maintaining that Christ had a Real Presence in the elements at Holy Communion, dangerously confused the sign with the thing signified.[11]

Another important theological difference between Conservative Evangelicals and Anglo-Catholics revolved around the question of authority. The Anglo-Catholics believed that Church's ministry was Apostolic. The apostles had exercised an authority in the Church which was derived from Christ, and their successors continued to rule, teach, ordain and serve with that authority. That authority was derived from 'above', not from 'below'; it was bestowed by Christ through consecration which was "a sacramental means of grace".[12] The Anglo-Catholic conception of the Church was hierarchical, not democratic: "To be a member of the Church meant from the first to be in communion with its officers, and in submission to their proper authority."[13] Authority flowed 'downwards' from the bishops who symbolised the continuity of the apostolic mission of Christ's Church and were the guardians of the Church's faith against erroneous teaching.[14] The Episcopate was also an assurance of a unity "by which we can be truly united with the whole Church from the beginning."[15] That made the Episcopate essential to the spiritual welfare of the Church: in short, "no Bishop, no Church".[16] Bishops were the authoritative custodians of God's spiritual gifts to His Church and therefore the only guarantee of grace: the non-episcopally ordained ministers were not apostates: but they were certainly not "stewards of the mysteries of Christ" and were "in great need of grace".[17]

The Conservative Evangelicals' power structure was more democratic. Conservative Evangelicals accepted the historical fact of succession in the episcopal ministry, but rejected the concept of the Episcopate as the *esse* of the Church. They maintained that the Episcopate was a purely functional order which was valuable for the proper administration of the Church, but not essential to it. Bishops were not the sole trustees of the Church's faith.[18] The authority from Christ came to the whole company of believers and not to any core of officials, the Episcopal Bench: "The power of the gospel was part of the experience of the *whole* church...Each Christian person, in virtue of his or her understanding, reception of the gospel, and readiness to proclaim it, must be held to exercise authority in the church."[19] Authority was, therefore, diffused. Nor did Conservative Evangelicals believe that the bishops were the only guarantee and channel of ministerial grace: the bountiful fruits of the non-episcopal churches gave evidence of spiritual blessings which made a mockery of the Anglo-Catholic assertion that these Protestant ministries were invalid.[20] Finally, Conservative Evangelicals believed that the unity of the Church did not depend upon the continuity secured by the apostolic succession. They were content with a spiritual union with the invisible Church to which all true believers belonged through Christ. The visible divisions between denominations did not trouble them: the ideal of one single visible Church of Christ unto whose authority every individual Christian had to submit was, to them, un-Scriptural.[21]

While Anglo-Catholics gave pre-eminence to the authority of the Church, the Conservative Evangelicals maintained that the Church's authority was subordinate to God's authoritative revelation to Man in Scripture.[22] Scripture was supreme over Reason which was a channel, not a source of Revelation, and over the Church, which was a witness to and a keeper of the Word, but not its maker.[23] The Bible alone was the only benchmark, the only test of faith and the only judge of controversy.[24]

These comparisons between Anglo-Catholic and Conservative Evangelicals schools of thought show the breadth of opinion held within the Anglican Church at its most extreme and demonstrate why the denomination has had an intrinsic propensity for dispute. Yet there were many other schools of thought which lay between these in the Anglican spectrum, and their inter-relationship was also not without tension. There was, for example, the crucial difference between the traditional High Churchman and the Anglo-Catholic. The traditional High Churchmen had an exalted conception of the authority of the Church, the claims of the episcopate, and the nature of the Sacraments.[25] While their services focussed more on the sacramental than those of their Evangelical brothers, and were more musical and beautiful, High Churchmen continued to uphold the Reformation and the formularies and beliefs of the Book of Common Prayer.[26] The Anglo-Catholics, on the other hand, were "overwhelmed by a vision of Christianity as a ministry of symbols, its channels of grace, its unending line of teachers from the Head: a sublime construction based on historical fact."[27] It was a sacerdotal vision which could not be satisfied by the existing formularies and beliefs of the Church of England. The Anglo-Catholics became "liturgical buccaneers" in their quest to express their theological principles in worship. They displayed little regard for the existing usages of the Church of England, which they either interpreted in the image of their own anti-Protestant ideal, sought to change, or simply ignored.[28]

There was also the distinction between Conservative and Liberal Evangelicals which emerged in the early twentieth century. The Liberal Evangelicals acknowledged that their roots were in the Evangelical tradition, but believed that the Evangelical message was in need of re-statement.[29] They showed a desire to embrace modern historical and scientific methods in order to effect that re-statement. Their attitude to the Authority of the Bible and the Atonement, two issues which were central to Conservative Evangelicalism, indicated the distinctiveness of the Liberal Evangelical position. First, Liberal Evangelicals argued that while the Bible was still authoritative, there was nevertheless a right of appeal to the historical records "in order to check the growth of traditional accretion, to correct errors of Church teaching, and to release continually new spiritual movements within the Church..." Although there was no one Liberal Evangelical view, none of them was a literalist: each argued that it was the mind of Christ, not the letter of Holy Scripture, which was authoritative.[30] Second, many Liberal Evangelicals departed from their Conservative Evangelical brothers on the question of the Atonement. They believed that salvation for themselves and for society was to be found at the Cross of Jesus, where God's Love in action was so supremely manifested. But for the Liberal Evangelicals that doctrine was "no longer related in (their) mind to a primeval Fall of Man, nor need it find expression in forensic terms...(They were)... dissatisfied with some of the older and cruder penal and substitutionary theories of the Atonement". Instead they sought to explore the impact of the Cross upon the personality of each individual.[31]

These brief descriptions of the doctrinal positions of Anglo-Catholics, High Churchmen, Conservative and Liberal Evangelicals do not exhaust the doctrinal distinctions within Anglicanism. There were several other identifiable schools of thought, such as Broad Church and Modernist.[32] Yet it is clear that the divisions between members of the same Anglican polity not only found expression in different interpretations of the common formularies and liturgy of the Church of England, but also in political activity. It is vital to understand that these tensions arose out of different doctrinal positions. A controversy over vestments was rooted in irreconcilable perceptions of Man's relationship to God; a disagreement about the Order of Holy Communion was based in differing interpretations of the sacramental principle; arguments over who decides matters of doctrine involve deeper cleavages over the nature and order of the Church and authority within it; and a dispute over the dating of the Book of Daniel, is not fundamentally about philology, but the authority of the Bible.[33]

II

This tension within Anglicanism was exacerbated in Australia because the doctrinal divisions were set in relief by its 'colonial' peculiarities. Whereas the Establishment in England was a force for compromise and conciliation, a liberal constraint to keep the centrifugal elements within the Church of England together for the sake of the national Church, no such cohesive element existed in Australia. It was the experience world-wide that unestablished Anglicanism tended towards uniformity rather than diversity within its ecclesiastical units, and a propensity towards conservatism rather than liberalism.[34] Establishment in England placed practical demands upon the Church of England to embrace all elements within that national Church, and, ideally, ensure their fair representation.[35] The absence of that constraint in Australia facilitated polarisation in that country. Few dioceses embraced the comprehensive ideal: Melbourne and Tasmania were notable exceptions.

It was not just a question of Establishment being a positive force for consensus and comprehensiveness, and its absence producing extremes. There were other, more immediate factors, which were peculiar to Australia. One was the fact that the diocese had always been the most important unit of church government in this country. National and provincial structures were slow to develop. Geographical isolation demanded that the diocese, and not the nation, province or parish, be the focus of church government in the nineteenth and early twentieth centuries. The Anglo-Catholic naturally felt that this discounted his cherished catholic ideal, but was usually content that, with a sympathetic diocesan, he had a liturgical freedom which had not been possible in England. The Evangelical E also found himself in an unfamiliar situation. Since the Gorham Judgment in 1847, English Evangelicals had increasingly looked upwards to the Nation and its agencies — the Parliament and the Judicial Committee of the Privy Council — as the dependable bulwarks of Conservative Evangelicalism.[36] They regarded Convocation and diocesan synods with great diffidence. But, after initial doubts and fears, Australian Evangelicals focussed 'down' upon the independence of those diocesan units in which they found themselves, defended them as the most efficacious form of church government, and did much to create and augment the power of the diocesan legislatures — the synod.

The dioceses in Australia were both the dominant church units and have also exercised self-determination: the result was a distinctive and independent tradition within each of them. Their very self-determination ensured that the churchmanship of the majority of opinion-makers was perpetuated, while the small size of the diocese was in direct inverse relation to the pressures and temptations upon the individual to conform to the predominant mode of churchmanship. "The smaller the community, the less willing public opinion is (in any field) to tolerate nonconformity."[37] The propensity of isolated self-determining dioceses to become narrowly monochrome in an unestablished context, was exacerbated in the Australian context by a second factor — the long episcopates of Australian bishops. Between 1836 and 1940 there were 90 bishops in the country. Five of these were translated to English dioceses and one to another overseas diocese. Twelve more were translated to other Australian dioceses. Thus no Australian bishop ever served as bishop of three dioceses, 93% of them served all their time in Australia, and 80% were bishops of only the one diocese. This resulted in long, formative episcopates. Adelaide, for example, had only four bishops from 1847 to 1940 with Augustus Short and Nutter Thomas each serving 34 years. Similarly, the first three bishops of Perth served 18, 17 and 35 years respectively. Most Australian dioceses have had similar experiences, and all have had at least one or two long and influential episcopates. In Sydney's first century the short five-year episcopate of Alfred Barry was exceptional. The other bishops — Broughton (17 years), Barker (28), Smith (19) and Wright (24) — died after long years at the helm.[38] The importance of long episcopates cannot be over-estimated. These bishops left indelible marks on their dioceses. This was most clear in the matter of personnel: after an episcopate of twenty years, the clergy who had been licensed by an earlier bishop were few. The vast majority had been licensed by that bishop, and his own predilections in matters of churchmanship were reflected in them. The impact of this was magnified by the fact that every bishop, marrying necessity with desire, sought to establish his own diocesan theological training hall where prospective ordinands could receive training under his watchful supervision. The size of the diocese and the standard of scholarship did not matter. There were nine theological halls in Australia by 1910, and many more ordinands were tutored personally under the supervision of the diocesan bishop. The theological institutions proved to be both a source of and a reinforcement for the peculiar theological tradition in that diocese. For example, when Bishop Barker died in 1882, only 12% (12 men) of the clergy in Sydney had been licensed before his Consecration, and of those who had been licensed during his episcopate, 42% (36 men) were graduates of the theological hall he had established in 1856, Moore College.[39] Similar situations were evident in other dioceses, so that when the time came for selecting the successor to such an influential bishop, the final choice was invariably conservative. The traditions and policies of the previous occupant of the see were upheld and perpetuated.

The point must be made that the development in the Diocese of Sydney of a predominant Conservative Evangelicalism was not extraordinary. To be sure, there were some unique characteristics of Sydney that contributed to it. Sydney had a large Roman Catholic population, with Archdiocesan authorities renowned for their conservatism and their strident, uncompromising legalism. Protestant/Roman Catholic sectarianism was clearly present until the 1950s.[40] The Church of England has traditionally reacted against the existing ecclesiastical environment: for example, against the Dutch Reformed tradition in South Africa and in the "paradise of dissent" of South Australia it has become strongly Anglo-Catholic.[41] Sydney was no exception: the Anglican Church there countervailed the very strong Roman Catholic influence with a powerful Protestant propensity. Second, this Protestant propensity was reinforced by the traditionally anti-religious, secular climate of the city. A message of Evangelical individualism proved more hardy in that hostile milieu of religious indifference.[42]

Despite these distinctive environmental factors, Sydney Anglicanism was not exceptional in its development of a predominant churchmanship. The majority of Australian dioceses have tended to extremes of churchmanship. The absence of the constraints of Establishment, the geographical and other more historical, factors which fostered the development of a robust and independent diocesanism, the long episcopates of bishops who left their indelible marks upon their dioceses, and the reinforcement within a see of a predominant theological tradition by the supply of clergymen from its theological college have all been factors in producing an Australian church characterised by diocesan distinctions rather than similarities. In this context, the Diocese of Sydney was not abnormally monochrome: it was peculiar only because it went the opposite way from the majority of dioceses. A Conservative Evangelical tradition developed within it, while many more dioceses became exclusively Anglo-Catholic or had distinct propensities in that direction. This dissertation examines the political forces behind the development of the distinctive theological tradition in Sydney, paying particular attention to the period between the election of Archbishop Wright in 1989 and the protest to Archbishop Mowll in 1938 by fifty clergymen against the allegedly monochrome character of the Diocese. Those political forces are best understood, however, in the evolution of power structures and party organisation in the fifty years prior to 1909.

NOTES - CHAPTER ONE

1. Peter Hinchliff, *The One-sided Reciprocity*, Darton, Longman and Todd London 1966 pp.108-208 *passim*; Stephen Neill, *Anglicanism*, Penguin Harmondsworth England 1965 p.427.
2. Neill, *op. cit.*, p. 427.
3. *C.S.* 15/9/1916 p.3; *A.C.R.* 25/6/1915 p.8; Ephesians 4:4-6.
4. *C.S.* 21/7/1916 p.6; Henry Wace, "The Church", in C.S. Carter and G.E. Weeks, *The Protestant Dictionary*, The Harrison Trust London 1933 (third edition) p.120.
5. H.S. Holland, "Faith" in Charles Gore (ed) *Lux Mundi* John Murray, London 1890 p.14.
6. J.R. Illingworth, "The Incarnation and Development" in *ibid.*, pp.211-212
7. *ibid.* p.183; F.L. Cross, "Anglo-Catholicism and the Twentieth Century" in G.L.H. Harvey (ed) *The Church and the Twentieth Century* Macmillan London 1936 p.327. See also A.M. Ramsey, *From Gore to Temple: The Development of Anglican Theology between Lux Mundi and the Second World War*, Longman London 1960 p.112.
8. *C.S.* 8/9/1916 p.8 (Thomas Quigley)
9. *ibid.* 8/10/1915 p.6; Commission on Christian Doctrine Appointed by Archbishop of Canterbury and York in 1922, *Doctrine in the Church of England, Report*, S.P.C.K. London 1938 pp. 126-129.
10. W.H. Griffith Thomas, *The Principles of Theology* Longmans, Green and Co. London 1930 p.360.

11. *ibid.*, p.399.
12. *C.S.* 11/12/1914 pp.25-26
13. Ramsey, *op. cit.*, pp.112-113,
14. Doctrine Commission *Report*, p.122; A.H.G. to D.A.G. 25/3/1935
15. *C.S.* 29/3/1913 p.8 (ed.)
16. Thomas, *op. cit.*, p.333.
17. *C.S.* 27/11/1914 p.6, 11/12/1914 p.6 (Hart)
18. *S.M.H.* 22/3/1928 p.12 (Hilliard); 14/6/1929 p.15.
19. *C.S.* 16/11/1917 p.6; *A.C.R.* 30/8/1918 p.8, 25/11/1926 p.6; Sykes et al., "Authority", p.11.
20. Thomas, *op. cit.*, p.337.
21. Henry Wace, "The Church" in C.S. Carter and G.E.A. Weeks, *op. cit.*, p.120.
22. *ibid.* pp.116, 284-285.
23. *ibid.* pp.124, 126.
24. Thomas, *op. cit.*, pp.265-290; T.C. Hammond, *In Understanding Be Men*, I.V.P. London 1976 (first printed 1936) pp.39-40, 153-159; J.C. Ryle, *Knots Untied*, Hunt London 1877.
25. F.L. Cross and E.A. Livingstone, *The Oxford Dictionary of the Christian Church*, Oxford University Press Oxford 1978, p.647.
26. Neill, *op. cit.*, p.46,
27. William Gladstone, quoted in James Bentley, *Ritualism and Politics In Victorian Britain: The Attempt to Legislate for Belief* Oxford University Press 1978 p.3.
28. *ibid.*, pp.2-4, 21ff.; John Gunstone, "Catholics in the Church of England", in John Wilkinson (ed.) *Catholic Anglicans Today* Darton, Longman and Todd London 1968 p.185.
29. T. Guy Rogers (ed.), *Liberal Evangelicalism* Hodder and Stoughton 1923 p. vi.
30. *ibid.*
31. *ibid.* p.vii.
32. Cross and Livingstone, *op. cit.*, pp.202, 926.
33. These issues come up in Chapters Four, Six, Seven and Eight respectively.

34. Hinchliff, *op. cit.* p.195.
35. See e.g. H.H. Henson, *The Bishoprick Papers*, Oxford University Press London 1946 pp.48-49.
36. Cross and Livingstone, *op. cit.*, p.581.
37. Hinchliff, *op. cit.*, p.197.
38. I am indebted to Associate Professor K.J. Cable for these statistics about Australian bishops, and for the biographical information found elsewhere in this dissertation.
39. Loane, *Hewn*, p.88; Loane, *The Centenary History of Moore Theological College* Angus and Robertson Sydney 1955 pp.176-177.
40. Broome, *op. cit.*, pp.95 ff.
41. David Hilliard, "The Anglican Church in South Australia: Towards a Portrait of an Institution". Transcript of a History Seminar at Flinders University 22/4/1983 p.18.
42. Broome, *op. cit.*, Chapter One; Edmund Campion, *Rockchoppers*, Penguin Sydney 1982 pp.59 ff.; Jill Roe, *op. cit.* pp.48-56.

CHAPTER TWO -

POLICIES, PARTIES AND POWER

I

When Bishop Frederic Barker arrived in Sydney in 1855 there was no one school of churchmanship which clearly dominated the Diocese. The Evangelical influence of the early chaplains had survived and was personified in the older clergy, but this enduring influence had been steadily overlaid by the High Church tradition which Barker's predecessor as Bishop, William Grant Broughton, had cultivated.[1] During Broughton's nineteen years as bishop the clerical ranks of the Diocese had been swelled by a growing number of disciples of the Tractarian movement, which had developed in Oxford in the 1830s.[2] Broughton's own sympathy with the Oxford Movement always remained conservative, critical, and dependent upon the consonance of its teaching with the Reformed tradition top which he remained loyal.[3] A number of the clergy Broughton patronised were, however, less cautious, and their enthusiasm for the vigorous advancement of Tractarian teaching raised Evangelical suspicions as to the eventual destination of this movement, suspicions which were seemingly confirmed when two Tractarian clergymen, Robert Sconce and Thomas Makinson, seceded to the Church of Rome in February 1848.[4]

The situation in the Diocese in 1855 was, therefore, confused. There were clear party differences, although there were no party organisations. Moreover, there was little to distinguish the services of worship in different parishes: Tractarian advancement in ritual at that stage only went as far as chanting the psalms, the musical enhancement of services, the wearing of a surplice in the pulpit and the erection of a cross on church buildings.[5] The Tractarians stood for the defence of the Church of England as a divine institution whose authority was secured by the Apostolic Succession of its bishops, and whose rule of faith was the Book of Common Prayer. Obedience to the teachings of the Church and submission to episcopal authority were the two themes of Tractarianism. Thus, the issues which divided those at the far ends of the ecclesiastical spectrum were matters of theology, not ritual, and attracted little attention from the large 'middle ground'. This middle ground comprised the bulk of the laity, most of whom were uninterested in the especial claims of the Tractarians and were uninspired by the piety and Gospel message of the Evangelicals. To complicate matters still further, the high turnover in the clerical force of the Diocese meant that the comparative strengths of different schools of thought were constantly shifting, and any suggestion of domination by one party was transitory. More than one quarter of the 57 clergymen in the Diocese in 1855 had served for less than five years and there was no indication that rapid changes in personnel would not continue.[6]

Bishop Barker has been justifiably regarded as the man responsible for transforming the Diocese from this: uncertain and unstable condition to one which was avowedly Evangelical.[7] It was a metamorphosis which was the 'product of both circumstance and Barker's own episcopal policy. That circumstance was Barker's appointment outside a tradition in which influential High churchmen secured colonial appointments for their friends, and supported these colonial bishops by supplying them with like-minded clergy. Bishop Broughton had been part of that tradition.

The Evangelical Barker, on the other hand, was without the same access to these sources of recruitment. He had to rely on the limited support that he received from the Evangelical missionary societies and his own friends in England and Ireland.[8]

The fact that Barker was not from that established tradition had attendant advantages. The absence of connections with the Society for the Propagation of the Gospel, which normally managed colonial appointments, and the comparative lack of strongly influential friends in the Church in England, meant that Barker was free from the inevitable pressures which accompanied such links. He was relatively free to chart his own course, make up his own mind, recruit his own clergy. He was free to reserve his judgement on matters about which he was uncertain or uninterested. It was an independence which allowed him to follow "a very distinct policy" with a single and undeflected mind. That policy was the supply of

> men of God, educated men divinely taught, mighty in the Scriptures, and men of much prayer, men who love the Saviour and the souls of men, who are true, whole-hearted members of the Church of England...and faithful to the order and discipline of their Church, men of a missionary spirit...[9]

Barker saw Australia as a mission field which required parish clergy-men to be able, evangelistic missionaries.[10] It was a dual role which was not without its problems but, to Barker, Evangelicals were best suited to the task. Although the exigencies of meeting the spiritual needs of a colony which was experiencing a population explosion demanded that Barker recruit able men regardless of their churchmanship, he always demonstrated a marked preference for men of Evangelical convictions.[11]

The supply from England of "sound, sensible sober-minded" Evangelicals was limited, and Barker was obliged to look to two other sources to provide clergymen who would form the stable core of his clerical force.[12] The first was the Church of Ireland. The Irish Church was a declining Anglo-Irish institution in which clerical opportunities were diminishing. Yet, the ministry continued to be a favoured vocation for the sons of Anglo-Irish families. The result was that many young, well-educated Irish clergymen emigrated, and the Dioceses of Sydney and Melbourne, with Barker and Charles Perry as their Evangelical bishops, were attractive destinations. Fewer Irish clergymen came to Sydney than to Melbourne, where their bishop considered that they constituted "an undue proportion", but, even so, nearly one quarter of the clergymen who served under Barker in Sydney were Irish, in a social context in which most Irishmen were Roman Catholic.[13] These Irish clergy strengthened the Evangelicalism of the Diocese. They were not all Evangelicals, but they were all staunch Protestants and emphatically endorsed Barker's general policies. Moreover, these men proved to be no mere sojourners: they usually had little desire to return to their homeland. They were in Sydney to stay and the Diocese gained for good an energetic and enthusiastic, if often volatile, group of clergymen.[14]

The second source of clergy — Moore College — was Barker's own creation. He established this training college one year after his arrival. It was absolutely fundamental to his overall policy of manning the Diocese with godly, educated men who were steeped in the Scriptures. Barker would have preferred close links with the University, but the staunchly secular University of Sydney had been deliberately "kept entirely free from the teachers of any religion" and Barker disdainfully disregarded it.[15] Nor could the facilities of the university's affiliated Anglican college, St. Paul's, be used as the college could only accommodate undergraduates or graduates, and few Anglican ordinands fell into those categories. Barker was left with only one alternative if his ordinands were to be provided with the theological training he believed they required: the establishment of a new and independent theological college.[16]

CHAPTER TWO - POLICIES, PARTIES AND POWER

Bishop Barker did not found Moore College in 1856 for the purpose of producing Evangelical clones. Both Barker and the College's first Principal, William Hodgson, were keenly aware that English theological colleges tended to be machines for the duplication of hard, narrow and overly, "ecclesiastical" viewpoints and they were anxious to avoid a replication of that "repulsive" model in Sydney.[17] However the two men did consider that, in the circumstances, this institution was the best means by which able men might be effectively equipped for their task of ministry. Moreover, both men perceived this task in essentially Evangelical terms: Hodgson's "decided Evangelical teaching" was designed "to guard those within the sphere of (his) influence alike from ritualistic innovations and from the old and oft-refuted objections of rationalistic infidelity."[18] The curriculum of the College, the appointment by Barker of Hodgson's successors, and the selection of ordinands were all consonant with that Evangelical perception. The Evangelical ethos of the College may not have been rigidly imposed upon its students but, nevertheless, the overwhelming majority of its graduates during Barker's episcopate were convinced and earnest Evangelicals.[19] During Barker's episcopate, Moore College trained 145 men for the ministry, one-third for the Sydney Diocese. This meant that when Barker died in 1882, nearly 40% (36 men) of the clergy within the Diocese had been trained at Moore College.[20] These locally-trained clergymen, together with the Irish clergymen, were important components of Barker's clerical force and became crucial factors in what has been called "the religious revolution in the Diocese of Sydney."[21]

There was another crucial factor in the renaissance of Evangelicalism in the Diocese: the strong and decisive leadership of Bishop Barker himself. Barker moulded his motley band of assorted High Churchmen, zealous Irishmen, sojourning Englishmen, and Moore College graduates into a distinctive and coherent group. A sense of clerical community developed with Barker as its undisputed head. Above all, Barker's leadership was based upon pastoring. Whereas Broughton had seen himself in prelatical terms, Barker saw the role of chief pastor as his essential function as bishop. Virtually all his ministerial life in England had been spent in a parish: he knew the life and difficulties of a parochial clergymen. Now, as bishop, he put that experience to good use, employing the principles and methods which had succeeded in similar situations in England. He was constantly on the move throughout the 'Diocese, overseeing and encouraging his charges. It was a continual visitation which meant that more central matters were sometimes left in abeyance, but it proved decisive for the ultimate character of the Diocese.[22]

This characteristic of Barker's episcopacy was exemplified in the monthly prayer meetings which Barker initiated soon after his arrival. At first these provided "a refuge from an unsympathetic environment and a source of inspiration" for Evangelical clergy who saw themselves as missionaries in a "barren, melancholy wilderness."[23] But soon they took on a more positive form. Regular district meetings were held which were in no way Evangelical conventicles but rather designed to promote mutual edification and support for men from all schools of thought. They were gatherings which fostered ministerial fellowship and collegiality.[24]

Barker's episcopate was co-incident with tremendous social changes which were promoted by the discovery of gold and successive waves of migrants into the Australian colonies, the small beginnings in New South Wales and Victoria of an industrial base, and the introduction of responsible government for the Australian colonies.[25] Yet, despite these social and economic developments, Barker left a diocese in 1882 which was smaller, more ordered, and had a greater institutional coherence than the one which he had inherited twenty-eight years earlier. The more unstable bush districts of the Diocese had been re-constituted as the new Dioceses of Bathurst and Goulburn leaving the Sydney Diocese more compact and manageable. Further, the clergy were a more stable and reliable group. The itinerants were fewer and there were more loyal, long-serving pastors.[26] The clerical ranks displayed a burgeoning homogeneity of churchmanship which was the direct result of Barker's vision of a Diocese pastored by spirit-filled men of God "mighty in the Scriptures... of much prayer, who love the Saviour and the souls of men..."[27]

II

The effectiveness of Barker's implementation of his Evangelical policy is evidenced by the comparative tranquillity of the Diocese throughout most of his episcopate. In the rest of the Church of England, the 1860s and 1870s were decades of enormous change and upheaval. Simple faith in the bases of Christianity — creator God, Christ divine, inspired Bible, eternal life — were being questioned.[28] Geology cast doubt on Genesis-time; modern textual criticism of the Scriptures raised a sense of insecurity in the Bible's authority; historians began to examine the extent of textual error or literary myth, and.the dating and authorship of various books.[29] In 1860, the publication of *Essays and Reviews* signalled the fact that there was a gap between Christian doctrine and the beliefs of some Anglican clergymen: indeed, when one of the authors of *Essays*, Frederic Temple, was elevated to the Episcopate in 1870, it meant that the Church of England had a bishop (and eventual Archbishop of Canterbury) who believed that the Bible contained legend, and who was prepared to ordain men who held liberal views on Biblical inspiration.[30] During the same period, the doctrine of evolution espoused by Darwin in the *Origin of the Species* (1859) and *The Descent of Man* (1871) was a direct assault on the concept of special creation and the very focus of Christianity: in short, if no Adam, no Fall; if no Fall, then no need for a Saviour.[31] It was believed that in the Saviour's place, Darwinism had introduced a natural process so apparently uniform that the miraculous was untenable.[32]

The turmoil generated within the Victorian Church by Biblical Criticism and Darwinism was only matched by the controversy over the development of ritual by the second generation of the Oxford Movement.[33] Ritual became more and more elaborate in a growing number of English churches. Its development was partly caused by the general ornateness of the age, partly as an attempt to attract the working class and partly as a doctrinal development. According to an 1882 survey, 64% of English and Welsh clergy took the Eastward position, 23% had candles on the altar, and 13% used vestments.[34] Protestant opposition to this development was fierce, and was fanned by the growing belief that the ritualists were a fifth column which intended to make England Roman Catholic.[35] Passions on both sides were raised even more by unsuccessful attempts to crush ritualism by legislation.[36]

These storms of theological dispute, historical and scientific debate and ritualist controversy lashed the Church of England throughout the 1860s and 1870s. Few of the colonial outposts were unaffected: in Melbourne, for example, the debates over the inspiration and authority of the Bible, the revisionist claims of liberal theologians, the ritualist controversy, the claims of the Spiritualists, and the conclusions of Charles Darwin were all subjects for earnest public debate which gravely affected the Church of England in that Diocese.[37] But, curiously, the storms of confusion which lashed other parts of the Anglican Communion between 1860 and 1880 passed Sydney by.[38]

There are three factors which contributed to this comparative tranquillity in Sydney. First, secular liberalism was far more developed in Melbourne and this movement happily allied itself with liberalism in biblical scholarship, Darwinism and ritualistic freedom.[39] Second, the intellectual calibre of the clergy in Sydney was probably lower than in Melbourne. Barker's clergymen were increasingly products of the local theological college rather than a British university, less well educated, and less sensitive than their predecessors to the intellectual issues of the 1860s and 1870s.[40] Leading Sydney laymen were, by comparison, far better educated and more concerned with these issues and figured conspicuously in Christian apologetic movements.[41] It was a sharp intellectual distinction which partly contributed to the division between laity and clergy in the 1880s and 1890s, a period in which the Evangelical laity were politically dominant.

The third and most important reason was that Barker's great practical emphasis upon the pastoral office promoted a church order in which controversy and division were discouraged and even suppressed.[42] Barker was not by nature autocratic, and his Evangelical convictions did not permit any high notion of the Episcopate. But his scant respect for the abilities of colonial clergy, and his disinclination to delegate, meant that he was obliged to exercise a firm, personal and intrusive control over the Diocese.[43] In addition, his organisation of regular district meetings of clergy, an innovation for those times, not only gave support and encouragement to groups of isolated professionals, but also "did something to promote a common approach to theological issues and a united stand on matters of churchmanship."[44] This was not because one school of thought was represented at these gatherings: far from it. But it was of immeasurable irenical benefit for the Church in Sydney to have issues discussed — and often resolved — in small private groups which elsewhere became the subject of heated public controversy.[45]

Whether it was due more to Barker's imposing pastoral role in the Diocese or more to the fact that contentious issues were privately defused Bishop Barker was able to keep the lid on tensions in Sydney for all but the last few years of his episcopate when, in his seventies, he began to lose his grip on the Diocese.[46] The only source of potential tension in Barker's time was the enduring cleavage between Tractarians and Evangelicals. This tension was in part a reflection of the party conflicts occurring in the English Church but it was also a legacy from Broughton's regime. Early relations between Barker and the Tractarian clergy were characterised by cool civility: the Tractarians were discomfited by working under an Evangelical bishop, while Barker quickly concluded "that the High Church clergy in Sydney were not to be trusted in co-operating in his religious policy."[47] Yet the potential for "open rupture" between the two schools of thought was never realised. Instead the Tractarians, who were not organised into any partisan society, steadily lost influence as Barker's own personal influence grew, and the number of Evangelical recruited by him increased.[48] This situation changed dramatically in the administration of Barker's successor, Alfred Barry. Barry, the fifty-seven year old former Principal of King's College, London, had been initially rejected by Sydney's Synod in a session in which party lines had been sharply drawn, but he was eventually elected by the five English bishops to whom the final choice was delegated.[49] Barry was pre-eminently a scholar who abhorred the factious spirit which church parties often engendered. He actively sought to uphold the plurality of opinion which the comprehensiveness of the Church of England allowed. To Barry, internecine squabbling over matters of churchmanship was counter-productive to the Church's major task of professing Christ for the good of humanity and "the higher life of the colony".[50] This "Broad Churchman" eschewed narrow definition in theology and sought to interpret Anglican formularies and beliefs in a broad and liberal spirit because he believed that, with the inevitable variety of development, character, temperament and background, "it would be vain to desire or hope to reduce to one uniformity. For all there is call, for all there is room."[51]

Barry was convinced that the conflict between secularism and Christianity was of far more pressing concern than matters of churchmanship.[52] Whereas his predecessor had only obliquely addressed himself to this question, and had envisaged church extension as the best means of countering secularism's challenge to Christianity, Bishop Barry quickly perceived that the assorted claims of the Freethinkers, Darwinians and

Spiritualists could no longer be quietly ignored, but had to be publicly refuted.[53] In late 1884 Barry brought Protestants of all denominations together to present a united front, the Christian Evidence society, against the growing secularist lobby. His articulate leadership of this Christian apologetic movement during the next five years won him the respect and admiration of many within the Christian community.[54] Ironically, however, this prominent position in the Christian apologetic movement also served to highlight to the Evangelical majority in the Anglican Church in Sydney that Barry was not one of them. The Evangelical leaders had specifically rejected Barry in the initial election synod in 1882 because of his "liberalism" and now they witnessed that liberalism being publicly promoted by Barry as he sought to reinterpret "the deep truths of Christianity" for the modern age.[55] Whereas Conservative Evangelicals had no inclination to assimilate sound modern research and thought with their existing theological system, Barry distinctly encouraged a critical tolerance of modern science and scholarship, and a re-examination of one's existing doctrinal position.[56] Barry was always at pains to cultivate respect and sympathy between believers and non-believers. This "liberalism" was in stark contrast to Barker's Evangelical piety which had so influenced the Diocese. Barker had eschewed the secular world; Barry encouraged his charges to meet secularism head-on, refute its error, and embrace its truths.[57] Barker had managed to contain many fractious tensions within the Diocese for most of his episcopate; Barry's consciously liberal policy indirectly cultivated these tensions and was the catalyst for party organisation and controversy.

These tensions were most clearly evident over matters of churchmanship. There is good reason to believe that, just as party tensions rose in England during this period, friction between Evangelicals and High Churchmen would also have increased in Sydney no matter who the Bishop had been.[58] But Bishop Barry's belief in comprehensiveness and desire not to alienate minority groups within the church polity was interpreted by Evangelicals, who were used to the uncompromising administration of Barker, as deliberate patronage of the traditional High Churchmen and the new school of High Churchmen, the ritualists (later identified as Anglo-Catholics).[59] They failed to make any distinction between legitimate exaltation of corporate worship and ritualistic innovation. They simply impeached the one with the other. They watched with alarm as the incidence of ceremonial increased under Bishop Barry: *Hymns Ancient and Modern*, styled by one extreme Protestant as "popery's poetical pioneer", began to be used in many of the fashionable churches; choral eucharists were now celebrated in a diocese where robed choirs had previously been rare; and Bishop Barry, convinced that music was "the handmaid of religion", founded the Church Choir Union to promote the study of music.[60] These were all legitimate developments but Evangelicals saw them as all of a piece with the more extreme innovations characterised by the introduction of altar lights, brass cross, mass vestments and processions with banners by the Rev. C.F. Garnsey at Christ Church St. Laurence in 1884.[61] At the Cathedral, Barry's encouragement of variety was expressed in changes of personnel. At the time of Barker's death, high churchmen had felt ostracised both from the pulpit and the chapter of the Cathedral. Under Barry, a wider circle of clergy were invited to its pulpit, a precentor and a minor canon were appointed and the daily offices of mattins and evensong were sung.[62] These were not radical changes, but sensitive Evangelicals nevertheless perceived in the new faces, new services and new music a campaign of infiltration of high church practices for which Bishop Barry was responsible. Even the secular *Daily Telegraph* attributed responsibility for these developments to Barry: "Under Dr. Barry, High Churchism has made rapid progress in the diocese, not because he has distinctly encouraged it, but because he has not distinctly discouraged it."[63]

III

The extent of party tensions became palpably clear by 1886. In that year a New South Wales branch of the Church of England Association was formed "to uphold the Principles of the Protestant Church of England, to protest against encroachment upon her Doctrines and Established Ritual, and to discountenance in every legitimate way Unauthorized Innovations."[64] Like its parent in England, it was a lay organisation out to stop the wicked ritualists. Its President was an Irishman, Judge W.J. Foster, a former attorney-general of N.S.W. who was on the eve of retirement from the Supreme Court, and a man who was perhaps the most powerful Protestant layman in Sydney.

The advent of the Church Association introduced an important new element into the ecclesiastical dynamics of Sydney. Previously, laymen had not been prominent in church affairs. The clergyman had been the focus and the driving force in church life. Able, interested laymen had been in short supply. The middle and upper classes which had traditionally supplied the Church of England with its active laity were under-represented in the Australian colonies and the clergyman had been obliged to fill the breach.[65] Moreover, the clergyman stepped into that position easily for he was invariably the natural social leader. In terms of education, for example, whereas tertiary educated laymen were rare in early Australia, more than half of the clergymen in Barker's early years were graduates.[66] That did not imply that they were intellectual giants, but it did mean that the clergy were a distinctive social group, which as much as churchmanship served to give them a sense of corporate spirit during Barker's years.

That situation began to change in the 1880s. There was greater social stability and a developing middle class in Australia at the very time when clergymen, their collective educational status slipping, were less obviously the natural social leaders.[67] Leading laymen seemed to be concerned with social and intellectual issues in a way in which the young, locally trained clergy did not.[68] In addition, laymen were becoming increasingly involved in the parishes and in the Synod, the Church's legislature. This was not just because the laity had become a more permanent and stable social factor in the life of the Church but also because the affairs of the Church were increasingly affecting the laymen's hip pocket nerve. The phasing out of state aid to religion from 1862 meant that while the State continued to support clergymen licensed before that date, the Church was increasingly obliged to ask its members to meet the stipends of the clergy. By 1886, only 16% of Sydney's clergymen received State aid.[69] The laymen, who were being asked to foot the bill for the stipends of the other 84%, quickly developed a I commensurate, critical interest in the affairs of the Church.[70]

The increased participation by laymen in the parishes and in the synod signalled the fact that the locus of power and authority was shifting. Before synods were established in 1866, the Bishop had been the only institution which had had any legal authority at all in the Church of England in Australia. Even after that date, such was the personal influence of Barker that he continued to be the focus of diocesan government.[71] Under his over-arching episcopal authority, the clergy led their people. Lay involvement was sought, but was subordinate to the exercise of clerical responsibility. Thus, despite Evangelical theory, power percolated downwards: the bishop had general authority, the clergy had local responsibility, and the laity co-operated.

This hierarchical power structure began to be broken down with the development in the 1880s and 1890s of effective deliberative assemblies at all levels of church government. The governing 1837 Church Temporalities Act, which had been modelled on entirely inappropriate English legislation, had hitherto restricted lay participation in parish affairs to the duties of the three wardens: there was no provision for parish councils. This came to be considered inadequate, and in 1897 the structure of parochial government was radically refashioned by the new Sydney Church Ordinance which not only defined the rights and powers of churchwardens and trustees, but also encouraged parishes to establish councils which could share with the wardens in the decision-making and administration of the parish.[72] At the Diocesan level, the 1837 Act had been partially repealed by an 1866 Act which had permitted diocesan synods to meet. During Bishop Barker's time, however, synods were never more than an opportunity for the Bishop to consult, inform and encourage the clergy and laity. They lacked legislative teeth: between 1866 and 1881 the Sydney Synod only passed eighteen ordinances, most of which were concerned with matters referred to it by General Synod.[73] The Synod's legislative potential for management and good government within the Diocese had not been developed. Diocesan government remained the domain of the bishop.[74]

Development of the legislative functions of the diocesan synod began to take place in these last two decades of the nineteenth century. First, the Property Acts of 1881, 1887, 1889 and 1897 vested the Synod with wide powers over church property: the legislature was now permitted to appoint trustees, and sell, mortgage or lease trust lands.[75] Next, preparations began for the introduction of a new Constitution which would facilitate more effective synodical government.[76] These moves came to fruition in the 1902 Constitutions Act which still governs synodical government in N.S.W.[77] synodical government developed still further in this period by the augmentation of the powers and authority of the Synod's executive, the Standing Committee. In 1895, the Standing Committee's defined powers and duties were limited: it was permitted to prepare the business paper for Synod, represent the Synod during its adjournment, and be a Council of Advice to the Bishop "in any matter in which he may desire their advice."[78] But the Committee had little scope for initiative until 1897, when the Standing Committee's responsibilities

were widened: in that year, the Synod bestowed deliberative powers upon
its Executive for "all matters affecting the interests of the Church...", and
power to initiate action without prior reference to the full Synod.[79] This
enabled the Standing Committee to act for Synod during the 51 weeks of
the year in which Synod did not sit: the Committee's authority grew as
it developed from being merely functional to being a deliberative body
as well. when Synod was in recess, diocesan government was no longer
the domain of the bishop, but of the clergy and laity as well.

The development of synodical government was dramatically demonstrated by the change in tempo at each session of Synod. Compared to
the relaxed deliberations under Barker where, on average, one ordinance
was passed each year, Synod in the 1880s and 1890s became a veritable
hive of activity: fourteen ordinances were passed in Barry's five years,
nine during the caretaker administration of Dean Cowper (1889-1890),
48 in the first nine years of Bishop Saumarez Smith's episcopate (1891-
1899) and 58 from 1900 to 1908. The wave of legislation continued in
Archbishop Wright's time when 99 ordinances were passed by Synod
from 1909 to 1919.[80] Of course, many of these ordinances were only
property ordinances to facilitate the rationalisation of the Church's real
estate, but their number demonstrated the increased administrative and
legislative oversight of the Diocese by the laymen and clergymen of Synod.

All of these developments — the encouragement of more lay participation in the affairs of the parish, the reconstitution of synodical
government, the assumption by Synod of effective legislative powers over
property, and the development of an authoritative executive of Synod —
accelerated the transference of power from the Bishop to the laity and
clergy. This did not mean that the Bishop of Sydney was being stripped
of inalienable rights and powers by grasping laymen and clergymen.
Rather it indicated that the colonial era in Sydney, in which the bishop
had extraordinarily wide, unilateral powers, was coming to an end and
the powers of the Sydney Diocesan were being pruned back closer to

the English norm.[81] It was a revision of the role of the Bishop which was in line with discussions throughout the Anglican Communion on the authority and independence of colonial Metropolitans, an issue which became all the more prominent after the 1897 Lambeth Conference recognised the custom of entitling all Metropolitans "Archbishop".[82]

Although this re-assessment and shift in the locus of power and authority was a natural part of the maturing process of a colonial church, it inevitably created tensions — or exacerbated existing ones — between party groupings. The rapid assumption of the legislative function by Synod, for example, could not help but be divisive. The Synod began to imitate the Westminster parliamentary model. Differences and not similarities of opinion amongst synodsmen were highlighted. Reflecting the secular development of organised political parties, de facto governments, oppositions and even Cabinets were formed within the Synod.[83] The Rev. H.N. Baker later observed that "A Synod, because it is a legislative body, splits its members automatically into parties, and creates antagonisms by generating in each party a desire to push its own views to triumph over others. There can be no doubt that Synodal government helps the cause of division, necessary as it is for legislation..."[84] The change in dynamic heightened the consciousness of party groupings in the Diocese because synod increasingly became the modus operandi by which those political groups achieved their goals. The prospect of forceful personalities in the mould of Barker exerting a formative influence on the Diocese did not disappear, but became less likely: synodical government necessarily meant "the routinization of charisma".[85] Henceforth the dominant force was the political group, not the charismatic individual.

The first demonstration of the power of a party organisation followed soon after the establishment of the Church Association in 1886. Towards the end of that year, Bishop Barry's long-planned project to replace the old reredos in the Cathedral with a new alabaster one, came to fruition. The centre panel of this reredos depicted the Crucifixion.[86] The

Church Association reacted strongly, and waged an effective propaganda campaign for the removal of the "crucifix" from the Cathedral. After an animated and often bitter debate in the 1897 session of Synod, the centre panel was replaced by a less objectionable work of art depicting the Transfiguration.[87]

The reredos controversy catapulted the fledgling Church Association into a position of prominence and influence. Its defence of the Church of England against the spectre of "Romanism without a Pope" was very popular at a time when the ritualist controversies in England were alerting Sydney churchmen to the possibility that similar developments could occur in their own backyard.[88] The Association quickly attracted the support of leading laymen: professional men, importers and merchants, government officials and pastoralists all sprang to the defence of a Protestant Church of England.[89] Whether all these men were Evangelicals, in the sense that they claimed a personal, saving relationship with Christ and considered the Scriptures were the final authority on all matters of faith and conduct, is impossible to determine. But they were all certainly "low churchmen", attaching relatively little importance to the claims of the episcopate, the priesthood and the sacraments. They were staunchly anti-Roman and most anxious to keep their religious services simple, Protestant and British.[90] With synodical government these men had the means to make their presence and their opinion felt; with Evangelical theory, they were able to legitimate their share in church government. Their Church Association made a strong and unapologetic push into Synod: by 1889, 34 of its governing committee were in Synod, and half of these were synodsmen of less than three years' standing. How many more Associationists were also synodsmen is unclear, but the Association quickly became an efficient, zealous party machine with a full-time organising secretary.[91] By 1889 its members had every confidence that they would be in u control of the Sydney Synod when the time came to choose a successor to Bishop Barry.[92]

IV

Bishop Barry resigned in May 1889 on the ground that the ill-health of his wife necessitated a return to England. There were murmured suggestions that the factious strife in the Diocese had got the better of him, and his resignation was in fact the strategic retreat of a defeated man.[93] But all the evidence indicates that his stated reason was genuine. The climate had adversely affected Mrs. Barry's health as early as 1886, and she was obliged to return to England in 1887. From that point Barry looked for an opportunity to return to England. His departure in 1889 after only five years as bishop may have surprised casual observers, but it was not an ill-considered, hasty action.[94]

Bishop Barry's short stay in Sydney saw the polarisation of the Diocese. His episcopal policy was in part responsible for this. He had encouraged his charges to come to grips with the challenges of secularism and modern Biblical scholarship, a policy which directly promoted debate. His own liberal apologetics provoked consternation among Evangelicals who became convinced that his professed desire for comprehensiveness implied active patronage of non-Evangelicals, particularly High Churchmen, with little regard for the views of the laity and Evangelical clergy. This was the catalyst for Evangelical party organisation. For their part, High Churchmen were angered by the successful Church Association campaigns, exemplified in the 1886 Reredos Dispute and the alleged victimisation of the Tractarian Thomas Hill, who was sacked as Principal of Moore College in 1888. It was only a matter of time before the High Churchmen matched the Church Association organisation.[95] However, the tensions unleashed by Barry's policies were considerably compounded by factors which had not been present for much of Barker's time, and over which Barry had little control: the increasing participation of the laity in church affairs and the development of synodical government, a forum in which differences within Sydney Anglicanism were permanently crystallised into party groupings.

These party tensions did not surface at the Diocesan Synod which met in June 1889 to nominate Barry's successor. There were no acrimonious debates; no verbal punches were traded. Instead the synod quickly settled upon three names to present to the Australian bishops. The lack of bitterness or dissent convinced the *Sydney Morning Herald* that the synod had displayed "Christian love and brotherly feeling" in its deliberations. In fact, it would be more accurate to describe the result as a short, sharp Evangelical victory. All three nominees were principals of Evangelical theological colleges in England: Handley Moule of Ridley Hall, Cambridge; Francis Chavasse of Wycliffe Hall, Oxford; and William Saumarez Smith of St. Aidan's, Birkenhead.[96] Their nomination clearly attested to the strength of the Evangelicals in the Diocesan Synod, but did not mean that party strife had happily dissipated. The High Church minority had not.disappeared; the potential for controversy and strife was still very much there.

That potential was realised in the confusion that followed. The method of election required both the New South Wales and Australian bishops to delete, consecutively, one name from the list: the surviving nominee was elected Bishop of Sydney, Metropolitan of New South Wales and Primate of Australia. The New South Wales bishops deleted Chavasse and the Australian bishops, by six votes to two, elected Handley Moule over Smith.[97] But the election became unsuccessful when Moule declined the offer. The initiative should have reverted to the Sydney Synod and the process begun *de novo*. The ageing, nearly senile, senior Australian bishop, Mesac Thomas of Goulburn, failed, however, to recognise this. Instead, before he telegrammed Moule, he enquired of his fellow bishops whether they would be willing to "transfer" their votes to Smith "in case" Moule declined. He received a number of affirmative replies so that, when Moule declined, he informed Dean Cowper, the President of the

Sydney Synod, that Smith had been elected. Cowper, unaware of the majority vote for Moule and his subsequent refusal, immediately offered the See to Smith, who accepted in August 1889.[98]

Bishop Kennion of Adelaide immediately protested to Bishop Thomas and Dean Cowper at this mode of appointment. Kennion's protest was not, as has been suggested, a "facade" for an attack upon Smith's churchmanship.[99] Rather, Kennion feared that this course of action could easily develop into a racket whereby Sydney could retain the Primacy with scant regard for the rights and opinions of the other Australian bishops simply by compiling a list of two straw men — of men they knew would decline — together with the nominee of their choice and the Australian bishops would be compelled to accept him as their Primate.[100] Neither Bishop Thomas nor Dean Cowper heeded Bishop Kennion's protest, which only made Kennion suspect that these two Evangelicals were in cahoots to deny the Australian bishops their rightful part in electing their Primate. Thus, Kennion promptly petitioned Archbishop Benson of Canterbury and the Colonial Office with the request that Smith not be consecrated until the election had been declared valid. A deadlock occurred which was only resolved when Smith eventually withdrew his acceptance and the Australian bishops, knowing that no gentleman would accept the position to the detriment of Smith, then unhappily concurred in his re-election.[101]

The unfortunate and protracted confusion which surrounded the election of William Saumarez Smith to the See of Sydney was the spark which re-ignited the enduring embers of party strife in that Diocese. Bishop Thomas of Goulburn had misled Sydney churchmen as to the nature of the bishops' ballot and they believed that Thomas had merely enquired of Moule whether he would accept the position before any voting had taken place. Dean Cowper and other Sydney Evangelicals had no idea that, as Moule himself later verified, Thomas' telegram had been in the form of an announcement of Moule's election and an offer of the Primacy.[102] Sydney Evangelicals were therefore convinced that the obstructionism of the bishops smacked of sour partisanship, and was an attack on Sydney's Evangelical tradition and the sort of manoeuvre they had come to expect from prelates who tried "to lord it over God's heritage".[103] They became defensive, and feared that the Australian bishops would force a non-Evangelical bishop upon them. Smith became a symbol of all that Sydney Evangelicals cherished: their self-determining independence, their integrity and honour, and the Evangelical tradition of their diocese. Their leaders made it virtually impossible for the Australian bishops to refuse to concur in Smith's re-election: if they had not, the Sydney Synod may well have withdrawn the Diocese from the General Synod, cut the See adrift from the positions of Metropolitan and Primate, and precipitated "a complete break-up of all corporate action by the church in Australia".[104]

For their part, the High Churchmen and the few Anglo-Catholics in Sydney supported Kennion's protest, and pressed for a fresh election. They believed that Smith's re-election had been cleverly orchestrated by the Evangelicals, and that Sydney was now doomed to have "a fifth rate, ultra-Low Churchman" as its Diocesan.[105] They were disconsolate and frustrated. The stubbornness of their Evangelical brethren, who seemed determined to risk the unity of the Australian church for the sake of getting their man, angered them. The frustration of the small group of Anglo-Catholics in Sydney found expression in counter-organisation. In August 1890, just one month before Bishop Saumarez Smith arrived in Sydney, the Rev. C.F. Garnsey launched *The Banner and Anglo-Catholic Review* and, at the same time, the English Church Union, which had apparently become moribund since its inception in 1880, was reconstituted as the New South Wales Church Union.[106] With its own paper, and with fresh life breathed into an old party structure, the Anglo-Catholics were back in business opposing the "philistinism" of the Evangelicals in Sydney.[107]

V

The forgotten centre of this confused election was the Principal of St. Aidan's, Birkenhead, William Saumarez Smith. He was in no way responsible for the controversy: indeed, after he first accepted the offer of the See in August 1889, he had been left in the dark for more than seven months, unaware of the details of the dispute which surrounded his election.[108] Yet the circumstances of his election limited Saumarez Smith's effectiveness as a bishop. He was a lame duck from the beginning. The dispute had alienated all but one of the Australian bishops.[109] More than this, the controversy had enflamed the already strong partisanship in the Diocese which he was to administer. It had strengthened the Church Association and prompted the formation of a rival party organisation and publication. It was a position that the most able of men would have found extremely difficult: he was unwanted by his brother bishops, and thrust into a Diocese which had witnessed a savage polarisation because of his election. On top of this, Smith suffered a final bitter blow when his wife died ten days before his consecration.[110]

Had Saumarez Smith been a charismatic leader of men, able like Bishop Barker to weld his ministers into a coherent clerical force, secure the co-operation of the laity, and command the respect of his episcopal fellows, he may have been able to overcome these formidable early difficulties. But the Sydney Synod had not demanded the election of a leader of men: its Evangelical majority had just been delivered from the "leadership" of Alfred Barry and they wanted a different kind of successor. They had no desire for a charismatic leader who concentrated power at the top. Instead, they sought a man who "would work quietly as an administrator of the Diocese."[111] Saumarez Smith filled that bill. He was primarily a scholar who had ably directed the affairs of St. Aidan's, Birkenhead for the previous twenty-one years. As Bishop of Sydney his administrative bent was demonstrated by the re-structuring of parochial and diocesan government, with such instruments as the Sydney Church Ordinance and the 1902 Constitutions.[112] But Smith was certainly not the man to tackle the formidable task of uniting an unhappy, polarised Diocese. He was not a forceful, imposing personality: he cultivated a "quiet unostentatious way, caring not for the limelight".[113] Faced with an Evangelical majority which was determined that the ritualism which had been condoned by Barry should be staunched, and a vocal Anglo-Catholic minority which was equally determined that the election of a Protestant scholar as Diocesan would not restrict the freedom they had lately come to enjoy, Smith appeared impotent, unable to ameliorate the divisive passions. The stage was set for more than a decade of continual party strife:

> "Just as diamond must cut diamond," the editor of *The Banner* declared, "so must organisation be met and checkmated by organisation. Even if the E.C.U. were a party Society, it has to contend against a party Society, and Similia, Similibus, Curantur... By every fair means, the pulpit, the platform, and the press, the Union is prepared to promote and defend the truth for which so many Martyrs have suffered and died.[114]

The Evangelicals were also unwilling to lay down their cudgels. They were satisfied by the confirmation of Saumarez Smith's election, but they were neither quietened nor mollified. As far as they were concerned, the news from England cast grave doubt over the long-term prospects for peace in the Church of England. The 1874 Public Worship Regulation Act had failed dismally to curb ritualism and the 1890 Lincoln Judgment, in which Archbishop Benson of Canterbury virtually acquitted Bishop King of Lincoln of ritualist irregularities, had only served to encourage Anglo-Catholics and dismay Evangelicals.[115] Clearly the Church of England was in a state of flux and the developments in England served notice on the

Sydney Church Associationists that, despite their recent success, they could not drop their guard. They had to remain alert and organised, lest self-satisfied complacency be responsible for ritualist gains in the Diocese.[116]

Partisan activity became a part of diocesan church life in Smith's episcopate. The extreme Church Association and the E.C.U. were soon joined by more moderate party groups: the High Church Churchman's Institute was founded in 1891, and the Evangelical Churchmen's Alliance appeared in 1893. What exactly prompted the emergence of these two organisation is unknown.[117] But their formation denotes the fact that considerable numbers of churchmen did not identify with the extremists at both ends of the ecclesiastical spectrum. The members of the High Church Institute consciously distinguished themselves from ritualism by demonstratively upholding the Prayer Book, and seeking to promote piety in the parishes; in the same way the Alliance had a more positive emphasis than the zealous vigilantes of the Church Association and preferred to propagate the ideals and principles of Evangelicalism rather than agitate against the beliefs and practices of others.[118] Both moderate groups seemed to attract groups of churchmen who had not been previously politicised: High Church laymen who had been under-represented in the E.C.U. swelled the ranks of the Institute; and Evangelical clergy, who had not been part of the exclusively lay Church Association, were prominent in the Alliance, which seemed to attract men who were dissatisfied by the extremism of the Association.[119]

The extent of support in the Diocese for the Institute and Alliance is unclear. Yet their emergence in the early years of Saumarez Smith's episcopate meant that by 1894 there were four political groups in the Diocese of Sydney. The E.C.U. branch at the 'extreme right' and the Church Association at the 'extreme left' closely corresponded to their parent societies in England. On the same continuum, the Churchman's Institute and the Churchmen's Alliance were at 'centre right' and 'centre left' respectively. There had developed an unprecedented awareness of church groupings at the same time as secular political distinctions had hardened.[120] It was a situation which provided the springboard for political action within the Church. Throughout the 1890s the Church Association waged campaigns against Anglo-Catholicism in its various actual or suspected forms; the Churchman's Institute published its propaganda in the *Churchman*; and the E.C.U. agitated for liturgical freedom.[121]

Despite the flurry of party activity in the early and mid-nineties, only the E.C.U. of these four party organisations survived into the twentieth century: the Churchman's Institute faded away after the death of its founder, the Rev. Spry Bailey; the *Churchman* was incorporated into the new national *Church Commonwealth* in 1900; and the two evangelical organisations merged into a new Protestant Church of England Union, which was founded in 1898.[122] This coalition was natural: although the two organisations had different emphases and different memberships, their merging made for more effective organisation and articulation of their Evangelical cause. It was, in fact, a coalition of familiar faces which imitated, in both name and sentiment, the English alliance of Evangelical forces which had formed the National Protestant Church Union in 1893. Yet its emergence was not totally prompted by an identification with English models: the Union was the product of local impulses as well. First, an enthusiastic Reformation Festival was held in October 1898 which resolved that such a Union must be established "to maintain and extend the efficiency of the Church of England as the original representative of evangelical truth and apostolic order in our country, and as a witness to the principles of the Reformation."[123] The second and far more significant local impulse in the creation of the P.C.E.U. was the presence in the Diocese of a growing number of Evangelical clergymen who were dissatisfied with the "moderation" of the Churchmen's Alliance. These clergy were more comfortable with the aggressive negativism of the Church Association, and the formation of the P.C.E.U. not only brought these two groups together but saw this group of clergy grow in prominence within Evangelical circles.

This is exemplified in the P.C.E.U.'s first President, the Rev. Mervyn Archdall, the Irish rector of St. Mary's, Balmain. Just as the Rev. C.F. Garnsey and Judge Foster were crucial figures in the formation of the E.C.U. and the Church Association, Archdall was central to this new Union. The P.C.E.U. was his baby and the means by which he extended his influence in the Diocese.[124] Indeed, for nineteen years the P.C.E.U. was in large measure the active extension of the convictions and beliefs of its excitable first President.[125] Under Archdall's leadership, the emphases and character of the P.C.E.U. were similar to those of the superseded Church Association. Whereas in the established milieu of England the Church Association had sought to use the secular courts to curb ritualism, its scion in unestablished Australia had resorted to exerting its powerful influence within the legislature of the Church, the Synod of the Diocese, for the purpose of enforcing its doctrinal and legal position. In the same way, the P.C.E.U. attempted to secure their anti-ritualist objectives through the Synod.[126] Its leaders were tenacious in their efforts in that forum to legislate belief and practice. Archdall unsuccessfully introduced an ordinance at the 1899 and 1903 synods to "regulate and define the vestments to be used in the Diocese of Sydney" — a move designed to ban the chasuble.[127] The attempts only failed because Archbishop Smith ruled that the ordinance was *ultra vires* because "there is too much doubt about the Synod's power to depart from the law as exercised in England to justify definite regulations being made here."[128]

When the ordinance failed in 1903, the P.C.E.U. continued to pressure Archbishop Smith by presenting him with a memorial on the subject signed by 43 clergymen. The memorial claimed that Smith's misguided tolerance of liturgical illegalities in the diocese was instrumental in the drift away from the church. They maintained that Smith had the power, if only he had the will, to ensure that lawlessness in the Church in Sydney was stopped.[129] Smith agreed that vestments were illegal and undesirable, but with no clear decision in England on their use, he refused to act independently, preferring "to wait for further light on what had become a very complicated matter."[130] The 1906 Royal Commission on Ecclesiastical Discipline, the anticipated source of that "further light", was to disappoint those like Smith who sorely sought elucidation.

Outside the synod, the P.C.E.U. disseminated its views by published word and public lecture. A young people's group was formed and its 300 members were well-drilled in the basics of Reformed doctrine. Membership of the Union itself peaked in the early years of the new century at about 600 with branches in twenty parishes. With its influence reaching far beyond this solid base of membership, the P.C.E.U. quickly became the principal church society in Sydney, assuming the position previously tenanted by the Church Association.[131] But, despite the similarities in emphasis between the two organisations, there was one crucial difference: although the P.C.E.U. had solid support from the laity, its leaders were clergymen, not laymen.

The P.C.E.U. sustained its campaign against ritualism and lawlessness throughout Smith's episcopate. Ironically, the words of Bishop Barry, that "the policy of inaction has already gone on too long, and is now morally impossible" became a slogan for Union members.[132] Indeed, in P.C.E.U. literature, Bishop Barry's words of 1887 were more than once pressed into Protestant service:

> The Church of England does not adopt the Congregational
> system. She has in her Prayer Book, with its rubrics and with
> the interpretation thereof by the ecclesiastical courts, a general
> law of public worship. If an appeal be made to the bishop on the
> ground of contravention of the law, clearly, so it seems to me, he
> must protect the law... (The Supreme Court) is the only existing

tribunal, ultimately determining what is Church law; and the alternative at present is between accepting its guidance, and leaving every bishop or clergyman to be his own law, or his own lawlessness.[133]

Law and order, not the Reformation, became the central issue for the P.C.E.U. That focus was the cause of its immediate success: the lawlessness of ritualism was an issue which every churchman could see and understand whereas the abstract distinctions between Evangelical and Anglo-Catholic doctrine were far more complex and unclear. Members of the P.C.E.U. alleged that illegal ritualism was spreading in their diocese and Archbishop Smith was doing nothing to prevent it. Eucharistic vestments, the emblem of Anglo-Catholic practice, had been used at Christ Church St. Laurence since 1884 and at St. James' King Street since 1900.[134] P.C.E.U. members were afraid that their use would spread to other parishes. Yet, the Evangelical Diocesan neither allowed their use, nor effectively banned them. Instead Smith ensured that the controversy continued unabated by announcing that although he believed vestments were illegal, he would not act until he had sought further advice from England.[135] For as long as Evangelicals believed that the law and order of their Church was being openly and unashamedly flouted by ritualists, the P.C.E.U. flourished, feeding on the anti-Catholic temperament of the larger Protestant community.[136]

The P.C.E.U.'s fear of a widespread eruption of ritualism in the Diocese was never substantiated: only two rectors ever wore vestments during Archbishop Smith's time and Anglo-Catholic practices only ever spread to one other parish, St. Saviour's, Redfern, under its idiosyncratic rector, Adam Maclean.[137] Yet the apprehensions of P.C.E.U. members were not fantastic: St. James', King Street and Christ Church St. Laurence were prominent city churches and the expectation that trends established at these centres would be imitated in the suburbs was not unreasonable.

Moreover, the 1898-1899 Kensitite campaign against popery in the Church in England, in which Protestant fanatics systematically disrupted Anglo-Catholic church services, the publication of the sensational anti-Anglo-Catholic *Secret History of the Oxford Movement* in 1897, and the unrestrained militancy of those in the Anglo-Catholic vanguard in England had not gone unnoticed by Sydney Evangelicals.[138] Together with many English churchmen they began to entertain "a genuine and uneasy feeling" that there was indeed a conspiracy to turn the Church of England into a popish church.[139] By association these Evangelicals condemned the entire High Church party and, with bad feeling rising on either side, and an Archbishop who undermined the intrinsic authority by his own position by his unwillingness to act, there was never any prospect of peace. Instead, the party antagonisms remained on the boil, the recipe for a far more unpalatable and explosive conflict which Archbishop Smith's successor would be obliged to resolve.

The significance of the incorporation of the Church Association and Churchmen's Alliance into the new P.C.E.U. was that it marked the beginning of an important shift in the ecclesiastical politics of Sydney. Previously the laity had led the Evangelical party organisations. The Church Association had been exclusively lay, and although the Alliance was strongly influenced by clerics in its ranks, Judge Foster had been chosen as its President, if only to assure the Associationists of the Alliance's friendly intentions.[140] But the appointment of Mervyn Archdall was the first formal indication of the clergy's assumption of leadership of Sydney's Evangelical party. In the fifty years after Archdall, only one layman led the Evangelical party in Sydney, Charles Richard Walsh from 1916 to 1920.[141] The clericalisation of the Evangelical leadership was a gradual process, sometimes masked by the presence of a few, quasi-clerical, laymen.[142] But from a high-water mark in the 1880s, lay participation and influence in the decision-making within Evangelical conventicles (and thus in the wider councils of the Church) steadily declined and, with it, there was a concomitant assumption of leadership by Evangelical clergymen.

After the laity's active participation in the affairs of the Church in the 1880s and early 1890s, the diminution in lay involvement from the late 1890s was surprising. But the simple explanation is that the majority of laymen lost interest in church government. In the 1880s participation in church government had been a novelty and the questions at issue were ones which directly involved the man in the pew: the financial requirements of parishes, the rationalisation of the Diocese's property, congregational participation in church building programmes and parochial policy generally. But towards the turn of the century the zeal of the laity as a whole for involvement in all councils of the Church began to flag. The financial and other mundane issues of the 1880s had been resolved and laymen began to localise their interests in the parish. Fewer of their number were willing to devote time and energy to diocesan councils and synods where the initiative in debates over less mundane, perhaps more eternal, questions was taken by those who claimed expertise and knowledge in those areas, the clergy. Significant numbers of laymen did not return to positions of influence within those wider decision-making councils until the 1960s when further rationalisation of the Church's property rapidly augmented its capital base and caused laymen to take a closer interest in the management of the Diocese, and to have their expertise in the areas of business, finance and commercial law acknowledged as valuable and essential components in the sound administration of the Diocese at the very time when theological and doctrinal knowledge was decreasingly the exclusive preserve of the clergy. But for the first sixty years of the twentieth century clerical influence, not lay, was the critical factor in Evangelical circles.[143]

VI

The 1880s and 1890s saw crucial developments in Sydney which transformed the political landscape of the Diocese. The first was the transference of power from the bishop to the laity and the clergy. Before the 1880s the locus of power had been the bishop. He was the dominant factor in diocesan government. His policies and his personal leadership abilities were the major formative elements in the development of the Diocese. This was exemplified in Bishop Barker. His avowedly Evangelical policies of recruitment and training and his strong directive leadership resulted in the development of a Diocese which was imbued with his Evangelical viewpoint.

That dominance of the bishop in diocesan government began to change from the 1880s. It was by no means a sudden or dramatic change: the authority of the bishop was still considerable. But the development of the legislative and deliberative functions of the Synod and its instrumentalities meant that the participation of the laity and clergy in the government of the Diocese increased. I This was the second crucial factor: power came to be shared by the clergy, the laity and the bishop. Bishop Barker had had a formative impact on the Diocese, but it was an influence made all the more imposing by the fact that his successors did not have the same unrivalled authority and free exercise of power which he had enjoyed.

The third vital element in these decades was a direct result of the growth of lay and clerical involvement in diocesan government, and the concomitant maturation of the institutional framework in which this transference of power could be expressed: the emergence of party organisations. The development of the legislative function of Synod in the 1880s and 1890s was essentially divisive and the product of this divisiveness was the emergence of no less than five party organisations. Henceforth, the exercise of power in the Diocese would become increasingly institutionalised and inextricably linked to the performance and fortunes of the respective political parties.

The growth of lay and clerical power, the maturation of synodical government and the concomitant emergence of institutionalised partisan activity all contributed to the propagation of division. But the high degree of party conflict during the episcopate of Archbishop Saumarez Smith can also be attributed to the fact that the Evangelical majority had chosen "a quiet administrator" and not a leader of men as the Bishop of Sydney in 1890. Smith lacked the strength of personality to achieve harmony within the Diocese. His refusal to act on a number of controversial matters exacerbated party strife and allowed divisions within the Diocese to grow deeper. The Evangelicals were particularly bitter that their chosen "good organiser" had not advanced their cause at all, but had, indeed, hindered them by his vacillating attitude to ritualist offences.[144] Ironically, when Smith died in April 1909, the call from these Evangelicals was not for a quiet organiser but for a leader of men who had vision, drive and initiative to succeed this faithful, pious "perfect non-entity" as the head of their Church.[145] Yet the archiepiscopal election which followed was the first public indication that there was no consensus within the Evangelical camp as to what direction this prospective leader should take them. It was a rift in Evangelical ranks which was the harbinger for the emergence of a new Evangelical leadership in Sydney, with interests which diverged significantly from the Protestant Church of England Union.

NOTES - CHAPTER TWO

1. Archdeacon William Cowper (77) at St. Phillip's, Sydney, Robert Cartwright (84) at Collector, and Thomas Hassall (61) at Cobbitty characterised this older Evangelical school; K.J. Cable, "Mrs. Barker and her Diary", in *B.A.H.S.J.* v.54,1,1968 pp.83-84; see tables of clergy in M.L. Loane, *Hewn From the Rock*, Anglican Information Office Sydney 1978 pp.62-63.
2. G.P. Shaw, *Patriot and Patriarch; W.G. Broughton* Melbourne Uni. Press 1978 pp.210-213, 222-228.
3. *ibid.*, pp.179-181.
4. *ibid.*, pp.209-214.
5. *ibid.*, p.179; Cable, "Mrs. Barker", p.87; The Rev. W.H. Walsh was the most advanced in ceremonial in 1855.
6. See Lists of Clergy in Loane, *Hewn*, pp.62-63, 72.
7. e.g. K.J. Cable, "Bishop Barker and his Clergy". First Moore College Library Lecture 17/4/1975. Transcript p.22.
8. Shaw, *op. cit.*, pp.84-85, 125-150, 177-178 *passim*; Cable, "Mrs. Barker", p.89.
9. 1877 Presidential Address, quoted in W.M Cowper, *The Episcopate of the Rt. Rev. Frederick Barker* Hatchards London 1888 p.346.
10. Cable, "Barker and his clergy", p.10.
11. *ibid.*
12. Charles Perry in 1850, quoted in A. de Q. Robin, *Charles Perry, Bishop of Melbourne* Uni. W.A. Press Nedlands 1967 pp.152; Cable, "Mrs. Barker", p.89.

13. *ibid.*, p.152.
14. Cable, "Barker and his Clergy", p.19.
15. Robin, *op. cit.* pp.128-129; Shaw, *op. cit.*, p.247; Cable, "Mrs. Barker", p.90.
16. M.L. Loane, *A Centenary History of Moore Theological College*, Angus and Robertson Sydney 1955 p.20.
17. Hodgson in 1855, quoted in *ibid.*, pp.19-20.
18. Loane, *Moore College*, p.32.
19. Thirty-two of Hodgson's students endorsed a testimonial on Hodgson's departure for England applauding his "decided Evangelical teaching" in "these days of doubtful disputation." See *ibid.*, pp.32, 180-183.
20. *ibid.*, pp.180-183.
21. Cable, "Mrs. Barker", p.91
22. Cable, "Barker and his clergy", pp.14-15.
23. Cable, "Mrs. Barker", pp.88-89; and "Protestant Problems in N.S.W. in the Mid Nineteenth Century", in *J.R.H.* III:2 pp.133-134.
24. Cable, "Mrs. Barker", p.88; Cable, "Barker and his clergy" pp.12-13.
25. See Frank Crowley (ed.) *A New History of Australia* Heinemann Melbourne 1976 pp.124-215 *passim* esp. pp.138-139, 148-149, 194-196.
26. See list of clergy in Loane, *Hewn* pp.90-93. 27% of all Sydney clergy in 1882 had served in the Diocese for more than 20 years; 42% more than 15 years; and of the 52% who had served 10 years or less, only one-third had been trained overseas, and all of these stayed in Sydney until they retired or died.
27. Cowper, *op. cit.*, p.346.
28. Owen Chadwick, *The Victorian Church* v.I Adam Black Sons London 1971 (3rd edition) p.527.
29. *ibid.*, p.559; vol. II (1970) pp.43ff.; 57-58.
30. *ibid.*, II, pp.75-83, 88-91

31. *ibid.*, pp.5,9; David Parker, "Fundamentalism and Conservative Protestantism in Australia 1920-1980" Unpub. Ph.D Thesis Univ. Qld. 1982 p.656.

32. Chadwick, *op. cit.*, II, p,9,

33. *ibid.*, II, p.25: Stephen Neill, *Anglicanism*, Pelican London 1965 PP.257-271.

34. Chadwick, *op. cit.*, II, pp.310, 318-319.

35. *ibid.*, pp.319-323.

36. *ibid.*, II, pp.324-325; James Bentley, *Ritualism and Politics in Victorian Britain* Oxford Uni. Press 1978 pp.80-97

37. Phillips, *op. cit.*, p.113; Robin, *op. cit.*, pp.131-147, esp. 142, 145-147; F.B. Smith, "Spiritualism in Victoria in the Nineteenth Century" in *J.R.H.* 3,3, 1965 pp.246-247, 250; Jill Roe, "Challenge and Response: Religious Life in Melbourne 1876-1886", in *J.R.H.*, 5,2, Dec. 1968 pp.158-160, 165.

38. Loane, *Moore College*, pp.31-33.

39. Robin, *op. cit.*, pp.140-143; Walter Phillips, *Defending "A Christian Country"* Uni. Queensland Press, St. Lucia 1981 p.118.

40. Cable, "Barker and his clergy", pp.5-6.

41. Phillips, *op. cit.*, pp.49, 119-122, 125.

42. Cable, "Barker and his clergy", p.15.

43. Cable, "Mrs. Barker", pp.83-84, 89; Cable, "Barker and his clergy", pp.13, 24.

44. Cable, "Barker and his clergy", p.13.

45. *ibid.*

46. See D.W.B. Robinson, "The Origins of the Anglican Church League". Second Moore College Library Lecture 9 April 1976. Transcript pp.2-3; Ruth Teale, "Party or Principle?" in *R.A.H.S.J.* v.55,2, June 1969 pp.146-147; Loane. *Moore College*. p.32.

47. Cable, "Mrs. Barker", p.84.

48. *ibid.*

49. E.D. Daw, "Electing a Primate: Alfred Barry and the Diocese of Sydney 1882-1883" in *R.A.H.S.J.* 66,4,1981 pp.252-253; Mathew

Hale to Benson 22/6/1883 v.10. f.376; Barry to Benson 30/9/1886, v.42. ff.110-111 Benson Papers.

50. quoted in Phillips, *op. cit.*, p.14; see also Daw, *op. cit.*, p.255.
51. quoted in Daw, *op. cit.*, p.237; see also Phillips, *op. cit.*, p. 100.
52. Phillips, *op. cit.*, pp.127-28.
53. *ibid.*, pp. 77, 117
54. *ibid.*, p.12, 127-128.
55. *ibid.*, pp.133-135; Daw, *op. cit.*, pp.246,253; F.B. Boyce, *Fourscore Years and Seven* Angus and Robertson Sydney 1934 pp.41-42.
56. Daw, *op. cit.*, p.237; Phillips, *op. cit.*, pp.133-136. For Barry's involvement in other Christian-secular organisations, see Richard Broome, *Treasure in Earthen Vessels* Uni. Qld. Press St. Lucia 1978 p.139.
57. Cable, "Mrs. Barker", pp.83-86.
58. See Bentley, *op. cit.*, pp.25ff., 80ff.
59. Cross and Livingstone, *op. cit.*, p.647.
60. Quoted in Phillips, *op. cit.*, p.46; Teale, *op. cit.*, p. 145
61. Teale, *op. cit.*, pp.144-145.
62. Phillips, *op. cit.*, p.46; Teale, *op. cit.*, p.145.
63. *D.T.*; 20/2/1888, quoted in Teale, *op. cit.*, p.148.
64. Rule Two of the *Rules of the Church of England Association of N.S.W.* (Sydney 188-), in the possession of Archbishop D.W.B. Robinson.
65. Cable, "Barker and his clergy", pp.3-5.
66. Half of all Barker's clergymen had attended university, but the proportion in his last years dropped markedly, *ibid.*, p.5.
67. See Crowley, *op. cit.*, pp.189-190; Cable, "Barker and his clergy", pp.5-6.
68. Phillips, *op. cit.*, pp.51,124, 159.
69. See List of Clergy, in Loane, *Hewn*, pp.90-91.
70. *ibid.*; Cable, "Barker and his clergy", pp.11-12.
71. K.J. Cable, "Good Government in the Church", The Inaugural Bishop Perry Memorial Lecture. April 1983. Transcript. pp.4-5.
72. Sydney's Diocesan Synod assented to the Sydney Church Ordinance in 1891 but it only came into force after the Church

Acts Repealing Act of 1897 was passed. See Robert Atkins; *Ordinances of the Synod of the Diocese of Sydney 1866-1908* Madgwick Sydney 1908. pp-111-112. and 119. For evidence of earlier dissatisfaction with Temporalities Act, see Phillips, *op. cit.* p.93.

73. *ibid. passim*

74. Cable, "Good Government", pp.4-5.

75. Atkins, *op. cit.*, pp.689-715.

76. R.A. Giles, *The Constitutional History of the Australian Church* Skeffington London 1929 pp.111-112.

77. H.L. Clarke, *Constitutional Church Government* SPCK London 1924 pp.130-136; W.G.S. Gotley (ed.) *The Inside Story* Sydney Diocesan Secretariat 1983 pp.111-117.

78. *Proceedings* of the 1895 Session of the Synod of the Diocese of Sydney pp.205-206 (my emphasis).

79. Atkins,*op. cit.*, pp.218-221.

80. *ibid. passim*; *Proceedings* of the Synod of the Diocese of Sydney 1866-1919; C.R. Walsh (ed.) *Ordinances of the Synod of the Diocese of Sydney 1908-1923* - Madgwick Sydney 1923.

81. As early as 1846, clergymen were querying the wisdom of the bishop's exclusive control of patronage. See Shaw, *op. cit.*, pp.197-98.

82. R.T. Davidson *The Five Lambeth Conferences* SPCK London 1920 p.200; Benson to W.S. Smith 28/8/1894 v.133 ff. 55-59; Smith to Benson 17/7/1894 v.133 ff.53-54 Benson Papers; *Verbatim Minutes of the Lambeth Conference* 1897 Conference v.41 ff. 107-109; 117, 120, 140-141, 145-146, 148.

83. For the concurrent politicisation of para-church institution such as the temperance movement, see J.D. Bollen: *Protestantism and Social Reform in New South Wales* Melbourne Uni. Press. 1972 esp. chapters 4,6.

84. *S.D.M.* June 1925 p.5. Baker's observation was particularly applicable for a large synod such as Sydney's.

85. For a discussion on "the routinization of charisma", see Sykes et al, *op. cit.*, p.8.

86. A reredos is an ornamental screen covering the wall behind the Holy Table.
87. M.A. Rodgers, "The Reredos Controversy", in *A.C.R.* 15/12/1980 pp.6-7. The substitute centre panel can still be seen today in the Cathedral.
88. Bentley. *op. cit.*, pp.97-114.
89. Mr. Justice W.J. Foster, Sir Albert Gould, Alexander Gordon, Hon. G. H. Cox, and William Beaver were just some of the prominent laymen of this period.
90. Cross and Livingstone, *op. cit.* p.839.
91. Teale, *op. cit.*, p.149; see Rules of the Church Association, *loc. cit.*
92. Teale, *op. cit.*, pp.150,156,157 Table One.
93. See Loane, *Hewn*, p.128 which implies that Barry's explicated reason was not the genuine or only cause.
94. Barry to Benson 14/5/1886, v.44.f.343, 30/9/1886 v.42. ff.110-111, 9/6/1887 v.10. ff. 376-425. Benson Papers. Barry became a Canon at Windsor in 1891, an office he held until his death in 1910, aged 84. His wife survived him.
95. Loane, *Hewn*, p.128; Loane, *Moore College*, pp.61-70; Robinson, A.C.L., p.4
96. *S.M.H.* 15/6/1889. p.6.
97. The Bishops of Goulburn, Grafton and Armidale, Perth, North Queensland, Adelaide, and Riverina voted for Moule; the Bishops of Melbourne and Bathurst voted for Smith, while Bishop Webber of Brisbane remained aloof and did not vote. Thus the vote was 6-2 in favour of Moule. Kennion to Randall Davidson 29/3/1890 v.92 f.133 Benson Papers.
98. Thomas to Kennion 31/7/1889 v.81 f.51; Thomas to Benson 25/9/1889 v.81 ff.84-85. Benson Papers.
99. Both Loane, *Hewn*, p.129 and Teale, *op.cit.* pp.151-153 infer incorrectly that Kennion'S protest was motivated by personal and churchmanship reasons, not legal reasons.
100. Kennion to Randall Davidson 21/10/1889 v.81 ff.92-93. Benson Papers.

101. Kennion to Thomas 19/8/1889 v.81. f.55; Kennion to Benson 23/9/1889 v.81 f.25; Kennion to Davidson 19/3/1890 v.92 f.133; Smith to Benson 20/3/1890 f.120. Benson Papers. See also Teale, *op.cit.*, p.153.

102. Kennion to Davidson 19/3/1890 *loc.cit.*

103. Alexander Gordon to Bishop Parry 29/10/1889 v.81 ff.103-106 Benson Papers. See also Teale, *op.cit.*, pp.152ff.

104. Montgomery to Thorold (Bp. of Rochester) 23/3/1890 v.81 ff.67-68. Benson Papers.

105. Spry Bailey in *Church of England Guardian* 22/2/1890, quoted in Teale, *op.cit.*, p.154.

106. *ibid.* The Banner ceased publication in 1892; Robinson, A.C.L., p.7.

107. Rodgers, *op.cit.*, p.7.

108. Smith to Benson 12/11/1889 v.81 ff.121-122; 18/11/1889 ff.126-127; 20/11/1889 ff.131-132; 4/12/1889 ff.150-151; 7/12/1889 ff.153-154; Benson to Smith 7/12/1889 ff.153-154.

109. Although Bishops Camidge of Bathurst and Field Flowers Goe of Melbourne voted for Smith in the first ballot, only Goe continued to support Smith after the dispute arose. Indeed Camidge was one of Bishop Kennion's most forceful supporters. Kennion to Davidson 29/3/1890 v. 90. f.133. Benson Papers.

110. Smith to Benson 17/6/1890 v.92 ff.147-8. Benson Papers.

111. Montgomery to Bp. Thorold (Rochester) 23/3/1890; Kennion to Davidson 29/3/1890. *loc.cit.*

112. See above, pp.64-67

113. *S.M.H.* 19/4/1909 p.6, 26/4/1909 p.15; Boyce, *op.cit.*, pp.141-142.

114. Teale, *op.cit.* p.154.

115. 15. Bentley, *op.cit.*, pp.119-120; Cross and Livingstone, *op.cit.*, p. 824; Chadwick, *op.cit.*, II, pp.353-354.

116. Robinson, A.C.L., pp.10-11

117. Robinson cogently suggests that the Alliance was generated out of the Evangelical enthusiasm of the 1891-1892 Grubb Mission, as an Evangelical counterpart to the Institute and from a sense of inadequacy of the Church Association. See *ibid.*, p.12.

118. *ibid.*; Teale, *op.cit.*, pp.154-155.

119. Teale, *op.cit.*, p.155.

120. See e.g. Bollen, *op.cit.*, pp.69-71.

121. Robinson, *op.cit.*, pp.10-ll; M.A. Rodgers, "The Kilburn Sisters" in *A.C.R.* 18/12/1980 pp.1,8.

122. Robinson, A.C.L., pp.12-13

123. *ibid.*, p.20.

124. Robinson, A.C.L., p.16.

125. *ibid.*; Broome, *op.cit.*, pp.87-91.

126. The affinity between the Church Association and the P.C.E.U. is illustrated by the fact that Archdall's book, *National Right and Liturgical Wrong* was published by the Association in 1899. See Mervyn Archdall, *National Right and Liturgical Wrong* Church Association London 1899. pp.307-308.

127. Broome, *op.cit.*, p.90.

128. *ibid.*

129. *ibid.* p.90. A memorial is a statement of facts as the basis of a petition.

130. *ibid.*

131. *ibid.*, p.87

132. quoted in M. Archdall, *op.cit.*, frontispiece.

133. 1887 Address, quoted in Robinson, A.C.L., p.23.

134. The Rev. Adam Maclean used vestments at St. Saviour's Redfern on occasions from 1915, and regularly from 1922. See Nigel Hubbard, *"Strive to be Faithful" The Life of Adam Robert Maclean 1869-1943* (Read before the Church of England Historical Society 1st April 1982) p.9; *S.M.H.* 18/5/1910 p.10.

135. Montgomery to Davidson 4/3/1904 B.2. Brisbane, Bishop of v.90. f.202-230; Smith to Davidson 8/2/1904 v.93 ff.246-250. Davidson Papers.

136. Broome, *op.cit.*, pp.87-88.

137. See Hubbard, *op.cit.*, pp.7-9, 15-17.

138. Chadwick, *op.cit.*, II, p.355.

139. William Sz. Smith *Memorandum ad Clerum* 11/6/1907 to 8/4/1909. Box 787 S.D.A.; Smith to Davidson 8/3/1904 B.1. 1904. Bathurst, Dean of. v.89. ff.235-240. Davidson Papers.

140. Robinson, A.C.L., p.11.

141. See A.C.L. *Minute Books* 1916-1927. 1929-1948.

142. Those laymen who became deeply involved in the affairs of the Church and spent considerable time in its service, sometimes at a cost to their businesses, could aptly be described as quasi-clerical, or "clericalised". Some examples are W.J.G. Mann,. W.R. Beaver, C.R. Walsh, and C.P. Taubman.

143. Robinson, A.C.L., p.18.

144. Montgomery to Bp. Thorold (Rochester) 23/3/1890. v.81 ff 67-68. Benson Papers

145. Sir Harry Rawson to Lord Elgin (Colonial Office) 3/3/1906. S. 24. Sydney, Archbishop of Sydney 1906. v.121. ff.251-261. Davidson Papers.

CHAPTER THREE -

A NEW LEADER FOR A NEW DIRECTION

I

In the early years of the twentieth century, Sydney churchmen were becoming increasingly concerned with the social problems which adversely affected the carrying out of an effective ministry in the city. In the nineteenth century, huge distances between country centres and a shortage of money and men had retarded the efforts of the Church of England to provide for the spiritual needs of its people. But the onset of the financial crisis of 1889 and the subsequent 1890 Great Strike demonstrated that new challenges were confronting all denominations. The colonial economy was depressed throughout the 1890s, and recovery was thwarted by the disastrous drought from 1895 to 1903.[1] These setbacks to the hitherto unbridled material progress of a young, self-conscious social democracy produced economic, industrial and social dislocations with which Sydney churchmen were forced to grapple. The difficulties of evangelism and pastoral care in the burgeoning urban environment of Sydney prompted debate on the structure of the social order, on economic inequalities and injustices, and on specific social and moral issues, such as the slums and alcoholism.[2] A nexus was extrapolated between these social and economic issues and the apparent religious indifference against which churchmen battled, and for which the empty pew bore silent testimony. In these times of perplexing social upheaval, churchmen began to acknowledge the palpable fact that the bulk of the population lived beyond the bounds of organised religion, and to conclude that the enigmatic "social question" was in large part responsible.[3] Although by 1909, social conditions had markedly improved, the anxiety of churchmen about social questions had not abated. They restlessly searched for a leader to provide them with answers.[4]

There was certainly no consensus amongst Evangelicals at this time over their approach to the perceived physical, intellectual and spiritual poverty of the masses which churchmen called "The Social Problem".[5] Men such as the rector of St. Peter's Woolloomooloo accused the Church of "quietly ignoring" the issue.[6] Others, notably Canon F.B. Boyce and the Rev. R.B.S. Hammond, responded to the problem by establishing in 1902 a special "Mission Zone" in the inner city, in which they worked for slum clearance, the material alleviation of the distress of poverty in that area, as well as preaching the Gospel.[7] But both critics and progressive activists were resisted by fellow Evangelicals who were unconvinced that the "Social Problem" could be solved by an improvement in environment, industrial reform, or a "Christianisation of wealth and property", however desirable these things might be. These opponents of the involvement of churchmen in social and structural reform were pietistic conservatives: they insisted that the only solution was Jesus Christ and the true development of the individual's personality in Him. Believers, they maintained, should devote their energies to effective evangelism, not dubious social salves.[8] Within the Evangelical school there were, therefore, significant differences of emphasis: was their primary task to preach, to heal, or could they practically combine the two? It was an issue on which no agreement could be found.[9]

The remains of William Saumarez Smith had barely been laid to rest in 1909 before the seriousness of this division within Evangelical ranks became evident. The division emerged as a disagreement over the credentials that Smith's successor should possess. Leading members of the P.C.E.U., led by Archdall and the Principal of Moore College, Nathaniel Jones, began to lobby for the nomination of a Conservative scholar, the Rev. W.H. Griffith Thomas, Principal of Wycliffe Hall, Oxford. Thomas was 48 and a regular speaker at the Islington Conference, and the Mildmay and Keswick Conventions in Britain. The pre-eminent concerns of Jones and Archdall were not social issues, but that the distinctive Evangelical tradition of the Diocese should be upheld, and that the Church in Sydney should be protected against the incremental incursions of ritualism.[10] They were confident that these concerns would be best advanced by the election of this strongly Protestant scholar and preacher.

Canon F.B. Boyce, the rector of St. Paul's Redfern, was not so sure. He had heard Thomas preach in England and "had not been impressed" with what he had heard.[11] In addition, Archbishop Saumarez Smith had been an academic and Boyce argued that the needs of the Diocese in the new century demanded a new style of leader. Boyce believed that a more practical and less bookish style of leadership would be provided by John Charles Wright, the newly-appointed Archdeacon of Manchester. Boyce believed that Wright's parish work at Bradford and Leeds and his administrative work in Manchester demonstrated a close acquaintance with the needs of a great city. Boyce made the inference that Wright was in tune with the social issues of the age and could lead Sydney churchmen in tackling these problems. Nor could Wright's Evangelical credentials be doubted: his appointment as Archdeacon indicated that Bishop E.A. Knox of Manchester, a mentor of Evangelicals throughout the world, had great confidence in Wright's abilities. Knox's 47 year old protege was a rising star in the English ecclesiastical firmament whom Boyce maintained was the modern Evangelical the Diocese of Sydney sorely required.[12]

Before the Election Synod met on the 25 May, the Evangelicals held four informal caucus meetings to discuss possible nominees. Such was the shift in power away from the laity since the 1880s that only clergymen participated in these decisive conclaves. Boyce recalled later that the first meeting backed Griffith Thomas solidly; he was the sole advocate of Wright. But, by the fourth meeting, Boyce had so powerfully argued Wright's case — by astute use of the public and church press as much as by private conversation — that the Evangelical clerics were evenly divided between the respective nominees of Canons Jones and Boyce.[13]

The failure of the Evangelicals to agree to support one candidate for the forthcoming election presented them with a danger. There was the real prospect that two nominations would split the Evangelical vote and thereby give success in the "first-past-the-post" election to a non-Evangelical. In order to obviate that eventuality this Evangelical clerical caucus agreed to submit the names of three Evangelicals to Synod: Wright, Thomas, and the Rev. F.S. Webster, of St. Thomas', Birmingham.[14] Webster's nomination was never a serious proposition but designed to ensure that the requisite three names on the Final List were all Evangelicals. Any prospect of an opportunistic non-Evangelical victory in the context of a divided Evangelicalism was thereby eliminated. There was, however, no doubt that the approaching Synod loomed as a tough, two-cornered contest between the respective backers of Thomas and Wright. The result settled the identity of the new Archbishop, and at the same time precipitated an important re-organisation of Evangelicals in Sydney.[15]

II

The election synod met on the 25 May 1909, little more than a month after the death of Archbishop Smith. This was the first time that the

Sydney Synod had been entirely free to choose its own Diocesan. The Archbishop of Sydney was no longer ex-officio Primate: in 1900, the General (national) Synod had reacted to the controversial election of Archbishop Smith in 1890 and the subsequent widespread dissatisfaction with Smith's leadership as Primate by freeing Sydney to elect its own Diocesan without reference to the Australian bishops, but, at the same time, stripping Sydney of its permanent status as Primatial See. From 1900, it was the responsibility of the Australian bishops to elect one of their number to be Primate. Now, in 1909, this change in the method of election came into operation for the first time. The 77 Sydney clergy and 130 lay representatives who constituted the Diocesan Synod were no doubt anxious to select a man who would retain the Primacy for Sydney but, by the same token, they welcomed the new autonomy they now had to elect one man to be their Father-in-God.[16]

Eight men were nominated for Archbishop. In addition to the three Evangelical candidates — Thomas, Wright and Webster — the names of one Broad Churchmen, O.T.L. Crossley of St. Kilda, Melbourne, and four High Churchmen, Bishop John Stretch of Newcastle, Archbishop Donaldson of Brisbane, and Canons Wakefield Willink of Great Yarmouth and S.A. Alexander of St. Paul's London, were also put forward. The significant feature of the nomination list was the fact that the High Church minority did not seize the opportunity presented to them by divisions in the Evangelical party and promote only one candidate. Instead they dispersed their votes over four candidates: Donaldson, Stretch, Willink and Alexander. That strategic error suggests that the High Churchmen were poorly organised and that consensus amongst them was as elusive as amongst the Evangelicals. It also meant that only the two principal Evangelical candidates Dr. Griffith Thomas and Archdeacon John Wright, had any real prospect of election.[17] The Evangelical majority was simply too large to allow the credentials of non-Evangelical nominees to be entertained for long.

A second element which became quickly evident in the debate was that the synodsmen, particularly the laity, were in no mood for a lucubrating academic. Their Archbishop had to be scholastically able, but it was clear that academic prowess was not the criterion by which they would choose their next leader. Rather, their ideal Diocesan would be a fine leader and preacher, able to command the attention of "the masses", particularly the young men who seemed to care so little for the Church's message. He had to come to grips with "the evident restlessness" outside the Church which threatened the peace within. He had to grasp the social problems of a city of more than 600,000 souls.[18] Synodsmen perceived that the need of the hour was a man who had demonstrated an ability to deal with the social issues which the growth and changes in their city over the past thirty years had precipitated. He had to be a man who, although loyal to their Reformation heritage, was a "modern" man with a breadth of outlook, which would enable him to promote concord and unity within the Church and, more generally, cause him to be "one of the moulders of the thought of our nation."[19]

These high, idealistic expectations implied, of course, an adverse judgment on the late Archbishop of Sydney, William Saumarez Smith. His lack of energy and charisma, his lack of determination and decisiveness, and his "positive horror of publicity of any kind" had denied his flock leadership.[20] Synodsmen respected his naturally retiring disposition, his humble-mindedness and his profound scholarship, but believed that the new age required a more active, vigorous leader. They wanted a man with "a new strength and a new insight: a new strength to control movements in one direction or another that may threaten the unity of the Church, and a new insight to discover eternal verities beneath forms that a democratic people may judge too harshly to be outworn."[21] Such predilections weighed heavily against the nomination of Dr. Griffith Thomas. Synodsmen vividly recalled that the late Archbishop had come to them as the academic, former principal of a theological college. How could they be certain that Thomas would be different? Would his election merely result in more of the same?

The supporters of Dr. Thomas were sensitive to this anti-intellectual backlash, and did not press Thomas' unquestioned academic qualifications. Instead, they argued that he was no introverted intellectual, but an effective communicator of the Gospel and Christian ideas. He had been a creative parish minister in London and, more recently, had edited the Churchman, which was increasingly the organ for younger Evangelicals. His supporters believed this activity clearly indicated that "while firmly attached to reformation principles, he is a man of broad outlook and catholic spirit."[22] It was a claim which was hotly contested by Boyce and other supporters of Wright. To them, Thomas was "an extreme Low Churchman" who would be unacceptable to a large body of the Australian Church, and thereby almost surely invalidate the claims of Sydney to remain the Primatial See.[23]

The supporters of Dr. Griffith Thomas were unable to convince their fellow synodsmen that they were not merely pressing for more of the same. They could not effectively refute the idea that their nominee was a Protestant academic, whose extreme Conservatism would alienate non-Evangelical churchmen. Canon Boyce and other supporters of Archdeacon Wright did not, on the other hand, have that problem. They were not swimming against the tide. They did not labour under any anti-intellectual backlash. They did not have to refute the suggestion that their man was ill-equipped for the needs of the present age: their man, they maintained, was the man for the hour. Wright had "shown in one of the great English towns... by great work personally done there, that he is an earnest powerful broadminded man... not the head of colleges or parishes or institutions so much as the maker of them."[24] The Archdeacon of Manchester, not the academic from Oxford, seemed best equipped to be the Diocese's "guiding voice...on the great questions of the day."[25]

Wright's experience in Northern English cities was attractive to synodsmen perplexed by the social, moral and religious condition of their "remarkable" age. But there was another factor which was fundamental to his election: Wright was not suspected of extreme Protestant views. The great majority of synodsmen were true sons of the Reformation. But they demurred at the extremism of many of the "red-hot Protestants" in their midst. They were all too aware the Church of England was facing a period of convulsive change in which the future character and form of worship of that Church would be determined. Men like Boyce recognised that "Evangelicals needed to close their ranks, and to avoid giving the impression of extremism."[26] Boyce was an astute politician. He realised that unless Evangelicals were unified and seen to be a positive, constructive force in the church polity, they would play little part in determining the shape of the Church of the new century. They would become defensive, occupying isolated ghettos, with little influence on the Church as a whole. To Boyce a young "modern" Evangelical such as Wright represented the best prospect for furthering Evangelical influence in the Australian Church. It was not, therefore, without point that he appealed to synodsmen to support a man who "might be described as a moderate, though indubitably loyal to the great principles of the Reformation."[27]

Dr. Griffith Thomas was too closely identified with the extremist "fighting Protestants of the vehement type".[28] Synodsmen did not question his Evangelical credentials: but they plainly perceived the need for a man "acceptable to all parties", an Evangelical who could influence the whole Church. They suspected that Thomas was not that man: indeed, one clergyman later recalled that "what killed Thomas was that the only photo (Canon Jones) had of him was with a collar and tie." That was simply too "Low Church".[29] Most synodsmen doubted that such a man could be elected Primate, that position of strategic influence which was no longer automatically held by the Sydney Bishop. Their hope for an influential

Evangelical presence in the Church of the new age was expressed by their election of John Charles Wright to the See of Sydney, by 222 votes to 76. Canon Boyce proudly beat his chest. From a position of lonely advocacy for Wright, he had secured a landslide win. He believed they had their leader at last.[30]

III

The basis for Boyce's conviction that Archdeacon Wright was the moderate modern Evangelical leader they needed can be found in Wright's leadership in England of "a kind of private movement on the part of younger and broader-minded Evangelical clergy to think and act for themselves."[31] The Group Brotherhood, as this movement came to be known, originated in late 1906 with a group of Liverpool clergymen who shared a common dissatisfaction with the condition of Evangelicalism in the Church of England.[32] Their discontent was heightened by the 1906 Report of the Royal Commission on Ecclesiastical Discipline which was the harbinger for change in the Church of England. With the very real prospect of liturgical reform, these younger Evangelicals believed there was a need for a "'newer' type of Evangelicalism which should be positive, active and liberal in its outlook."[33]

In January 1907 the "Liverpool Six" called a conference of clergymen who shared their "serious misgivings...as to the present position of Evangelicals".[34] Canon J.C. Wright was among the score who attended this meeting at which the movement was launched.[35] It was decided to establish prayer and study groups throughout the country. Study was the immediate object of the individual groups' existence because "the need to think afresh the doctrinal position of Evangelicals and to state in new terms the contribution which they had to offer the contemporary life and thought was felt to be most urgent. Our feeling", wrote the

Brotherhood's secretary, "is that the need of the moment is definiteness of teaching and unity of action on the part of younger Evangelicals." Confronted by perplexing social and moral issues, and in the face of the theological question raised by Higher Criticism, these men sought to develop a new Evangelical apologetic for the new age.[36]

Canon Wright was chairman of this Movement until he became Archbishop of Sydney in 1909. He envisaged the Movement as "an effort to increase the power and value of Evangelicalism. He deplored the fact that Evangelicalism was too often wholly negative, involving incapacity to inspire, and that it was often misrepresented in its attitude to criticism, to definite church life, and to social questions".[37] To Wright, the Brotherhood was first and foremost an attempt to examine and re-state basic Evangelical beliefs, and, then, on that basis of common doctrine, take common practical action to make Evangelicalism a more lively and influential force in the Church of England.[38]

The Brotherhood's re-statement of Evangelical doctrine distinguished its members from their more conservative fathers and brothers. The Conservative Evangelicals, for example, attacked liberal scholarship, particularly the Higher Criticism movement. The Liberal Evangelical Brotherhood, however, defended the enquiring scholarship of the age. Although they affirmed that Scripture was the basis of essential Christian Truth, they nevertheless asserted "that the serious and reverent examination of the text and origins of the books of Holy Scripture is lawful for Christian men, and cannot fail ultimately to help to a better understanding of its meaning."[39] Members of the Brotherhood firmly nailed their colours to the mast of liberal scholarship. They were confident that the Bible was the Word of God, and was *ipso facto* able to stand up to any searching, critical examination. It was only the faithlessness of men that made some fear such scholarship: "serious and reverent" learning would in fact help men to understand all the more God's revelation to them. On the question of authority, the Brotherhood re-asserted the

Reformation principle of the right of individual judgment: all external forms of authority in religion were only valid if they corresponded with an individual's spiritual experience, conscience and reason. These three elements, they maintained, could not be simply ignored by a blind insistence upon the verbal inspiration of Scripture and its absolute inerrancy.[40]

The practical measures which the Brotherhood took "to make (their) thought felt in the wider circle of church life" were modest.[41] Popular books on doctrinal, devotional and social questions were published, lectures were delivered. But the Movement's greatest influence came from what was always its focus — the private small groups. These brought like-minded clergymen together to study questions of doctrine, church order, Biblical criticism, and social problems. They were certainly not spectacular. But Wright, whose Shakespearian allusion in 1907 to "We few, we happy few, we band of brothers" inspired the name "The Group Brotherhood", perceived that these small bands of clergymen had a great mission as Liberal Evangelical Churchmen.[42] Theirs was not just a loose affiliation of small study groups. Rather they were the leaven for the whole lump, and would provide the stimulus for a period of renewal, and become the catalyst for the transformation of the character of Evangelicalism. Wright's assessment was astute, for from their number emerged the Liberal Evangelical leaders who were to be so influential in the Church of England in the 1920s and 1930s.

Wright's leadership of the Group Brotherhood in its formative years was significant for the Diocese of Sydney. It was a signpost to his concerns and attitudes as an Evangelical Churchman, attitudes which were all too infrequently articulated when he became Archbishop, but which were implicit in some of his appointments and actions. It also firmly identified his position in the Church of England. Wright may well have been a protege of the staunchly Protestant and anti-Modernistic Bishop Knox of Manchester, but his involvement in The Brotherhood demonstrated that he was no blind disciple of the old Bishop. He identified with Knox's conservatism in theology, but shared the conviction of other Liberal Evangelical members of The Brotherhood that there was a need for Evangelicals to embrace the valuable attributes of modern scholarship.[43]

Wright's influence as Chairman undoubtedly provided a constraint upon theological liberalism in The Brotherhood, and it is open to speculation to what extent his departure to Sydney was a factor in the progressive shift of the Brotherhood away from a theologically Conservative Evangelical position, and towards the theologically incoherent and indifferent position which characterised English Liberal Evangelicalism in the 1920s.[44] But even that trend did not alter Wright's affection, loyalty and attachment to the aims and ideals of the Movement which he had been instrumental in founding. He remained a member of the Group Brotherhood, and the Anglican Evangelical Group Movement which succeeded it, until his death in 1933. He was an active supporter of the affiliated group in Sydney, and, as late as 1932, proposed Sydney clergymen for membership of the A.E.G.M.[45]

IV

The election of John Charles Wright as Archbishop was a watershed for the Diocese of Sydney. It was an acknowledgement that there were tremendous social questions which churchmen had to answer, questions which directly affected the welfare of the Church and the effectiveness of its ministry. There was, after all, a clearly perceived nexus between these social, moral and religious issues and the recognised fact that a significant proportion of Australians were unchurched and religiously indifferent.

Sydney Synodsmen elected Wright in the belief that he might provide answers to these questions, and the leadership to do something about them. Events were, however, to prove that these expectations were at odds with Wright's own perception of leadership and his role as bishop: Wright had shown as chairman of the Group Brotherhood that he was pre-eminently a moderator, not a directive leader. His leadership in Sydney was substantially the same: "to make churchmen individually and the diocese as a whole rise to a sense of their own responsibilities and find their own way" of solving their problems." That meant that he regarded the bishop of a diocese "as its constitutional administrator — to administer the law and not to make it." (46) Sydney churchmen who expected him to be a charismatic, leader who had the answers were to be disappointed. In particular, Canon Boyce, Wright's main promoter, was sorely disappointed with Wright. Decades later Boyce wrote that Wright had "nothing of Bishop Barker's fighting qualities and failed to lead the Church forward on any great spiritual or moral enterprise."[47] Boyce, together with many other Sydney churchmen, failed to recognise that Wright refused to exercise power in a directive or authoritative manner, but was content for it to develop under him.

Wright's election also denoted a re-alignment of Evangelicals in the Diocese. It was the first indication of a swing away from the Conservative Evangelicalism which had dominated the Diocese for the previous two decades. The preferred nominee of the P.C.E.U. had been roundly defeated. Synodsmen had rejected a Conservative Evangelical theologian and plumped for a moderate "modern" Liberal Evangelical. It was the first tangible expression of a feeling in Sydney Evangelical circles that the Evangelical cause in the new century would not be best served by the negative belligerence typified by the Church Association and the Protestant Church of England Union. The election of an Evangelical bishop who was conservative in theology but liberal in scholarship was at once a bold and politically astute bid to keep Sydney as the Primatial See and also the product of a swing to the Evangelical centre in Sydney.[48] That trend was confirmed when a new party organisation emerged to eclipse the P.C.E.U. and harness that Evangelical impulse for consensus and conciliation. The dominance of that party, and its development into the most powerful political organisation the Diocese had ever seen, was greatly expedited by the early policies and actions of the new Archbishop.

NOTES - CHAPTER THREE

1. Crowley, *op. cit.*, p.227.
2. Bollen, *op. cit.*, pp.3, 114f, 127, 130, 134-5
3. *Census* of the Commonwealth of Australia, 1911, pp.764-771, 826-827
4. Broome, *op. cit.*, pp.2,4.
5. *ibid.*, pp-36-42: Boyce, *op. cit.*, pp. 87-111
6. *C.S.* 20/9/1912 p.15 (H.N. Baker).
7. Broome, *op. cit.*, pp.36-42.
8. *C.S.* 22/8/1913 p.4, 5/9/1913 (A.A. Yeates).
9. See Matthew 4:23.
10. For Thomas' activities and views in North America, see George M. Marsden, *Fundamentalism and American Culture: Shaping of Twentieth Century Evangelicalism 1870-1925* Oxford University Press N.Y. 1980 pp.148,168; and "Fundamentalism as an American Phenomenon: A Comparison with Evangelical Evangelicalism" in *Church History* 1977 p.222.
11. Boyce, *op. cit.*, p.145.
12. *ibid.*, pp.145-146.
13. These meetings were not held under the auspices of the P.C.E.U.; F.B.Boyce, *op. cit.*, p.146; cf. e.g. *S.M.H.* 15/5/1909 p.14, 28/5/1909 p.7.
14. Boyce, *op. cit.*, p.147.
15. Interview of John Bidwell with D.W.B. Robinson and B. Ballantine-Jones 7/8/1972. Transcript, p.14; Standing Committee Special Meeting 30/4/1909. S.C. *Minute Book IV* pp.342,345-46;

Proceedings of the Special Session of the 14th Synod of the Diocese of Sydney 25/5/1909 - 27/5/1909; *Minute Book of Synod* 1906-1920 25/5/1909 p.89.

16. Minutes of the meeting of Synod of 25/5/1909. *Minute Book of Synod 1906-20* p.90; *Proceedings* of a Special Session of the 14th Synod of the Diocese of Synod 25th May to 27th May 1909 p.17; *S.M.H.* 26/5/1909 pp.9-10.

17. *S.M.H.* 27/5/1909 p.7; 13/11/1909 p.12. These nominations were all made without the consent of the nominees.

18. *S.M.H.* 24/4/1909 p.12, 27/4/1909 p.6, 25/5/1909 p.6, and 27/5/1909 p.7.

19. *S.M.H.* 26/5/1909 pp.9-10, 27/5/1909 p.7, 28/5/1909 p.7, 13/11/1909. p.12; *C.C.* 30/6/1909 p.915.

20. Boyce, *op. cit.*, pp.142-43.

21. *S.M.H.* 19/4/1909. p.6.

22. *S.M.H.* 15/5/1909 p.14. Griffith Thomas succeeded Dean Henry Wace as editor of the *Churchman* in May 1905. His editorship was the harbinger for a distinct shift in the emphasis and outlook of this influential periodical. Its tone was still staunchly Protestant but the contributors included men who belonged to the Group Brotherhood (of which Thomas was a member): Dr. Tait, Harrington Lees, Watts Ditchfield, J.A. Harriss and F.S. Guy Warman and others, who were to lead the intellectual side of the Liberal Evangelical movement in England in the years to come. When he relinquished the editorship in September 1910, it is significant that two prominent members of the Brother- hood, Dawson Walker and Guy Warman, took over the editorship. See The *Churchman* 1898-1924.

23. 23. Boyce, *op. cit.*, p.147.

24. *S.M.H.* 27/4/1909. p.6.; 28/5/1909 p.7; 27/5/1909 p.7.

25. *S.M.H.* 26/5/1909. pp.9-10.

26. D.W.B. Robinson, A.C.L., pp. 26-27; Boyce, *op. cit.*, p.150.

27. Boyce, *op. cit.* p.146. See also *S.M.H.* 12/5/1909 p.11 and Bidwell Interview Transcript p.14.

28. Reference to Mervyn Archdall in H.M. Montgomery to R.T. Davidson 3/4/1914 1914 A.8. Archdall. Davidson Papers;
29. Bidwell Transcript, p.4.
30. *S.M.H.* 12/5/1909. p.11; 28/5/1909 p.7; 29/5/1909 p.13; Boyce *op. cit.*, p.150; The final vote was as follows:

	Clergy	Laity
WRIGHT	89	133
THOMAS	20	48
WEBSTER	4	4

31. Eugene Stock to Davidson 5/6/1909. 1909. S.27. Davidson Papers. (Stock had married Mrs. Dorothy Wright's mother, Mrs. Ivo de Vesci Fiennes, the widow of the son of the 16th Lord Saye and Sele).
32. The six Liverpool clergymen were Dr. Tait, Lisle Carr, and the Revs. B.C. Jackson (St. Bride's), A.F. Thornhill (St. Michael's-in-the-Hamlet), F.S. Guy Warman (St. Mary's Birkenhead, and Lecturer at St. Aidan's), and the vicar of Toxteth, H.E.H. Probyn. See *Minutes* of the Group Brotherhood, A.E.G.M. Papers The University Archives, Brynmor Jones Library, The University of Hull, DEM 1/14.
33. L. Hickin, Unpublished Draft of a History of.the Anglican Evangelical Group Movement p.4. A.E.G.M. Papers, Ref. No. DEM 7/24. *loc.cit.*
34. F.S.Guy Warman to _____ (Confidential Circular) n.d. (Jan 1907). *loc.cit.*
35. *Minute Book* of the Liverpool Six 1907-1911, Minutes of 1/12/1906. Ref. No. DEM 1/14. A.E.G.M. Papers. *loc.cit.* Others present at the inaugural meeting included J.E. Watts-Ditchfield, F.E. Murphy, F.T. Woods, H.V. de Candole, Cecil Wilson, Dawson Walker and Foster Carter. See also Hickin, *op.cit.* pp. 4-5.
36. Guy Warman to _____ (Confidential Circular) January 1907. A.E.G.M. Papers *loc.cit.*

37. quoted in Guy Warman, "Confidential Report of a Conference" of Clergy held at Woolton Hall, June 27-29, 1907. DEM 10/1 A.E.G.M. Papers.

38. *ibid.*

39. *ibid.* p.3.

40. *ibid.*

41. *ibid.* p.3.

42. *Henry V* Act IV, Scene III; The Liverpool Six recognised that nomenclature rapidly institutionalises movements and therefore decided against assigning a name to the gatherings they promoted. See *Minute Book* of the Liverpool Six, 2/2/1907. A.E.G.M. Papers REF. No. 1/14.

43. See E.A. Knox, *Reminiscenses of an Octagenarian* Hutchinson London 1934 pp. 324-330.

44. See Hickin, *op.cit.*, pp.8-9.

45. *A.C.R.* 14/11/1935.p.12; 28/11/1935.p.10; 9/1/1936. p.3. See Knox's obituary of Wright in the English *Record* Cited in *A.C.R.* 4/5/1933 pp.7 and 10, where Knox says the Group Movement "has diverged signally from his (Wright's) aims and intentions."

46. *S.D.M.* April 1933 p.8 (S.M. Johnstone); *S.M.H.* 10/5/1910 p.4.

47. Boyce, *op.cit.*, p.151.

48. *ibid.*, p.150; In the event, Archbishop Wright was elected Primate in 1910 by the smallest of margins. The Australian Bishops voted 12-11 to keep Sydney as the Primatial See. Wright was only elected after the other candidate, Archbishop Donaldson of Brisbane, voted against himself. I am grateful to Assoc. Prof. K.J. Cable for this information. See also *C.C.* 31/3/1910 p.3, 30/4/1910 p.9.

CHAPTER FOUR -

A CONSTITUTIONAL ADMINISTRATOR

I

The first two years of Wright's episcopate were critical to the future political environment of the Diocese of Sydney. It was a period in which it became quite clear that Wright's consciously positive Liberal Evangelicalism departed markedly from the controversial and negative style which had characterised Sydney Conservative Evangelicalism in the 1880s and 1890s. In addition, Wright made key appointments in this early period which underlined his Liberal Evangelical ethos, and these appointments had far-reaching implications for the administration and character of the Diocese in the years ahead. But above all, the first two years of Wright's episcopate were significant for a definite and declarative action on the part of the Archbishop which, in one stroke, determined the parameters of liturgical development in the Diocese for the next three decades and, with that, sealed the political fortunes of the rival church parties in the Diocese.

Archbishop Wright was commendably prompt in assuming his new duties. He was consecrated in St. Paul's Cathedral London, on the 24th August, 1909 and sailed into Sydney in November 1909, just six months after his election.[1] The election was still fresh enough in the minds of Sydney churchmen for them to be warmly enthusiastic at his coming. His supporters were excitedly expectant and even non-Evangelicals were encouraged by the flow of positive intelligence from England that Wright belonged "to that new and constantly growing group of Evangelicals which, with its more comprehensive outlook and broadened sympathies, seems likely to exercise considerable influence upon the future of religion throughout the Empire."[2] High Churchmen were heartened to know that Wright's previous service evidenced courtesy and tact: "Everywhere his influence seems to have made for peace. We hope, therefore, that even the troublous waters of the Sydney world may be calmed by his generous influence."[3]

The editor of the *Sydney Morning Herald* also had high hopes that Wright would combine his own views with "a breadth of outlook and a tolerance which enabled him to look with sympathy on convictions to which he cannot himself adhere." This, the editor adjudged, "was the secret of his election." Indeed, Wright's much-vaunted "moderation" would "temper the desire for too energetic measures to which he will be urged by extremists, who... forget that the heresy of to-day often becomes the orthodoxy of to-morrow."[4] The only apparent want of confidence in Wright came from the supporters of Griffith Thomas. Nathaniel Jones and Mervyn Archdall were noticeably silent. They had been confident that Thomas would defend the Protestantism of their Church against the ritualistic innovations which they believed threatened it. They now seemed to reserve their judgment of Wright lest this young Archbishop, highly acclaimed for his familiarity with the social needs of the age and eagerness for the cultivation of liberal scholarship, should prove soft on ritualism.

Archbishop Wright made a declarative and confident statement of his personal attitudes and intentions as Archbishop in his first Synod charge in December, 1909. He made it clear to the Synod that he was an Evangelical Churchman who was attached to an Evangelicalism

"in its positive and constructive aspect, with little stress upon the negative and controversial side inevitable to any earnest thinker, but allowed disastrously to bulk too largely in evangelicalism to the overshadowing of the great principles of the school. I claim to be an evangelical partly by heritage, but far more largely through conviction, wrought chiefly by intimacy with men of other schools of thought.."[5]

"True Evangelicalism", Wright maintained, was concerned with great truths: the direct access of every believer to God, the supremacy of the Bible, and the right of private judgment. "It is no part of true Evangelicalism," he added, "to object to surpliced choirs, to the turning to the east during the creed, or to the introduction of many small brightnesses amongst the accessories of worship." Wright was concerned that Evangelicals focus on positive essentials, not mere Protestant proclivities.[6]

The significance of this declaration was perhaps lost on his Conservative Evangelical listeners. Their new Archbishop conceded that he was not merely an Evangelical by conviction, but acknowledged that his background was a significant factor as well. Moreover, while he declared that he had independently arrived at a position of Evangelical churchmanship, he had not come to that position by some cerebral process conducted in an isolated vacuum, nor by the peer pressure of other Evangelicals, but by his intimate knowledge and contact with men of other schools of thought. It was not a conviction determined by an identification with a monochrome religious group, but one fashioned out in the midst of a plurality of opinion and beliefs.

This belief was critical to Wright's intended episcopal policy. Wright was avowedly Evangelical, but he believed in an Anglican order which permitted the expression of the wide breadth of opinion which the parameters of that order permitted. other non-Evangelical schools of thought were to be accommodated and encouraged under his administration: "It is a blunder for any man, and for any school of thought, to assume infallibility and to speak as though one expression of thought contained the whole counsel of God. In all probability it described only one side of the shield....I should regard it as lamentable", he concluded, "if a diocese found room for none but evangelicals...".[7]

The clear implication of these words was that *Evangelicals* would be the poorer without that plurality. Wright believed there was an undoubted need for the "intellectual robustness" of the Broad Churchman and the High Churchman's "emphasis upon the sacramental system of the Church, his love for the old historical order, (and) his valuable teaching of the corporate side of Church life", despite the discomfort they sometimes caused their more conservative brethren. Wright promised to try to meet that need by securing "an adequate share of representation" for different schools of thought although, he added tartly, not necessarily at each school's own estimate of itself.[8]

Wright's appointments in the first few months of 1910 were indicative of this even-handedness. In February, he appointed Canon Nathaniel Jones, and Dr. Lewis Radford, the Warden of St. Paul's College, as his examining chaplains. (Jones had backed Griffith Thomas at the election Synod, while Radford, a High Churchman, had sponsored John Willink.) In March, he made Canon Boyce the first Archdeacon of West Sydney. Thus, both ends of the ecclesiastical spectrum were recognised in the matter of judging the fitness of candidates to serve in the Diocese, while Boyce's appointment gave preferment to a man eager to see a positive and vital Evangelicalism put into practice in the city of Sydney. Later, Wright's Liberal Evangelical predilections were reflected in his appointment in 1911-1912 of two members of the Group Brotherhood, the Rev. D.J. Davies to succeed Nathaniel Jones as Principal of Moore College, and the Rev. A.E. Talbot as Dean of the Cathedral.[9]

Wright's promised even-handedness was not, however, an invitation to licence. He promised to be a bishop of a comprehensive Church, and not of one party, but he was keenly aware that the concept of comprehensiveness had been abused in England, particularly concerning liturgical variations, ritual and vestments. He was determined that the same trend should not occur under his administration. First and foremost, Wright was a constitutionalist. In England, he declared,

> Comprehensiveness has been allowed to degenerate into license.
> A parish has too often been permitted to rule a diocese...
> Comprehensiveness has its limits. The vestiarian rules of the
> Church were formulated as a compromise between those who
> wanted too much and those who would have been content with
> too little..." Wright was convinced that his role was to enforce
> those rules: "I regard the Bishop of a diocese as its constitutional
> administrator — to administer the law and not to make it.[10]

Wright's first Synod Charge was a clear expression of the attitudes and intentions of Sydney's new leader. He had openly proclaimed his own Evangelical beliefs and articulated his appreciation of the historical Anglican order, with its generous accommodation of men of differing schools of thought within comprehensive parameters. It was a declaration which gladdened the hearts of those who had hoped for moderation, and allayed High Church fears that he would not welcome their presence in the Diocese. Again, only the Conservative Evangelical P.C.E.U. members seemed to be uneasy. They appeared to be anxious lest their new Father-in-God was strong on Anglican unity, but weak on Reformation fundamentals. But, despite the anxiety of these churchmen, who seemed unconvinced by Wright's declaration that he would not tolerate illegality, there seemed every prospect that under Archbishop Wright's leadership Sydney would experience a "truce of God", a diminution of party conflict and the beginning of a new era of harmony and reconciliation with Wright as the centre of diocesan unity.[11]

That hope was quickly dashed. By late 1910, High Churchmen who had earlier praised Wright as "...a concrete example of the New

Evangelicalism which is rapidly displacing the older school of narrow Puritanism", were lampooning the same man as "the autocratic 'Pope' of Sydney".[12] Concomitantly, the P.C.E.U.'s initial wariness of Wright was replaced by thunderous applause.[13] The dramatic change was caused by Wright's refusal to accept unconditionally the clergyman nominated to him for the vacant incumbency at St. James', King Street. It was and incident which demonstrated the full implications of the Archbishop's understanding of his role as a constitutional administrator.

II

St. James' was the oldest Anglican church building in Australia, and early in Bishop Broughton's time had served as pro-cathedral. Its incumbent from 1840 to 1884, Robert Allwood, had distinct Tractarian sympathies but, in keeping with the ceremonial conservatism of the first generation of the Oxford Movement, introduced only minor liturgical changes. More ritualistic developments occurred during the ministry of Allwood's successor, Henry Latimer Jackson. By the 1880s when Jackson came to St. James', the parish was experiencing the problems associated with the demographic shift to the suburbs: attendances were diminishing; the offertories falling. Jackson's main emphasis was scholarship and the promotion of a modern message to the growing city of Sydney. But, pressed by his congregation, he also increased the range of services and brightened them, installed a robed choir, and added flowers, candles and a brass cross to the Holy Table. These minor ceremonial changes were incidental to Jackson's basic pulpit-oriented sense of mission for St. James', Yet they nevertheless forwarded the slow development of ceremonial at the church.[14]

Jackson's successor, William Carr Smith, dramatically accelerated these developments in ritual by renovating the interior of the church in

1900-1901. The huge-box pews and overhanging galleries were ill-suited to ceremonialism; they gave way to open seats, a single gallery and a new apse. Servers were introduced.[15] The transformation was complete when, in 1900, the badge of Ritualism, the chasuble, was introduced. These changes, together with the "Social Gospel" preached and practised by Carr Smith, a self-professed socialist, had a marked impact on the church. Attendance increased markedly, offertories doubled, and the number of communicants increased tenfold. The chasuble had been worn at Christ Church St. Laurence since 1884, and had been the subject of a proposed ordinance to ban its use in the Sydney Synod in 1899 and 1903. Its introduction at St. James' indicated to Evangelicals that the ritualists were on the move.[16]

The chasuble, a large round seamless garment worn by the priest, was the most distinctive of those vestments which the Church of England had discarded at the Reformation. It symbolised the priest's pre-eminent role in the sacrifice of the Mass and therefore implied the localised Presence of the Body and Blood of Christ in the bread and wine of the sacrament.[17] In addition, Anglo-Catholics expressed strong attachment to the vestments as symbolic of the continuity of the whole Catholic, or universal, Christian Church. The vestments were, in sum,

> "a sign to the world that the Eucharist of the Church of England was no bran-new (sic) Zwinglian rite, neither was it any fancied New Testament commemoration, but it was the ancient Holy Communion, Lord's Supper, Mass, or Liturgy of the whole Catholic Church. Their present use in the Church is avowedly expressive of doctrine: the vestures are only symbolic, but they enshrine the doctrine...the beautiful frame to the heavenly picture."[18]

Evangelicals rejected this view of Holy Communion. They believed that the only sacrifice at the Communion was one of praise and thanksgiving and the "living sacrifice" of the worshippers themselves; Christ was not present in the elements, but in the hearts of believing communicants. Any other assertion, they maintained, cavilled at the sufficiency of Christ's sacrifice on the Cross which gave every believer direct access to God. Christ was his mediator and advocate; he had no need for a sacrificing, mediating priest. Lastly, Evangelicals admitted that vestments were symbolic of an historical continuity: but rejected them on that very ground, because they were links with doctrines and practices which the Reformation had rejected and which, they maintained, were illegal. The issue of vestments was, above all, a matter of doctrine, not dress.[19]

III

The resignation of William Carr Smith as rector of St. James' just before Archbishop Wright arrived in November, 1909, was the harbinger of a struggle between the Anglo-Catholics and Evangelicals over the ritualist practices at that church. The number of Anglo-Catholics in Sydney was still small and only the services of Christ Church, St. Laurence and, lately, St. James' gave liturgical expression to their doctrinal position. But both Anglo-Catholics and Evangelicals saw the appointment of a new rector to St. James' as a test case. The Anglo-Catholics at St. James' — and they were by no means numerically dominant — were beginning to flex their muscles, while the Evangelicals saw the growth of Anglo-Catholic practices at the church as the thin end of the wedge for the Diocese as a whole. The Evangelicals were determined to keep Anglo-Catholicism out of Sydney, while the Anglo-Catholics were just as determined to retain and extend the usages and practices at St. James' which had begun to make it a centre of Anglo-Catholicism. The symbol of the struggle was to be the chasuble.[20]

CHAPTER FOUR - A CONSTITUTIONAL ADMINISTRATOR

The struggle over St. James' began when the Presentation Board — the five representatives of the parish and four nominators elected by Synod — were unable to agree upon one name to present to the Archbishop for appointment. The parochial nominators, on the advice of Carr Smith and others in England, had proposed the Rev. Harry Darwin Burton, of St. Alban's. For this nomination to have been successful at least one of the four synod nominators had to agree. But the synod nominators — Canons Boyce and John Vaughan, William Beaver and Charles Walsh — unanimously rejected the nomination of Burton. The parish nominators had portrayed Burton as a very "Moderate" man, but the advice which the synod nominators received from Eugene Stock, an elder statesman of the C.M.S., was to the contrary.[21] Burton, they maintained, was an extremist:

> "The question is," said Canon Boyce, "shall an extremist be appointed, and one quite different in the conduct of church services to the ordinary High Church clergymen? I draw a distinction between a high churchman and a Ritualist. I consider the gentleman desired by St. James to be a Ritualist, as he wears vestments, uses lighted candles in daylight on the Holy Table, and burns incense.[22]

The decision of the synod nominators provoked a wave of obloquy in the secular and church press. They were accused of partisanship and hypocrisy: these Protestant obscurantists, it was alleged, ignored the illegal use of the "individual cups" at Communion, a practice at two Sydney parishes, yet were intransigently legalistic in the matter of vestments.[23] One of the parochial nominators, Canon Hey Sharp, accused the Evangelical oligarchy of deliberately stacking the Presentation Board in "shamelessly intolerant" elections for the express purpose of putting "a veto on the accustomed ritual at St. James'"[24]

Sharp's complaint was legitimate. The complexion of the Presentation Board had changed so dramatically in the last year that whereas previously most nominations by parochial representatives had stood a good chance of success, now it was impossible for any nomination to succeed in which Evangelicals did not concur. In 1908, Allan Uther, a Synod representative from St. Paul's College, where Sharp was Warden, lost his seat on the Presentation Board to E. H. Rogers, of St. John's Ashfield, the Chairman of Committees of Synod. At the next session of Synod, just after the St. James' vacancy occurred, Rogers made way for C.R. Walsh, Prothonotary of the Supreme Court, an active Vice President of C.M.S. and a future President of the Anglican Church League, while the Rev. H.W. Mort, of All Saints', Woollahra, was defeated by Canon John Vaughan, of Summer Hill.[25] The synod nominators were by the end of 1909, therefore, all members of the Anglican Church League, the new Evangelical party which Boyce had been responsible in establishing. They were, in fact, its President and three of its Vice Presidents.[26] While the founders of the Anglican Church League aimed to bring Evangelicals together and project a more moderate and reasonable image, that objective was clearly not, in their eyes, inconsistent with a rapid assumption of power within the Diocese.

The deadlock at the Presentation Board was temporarily broken when Burton accepted a position in Christchurch, New Zealand, and withdrew his name from consideration for St. James'. At the second attempt the parochial nominators proposed Canon Percy Wise of Goodwood, Adelaide, whom they described as "one of the ablest preachers in Australia, (and) a splendid organiser...."[27] It was a nomination which had little chance of success: Percy Wise was at the forefront of the Anglo-Catholic movement in Australia and a man whose militant disobedience to episcopal authority proved an "almost constant source of anxiety" to Bishop Thomas of Adelaide. The synod nominators of Sydney flatly rejected Wise's nomination.[28]

CHAPTER FOUR - A CONSTITUTIONAL ADMINISTRATOR

The impasse was broken in April 1910 when the name of Joseph Kite, the Dean of Hobart, was proposed. Kite, an orthodox High Churchman, had never worn vestments. His nomination was carried by the joint Presentation Board, and his name presented to the Archbishop for appointment. The sighs of relief were many: it seemed that the controversy was over and an appointment would take place in which both parties would concur. The relief was, however, premature. Archbishop Wright, who had until now maintained a rigid silence, refused to appoint Dean Kite unless he agreed "to undertake that he would suspend the use of Vestments until in the judgment of the Archbishop of Sydney for the time being they had become *legal*."[29] Dean Kite objected to this request for a guarantee. He refused to give any such undertaking and, after further correspondence, withdrew his nomination.[30] The former incumbent, William Carr Smith, then offered to return in order to resolve the issue, but his offer was firmly rejected by the synod nominators.[31]

Wright's demand of Dean Kite was extraordinary and the Dean's umbrage was understandable. A conformist to the law, he was being required to undertake not to do something illegal. One observer caustically remarked that Wright would have been "equally justified in asking Dean Kite if he proposed to bring more than one wife with him."[32] Yet it was not an imprudent request. Wright knew that the new rector of St. James' would experience strong pressure to maintain the existing ritual and practices at the church. He was convinced that there was a push to make St. James' a centre of advanced Anglo-Catholic practice in Sydney and his hardline stance was intended to pre-empt that development. Bishop Knox of Manchester had refused to license any curate to a parish who proposed to use vestments. Knox's former Archdeacon had now gone much further than that. Free from the constraints of English patronage laws and the risk of prosecution, Wright acted against *incumbents*, not just curates. Bishop Knox could inhibit but not prevent the use of vestments;

Wright's action against Kite clearly indicated his determination to ban vestments altogether.[33]

The Archbishop's action provoked a storm of controversy. The supporters of St. James' felt cheated. They had thought that a "Tolerant Moderate Evangelical" would acquiesce in the status quo at St. James'. They had ignored Wright's long-established opinion on vestments and now, bitterly disappointed, they accused him of inconsistency, hypocrisy, and even simony.[34] They pointed the finger at Evangelicals who did not conduct daily services or celebrate Holy Communion on Holy Days, abbreviated their services, and used individual cups at Communion.[35] "Legalistic scrupulosity", these Anglo-Catholics argued, worked both ways. Wright could not "penalise one party of men and smile at the omission and active disobedience of another."[36]

The vehemence with which the St. James' lobby attacked Wright revealed the strength of personal feeling of their leaders. These sentiments were not entirely altruistic. Wright's most vocal critic, Sidney Marston, the acting rector, entertained a vain hope that he was a possible candidate for the vacant incumbency.[37] Canon Hey Sharp, the senior parochial nominator, obviously saw St. James' as a test case for parish rights against "the obscurantist tyranny of a party-controlled Synod." But it was more than just that for Sharp. After thirty years of influence in the Diocese as Chaplain to Bishop Barry and Smith and Warden of St. Paul's College, Sharp had developed in his retirement another sphere of interest, influence and ministry at St. James', King Street. It was a position which could have become tenuous if the parish's nominee was not appointed.[38]

The role of Bishop Montagu Stone-Wigg, the third 'parish leader', was more intriguing. Stone-Wigg had only retired from the Diocese of New Guinea, the stridently Anglo-Catholic missionary diocese which he had established, because of severe asthma.[39] In 1910, he was only 48, a zealous, evangelistic Anglo-Catholic, and simply not ready for an inactive retirement. Instead, he was seeking another centre of ministry, another mission field in which he could continue to promote the "rightful heritage" of Anglo-Catholicism. "The parish church of Australia", St. James' King Street, seemed the ideal centre for that ministry.[40]

That prospective situation would have been intolerable. Archbishop Wright would have found himself confronted by a rival bishop operating out of a prominent city church, whose whole propensity in doctrine and ritual were antithetical to his own. Party tensions in Sydney would have been exacerbated and the Diocese polarised under the respective leadership of the two Bishops. This prospect of episcopal confrontation was by no means improbable: Stone-Wigg had already volunteered to become the rector of St. James' in order to wear vestments and challenge Wright to prosecute him. Wright, wisely, declined to be dared.[41]

The acrimony of his opponents wounded Wright. But the "very scurrilous newspaper attacks" and the "attempts to rally all High churchmen on the plea that the rights and gains of all alike were endangered" did not surprise him. He had seen it all before in England. What hurt him most, however, was "the employment of social ostracism, so far as it will go." The newly-arrived Wright family were snubbed by people who disapproved of his action against St. James', King Street.[42]

It was a social pressure which only strengthened Wright's resolve. His experience in England had convinced him that conciliation and accommodation with those "purposeful, relentless, and never-swerving men... who have set themselves quite honestly, at any cost, to bring back the doctrine and ceremonial held in the Church of England before the Reformation" simply did not work.[43] He believed that respect for and continuance of order and authority in the polity of the Church of England demanded strong episcopal action: "With firm action then," Wright concluded, "there is no danger though there will be noise."[44] The Archbishop was, however, concerned that he had been misunderstood and misrepresented. He resolved to remedy that situation by preaching at St. James' on Sunday evening, the 5th June, 1910. There, and not in the press, he would put the record straight.

The atmosphere was highly charged that night. The church was packed, and the winter's cold did not deter a crowd of 800 from pressing up to the windows outside in the hope of hearing the Archbishop's pronouncement. Wright, despite a dose of laryngitis, delivered a powerful, unequivocal message. From the outset he tried to distinguish — and drive a wedge — between Sydney's High Churchmen and Anglo-Catholics. He dismissed the notion that he meant to "transmogrify" St. James' into a "low" church. That suggestion, Wright said, "is a deliberate falsehood. It is as a high church that I want to preserve St. James. It is only an excrescence upon true high churchmanship with which I ask you to dispense."[45] Wright perceived St. James' as a strong High Church in the tradition of Hack, Keble and Church. He denied that he wanted to sweep away their "beautiful musical service" or remove their 'Eastward Position', a practice he disliked, but considered legal. He wanted the church to be the best example of Oxford Movement churchmanship, but in strict accord with the Prayer Book.[46]

The Archbishop then explained his position on Eucharistic vestments. He rejected them on his understanding of the Act of Uniformity of 1559 *in conjunction* with the Ornaments Rubric of the Prayer Book. Each party interpreted the Rubric differently but Wright contended that vestments had been swept away by the power of the Act, not by the implications of the Rubric, and could not, therefore, be re-introduced until that Act was amended or repealed.[47]

Finally, Wright dismissed the idea that he was acting in the interests of or at the behest of a church party: "I do not do this", he assured the congregation, "under the influence of any 'counsellors' in Sydney, as some of your friends would have you believe. I have acted independently, and shall continue to do so". He was not there as the Bishop of a Party, but as the Father-in-God of them all, who had a bounden duty to uphold the law. They had a perfect right to agitate for reform, but they were not at liberty to break the law first in order to mend it afterwards."[48]

Wright was satisfied that his sermon allayed the fears of High Churchmen and conveyed to everyone that "I was standing for legality." He believed he had succeeded in isolating the Anglo-Catholics from the High Churchmen in the Diocese and that now "the Church as a body are (sic) with me."[49] The Anglo-Catholic "bitter partizans of vestments" were, however, unimpressed by Wright's legalistic stand and continued their vitriolic public campaign.[50] Wright's call for St. James' to be sweetly "nice and High Church", with lovely little services of mattins, evensong, and glorious anthems, angered them. "Churchmen", they cried, "are fighting for essentials and not for toys!" They were not to be fobbed off: "This is no question of pretty clothes, or pretty music, but of ... doctrine."[51] On that score, their Evangelical Archbishop entirely agreed. But to Wright the rejection of vestments at the Reformation was crucial: it signified "a renunciation of mediaeval theology in the cause of primitive truth."[52] Wright's position as a constitutionalist was clearly not disinterested. His legalism was reinforced by an Evangelical affirmation of the Reformed character of the Church of England.

After Wright's sermon at St. James', the parish nominators refused to co-operate with the synod nominators or the Archbishop, and the appointment lapsed to the Archbishop. Wright, however, found that the appointment of a High Churchman as rector was no easy matter. His efforts were continually frustrated by rearguard guerilla tactics by unhappy Anglo-Catholics: "...many attempts were made to preclude an appointment of a High Churchman", Wright wrote, even "several likely men being told that their life would be (made a misery ??) if they accepted."[53] Finally, Wright "called the Wardens, and frankly told them that if they would help me by not making difficulties as to payments etc., I would, as I said, appoint a good High Churchman. But," Wright warned them, "if difficulties' continued I *should* appoint — a Churchman."[54] The implication was clear. The wardens either co-operated in the appointment of an orthodox High Churchman, or found themselves lumbered with an Evangelical. They decided to "co-operate", and the Archbishop appointed the Reverend Wentworth Francis Wentworth-Sheilds, an Englishman who had lately served as Archdeacon of Wagga.[55]

The Anglo-Catholics remained resentful and muttered bitterly that Westworth-Sheilds, who promptly replaced the chasuble with the surplice but made no other liturgical changes, had sold them out.[56] Sidney Marston retreated to England, some members of the congregation joined the worshippers at Christ Church St. Laurence, and the surviving Anglo-Catholic remnant briefly vented their frustration by organising a Church Defence League to promote their Anglo-Catholic cause.[57]But "the great mass of the congregation" was relieved that the bitter struggle was over.[58] Indeed the speed with which St. James' settled down after the controversy, and the ready appreciation of Wentworth-Sheilds' ministry, was demonstrated by larger congregations, more communicants and larger collections than ever before.[59] The rapid recovery of the parish after the dispute indicated that the impulse for an acceptance of Anglo-Catholic churchmanship had not come primarily from the pew, but from the chancel. Wright's action meant that this attempt by Anglo-Catholic clergy to make St. James' a centre of advanced churchmanship was thwarted. Despite the sacramental theology and elaborate choral ritual which emerged at the church under Philip Micklem, Wentworth-Sheilds' successor, it was a blow to Anglo-Catholicism in Sydney from which it never recovered.

IV

The dispute at St. James' was significant in three ways. First, it was an early indication of the central tenet in Wright's episcopal policy: his intention to act constitutionally. Those churchmen who had hoped for charismatic initiative and leadership were quickly forced to recognise that personal inspiration and preference played little part in determining Wright's policy. He was committed to administering the law, not making or circumventing it. His benchmark for episcopal action was his understanding of the law of the Church of England: the Prayer Book, its rubrics, and the interpretations thereof by the ecclesiastical courts. These constituted a general rule of public worship which Wright would always uphold. He did not believe that a bishop had any discretionary powers beyond that law. He was, therefore, critical of English bishops who condoned incense, vestments and reservation of the sacrament, but prosecuted clergymen for conducting the service of Benediction. Wright believed that these bishops acted without authority in setting an arbitrary line between what they ignored and what they prosecuted. To Wright all the law, or none of it, had to be enforced.[60] Wright was free from the constraints which shackled his brother bishops in England and emboldened by a wide discretionary power under the Sydney Presentation Ordinance. The St. James' dispute was an early demonstration of his determination to use that position of strength in order to enforce that law. Clearly, the advent of constitutional government had come.[61]

Second, the St. James' dispute marked a crucial change in the political situation in the Diocese. Before, under Bishops Barry and Smith, Anglo-Catholics had been a small but growing force in Sydney. There had been every prospect that Sydney's High churches would imitate the trend in England and other parts of Australia in the adoption of more elaborate ritual and the nomination of more advanced Anglo-Catholic rectors. If that had occurred a significant and militant Anglo-Catholic clerical minority would have arisen in Sydney. This minority would undoubtedly have crossed swords with the Evangelical majority which, in reaction, would have rejected any suggestion of moderation and remained happily captive to a Conservative Evangelical leadership.

But the action of the synod nominators in refusing to nominate an Anglo-Catholic to St. James', together with Wright's demand that the rector not wear the chasuble, the emblem of Anglo-Catholicism, effectively stalled the development of ritualism in the Diocese. Anglo-Catholicism was nipped in the bud. Nor was Archbishop Wright's stand at St. James' an isolated case. From 1910 Wright required an undertaking from all clergymen who wished to be licensed in Sydney that they would not wear vestments (nor use separate cups at Communion).[62] The full weight of this requirement immediately fell upon the Anglo-Catholic church of Christ Church St. Laurence whose rectorship became vacant in 1911. The new rector was obliged to dispense with vestments, which had been used in that church for twenty-seven years.[63] Thus, within two years of Archbishop Wright's arrival in Sydney, Eucharistic vestments had all but disappeared from the Diocese; never to return.[64]

The prohibition of vestments did not, of course, mean that Anglo-Catholic clergymen disappeared from the Diocese. Successive rectors of Christ Church St. Laurence and the rector of St. James' from 1917 to 1938, the Rev. Dr. P.A. Micklem, were Anglo-Catholics. Nor did the ban mean that such men no longer gave ceremonial expression to their beliefs; in fact, it was often all the more elaborate at Christ Church St Laurence and St. James' King Street in the 1920s as if to compensate for that constraint. But the Archbishop's requirement effectively reduced the number of Anglo-Catholics who were willing to work in Sydney. Vestments were not optional extras for convinced Anglo-Catholics, but essential doctrinal accoutrements of their priestly ministry. Some 'mission-minded' Anglo-Catholics were willing to forego them in order to minister in the important parishes of Christ Church and St. James' but, generally, few Anglo-Catholic clergymen were happy to serve in an ordinary Sydney parish under such conditions. Their natural preference was a parish in another diocese in which they could give full liturgical expression to their doctrinal beliefs.

Third, the St. James' dispute was also crucial for Evangelicalism in the Sydney Diocese. After it, the swing to the Evangelical centre, which was evident in the election of Dr. Wright, became even more pronounced. Previously, Conservative Evangelicals had prospered because they could focus on the inroads that Anglo-Catholicism had made in the Diocese during the episcopates of Barry and Smith. The practical, tangible issue of ritualism was always at the centre of their campaign. But the advent of a regime of constitutional government and its triumph over ritualism denied the P.C.E.U., the Conservative Evangelical party whose *raison d'etre* was a legalistic anti-ritualism, the very conditions upon which its political influence depended. The swing to the Evangelical centre was not therefore hindered by a polarised political context. Moderate Evangelicals were not transformed into Conservative Evangelical extremists in reaction to a growing Anglo-Catholic presence. Instead the trend towards Evangelical consensus continued unencumbered as the conservative laity quickly accepted a less extreme Evangelical leadership. It was a political climate in which a party which sought to be the focus and expression of Evanglical consolidation prospered. The evolution of that new party, the Anglican Church League, was not only fundamental to the history of the Sydney Diocese, but also provided a unique opportunity for study of the concept, practice and development of a party organisation in the Anglican polity.

NOTES - CHAPTER FOUR

1. Wright to Davidson 9/6/1909; Wright to Davidson 18/6/1909; Davidson to Wright 13/6/1909; Wright to Davidson 28/8/1909. *loc.cit.*
2. *C.C.* 31/7/1909,p.934, citing *The Guardian*.
3. *C.C.* 31/8/1909 p.949.
4. *S.M.H.* 13/11/1909 P.12 (editor)
5. *S.M.H.* 7/12/1909 p.10. *Proceedings* of Synod of the Diocese of Sydney December 1909 p.36.
6. *ibid.*, pp.36-37.
7. *ibid.* PP.37-39; *S.M.H.* 7/12/1909 p.10.
8. *S.M.H.* 7/12/1909 p.10; *Proceedings* of Synod of the Diocese of Sydney December 1909 pp.36-39.
9. Loane. *Moore College* . pp.113-114.
10. *S.M.H.* 7/12/1909 p.10.;*Proceedings* of Synod of the Diocese of Sydney December 1909 pp.36-39.
11. *C.S.* 14/5/1912 pp.1, 6; 25/7/1912 p.1; 16/8/1912 p.7.
12. *C.C.* 31/3/1910.p.3; 29/4/1911 p.7.
13. Robinson, *A.C.L.*, pp.23-24.
14. K.J: Cable, "St. James' King Street 1819-1894 Pt. II" in *R.A.H.S.J.* v.50. pt.5, p.358; and "Liturgy at St. James', King Street", Transcript of Lecture given at the Church on 28 June 1981 p.3.
15. Teale, *op. cit.*, p.145; "Former Parishioner" (Lr to ed) *S.M.H.*; 18/5/1910. p.11; K.J. Cable, *St. James' Church, Sydney*. The Churchwardens. Sydney 1982 p.38.
16. *ibid.*

17. Cross and Livingstone, *op. cit.*, pp.271-272, 475-478.
18. *C.C.* 31/5/1910.p.5.
19. Cable, "Liturgy", p.4; Owen Chadwick *The Victorian Church* vol. II, Adam and Charles Black London 1980 p.317. Chadwick clearly believes that vestments were legal; Cross and Livingstone, *op. cit.*, p.1012.
20. *C.C.*, 30/10/1909 p.985, 31/1/1910 p.9.
21. *S.M.H.* 12/5/1910 p.10.
22. *D.T.* 18/2/1910 p.4. The parish representatives of St. James' were Dr. Cyril Corlette, Messrs. S.H. Young, T.L. Grainger, and A.H. Bird and Canon William Hey Sharp.
23. *S.M.H.* 18/2/1910 p.5, 19/2/1910 p.5, 25/2/1910 p.8.
24. *ibid.* 18/2/1910 p.5, 22/2/1910 p.9.
25. See Sydney Diocesan *Year Books* 1908-1909; *S.M.H.* 18/2/1910 p.5. This was, I believe, the first electoral success of the A.C.L. which had only been established in 1909. It was a stunning inauguration.
26. See A.C.L. membership records. The papers of Hugh A. Corish, Moore Theological College Library.
27. *S.M.H.* 24/3/1910 p.10.
28. A. Nutter Thomas to Davidson 5/3/1920. 1926.A.27. Davidson Papers; Thomas to Clergy "Ad Clerum", 20/4/1921, in which he hoped the Goodwood parish would relinquish its attitude of aloofness of the last 12 years. *loc.cit.*
29. *S.M.H.* 20/4/1910 p.8.
30. Wright to Davidson 15/1/1911. 1911.S.34. Sydney. Davidson Papers.
31. *S.M.H.* 12/5/1910. p.8; 14/5/1910 p.8; 27/5/1010 p.8; *C.C.* 30/7/1910 p.11.
32. *S.M.H.* 11/10/1910 p.10.
33. E.A.Knox, *op.cit.*, pp.303-308. The patronage laws in England meant that bishops had far less authority and influence over incumbents. Knox could have been sued if he had acted against incumbents; he could only prevent curates wearing vestments by refusing to license them. Wright had far greater discretion under the terms of the Presentation Ordinance.

34. *S.M.H.* 17/5/1910 p.12; 26/5/1910 p.6.
35. *S.M.H.* 21/5/1910 p.8, 26/5/1910. p.6, 13/6/1910.p.7, 28/5/1910. p.11; C49; 31/8/1910. pp.8-9.
36. *C.C.* 31/8/1910 pp.8-9.
37. *S.M.H.* 17/4/1909.p.11, 22/2/1910.p.9, 13/6/1910. p.7, 21/5/1910.p.8, 26/10/1910.p.11, 12/10/1910.p.15.
38. *ibid.* 18/2/1910.p.5.
39. For a good portrait of Montagu Stone-Wigg, see David Wetherell, *Reluctant Mission: The Anglican Church Papua New Guinea 1821-1942*, Uni. Qld Press St. Lucia 1977 pp.40-94.
40. *C.C.* 30/9/1910 pp.12-15; *S.M.H.* 17/4/1909 p;11, 22/2/1910 p.9, 17/5/1910 p.3. Stone-Wigg became parochial nominator at St. James' in 1912, succeeding Canon Hey Sharp.
41. *Australian Churchman* 9/7/1910 p-8; Stone-Wigg finally found a larger sphere of influence in launching the *Church Standard* in 1912. He edited this national Anglo-Catholic paper until his death in 1918. The *Church Standard* had a circulation of 6,000 in 1913. *C.S.* 14/5/1915. p.4; 22/8/1913.
42. Wright to Davidson 15/1/1911, Davidson Papers.
43. *D.T.* 18/5/1910. p.11.
44. Wright to Davidson 7/6/1910. 1910.S.34. Sydney, Bishop of. Davidson Papers.
45. *S.M.H.* 6/6/1910 p.7.
46. *ibid.*, *D.T.* 6/6/1910 p.7.
47. *ibid.*
48. *ibid.*; Wright to Davidson 7/6/1910; Wright to Davidson 15/1/1911. *loc.cit.*
49. Wright to Davidson 15/1/1911. Davidson Papers.
50. *ibid.*
51. *C.C.* 30/6/1909 p.920, 30/6/1910. pp.5-6.
52. *Australian Churchman* 6/8/1910. p.10; Wright to Davidson 15/1/1911 *loc.cit.*
53. Wright to Davidson 15/1/1911 *loc.cit.* (three words unclear)
54. *ibid.* (Wright's emphasis).

55. *ibid.* 30/7/1910.p.11.
56. *C.C.* 31/8/1910 p.5.
57. *S.M.H.* 11/10/1910 p.10. Marston returned to the West Country in England, was chaplain to Earl Beauchamp (who as Governor of N.S.W. had given St. James' its first eucharistic vestments) for a year, before becoming the rector of Dymock in the Diocese of Gloucester for 26 years, until the parish was sequestered in 1937.
58. Wright to Davidson 5/9/1910 *loc.cit.*
59. *ibid.*; Cable. *St. James' Sydney*, p.42
60. *Proceedings* of the Synod of the Diocese of Sydney. December 1910. pp.36-7.
61. *ibid.* Robinson, A.C.L., pp.23-24; Wright to Davidson 7/6/1910; 11/4/1911. Davidson Papers.
62. Re: the regulations which Wright required all clergy to sign, see Wright to Davidson 11/4/11, 13/5/11. 1911. S.34; Montagu Stone-Wigg to Davidson 18/3/1913 1913.A.20 Australia. Davidson Papers.
63. Re: Christ Church dispute, see *S.M.H.* 5/4/11 p.11, 6/4/11 p.8, 15/4/11 p.6, 17/1/11 p.11, 29/4/11 p.9, 22/5/11 p.8, 26/5/11 p.7, 27/5/11 p.7, 22/6/11 p.24; *C.C.* 31/7/11 p.5, 31/8/11 pp.4,9.
64. The Rev. Adam Maclean, the Irish rector of the struggling parish of St. Saviour's, Redfern, had been licensed by Archbishop Smith in 1906, and wore the chasuble in that parish occasionally from 1915 and invariably from 1922 until his death in 1943. See Nigel Hubbard, *"Strive to be Faithful": The Life of Adam Robert Maclean 1869-1943.* Read before the Church of England Historical Society 1/4/1982. p.9.

CHAPTER FIVE - THE "VERY
WONDERFUL WAY" TO POWER

I

Political parties occupy a singularly prominent position in secular polities. In a totalitarian state, the party constitutes the decision-making caucus of the State: the State becomes a larger manifestation of the will of the Party, and causes that will to be implemented. By contrast, the political party in the West is a mere private association to which the law gives no more rights or duties than it bestows upon any other private organisation. Yet these private associations are fundamental to Western civil order and government. The democratic polity necessitates the existence of political elites in and around which the effective organisation of opinion can take place. The very need to govern implies the existence of decision-making elites and the presence of "opposing" outer rings which would govern but for the superior power of the dominant elite.[1]

A party derives that power through a representative function which is expressed in two ways. First, the party pre-selects candidates who thereby owe loyalty — and their seat — to the party. Second, the party adopts policies and articulates opinions which these candidates, and the party as a whole, present to the constituency as the party's platform. Theoretically, this platform represents the opinion of its supporters, but in practice the political party seeks to win the support of the constituency to its point of view.[2] This method of exercising power is not confined to the political system of the state. Parties facilitate decision-making by the effective organisation of opinion in trade unions, schools, businesses, and even university faculties. They may not have a name or official membership — and their power may be all the greater because of that — but they certainly exist, representing a wide range of opinions, and testifying to the pluralism of many of our social institutions.[3]

In a comprehensive polity such as the Church of England, in which men with definite theoretical differences uneasily co-exist, parties have long existed as the means by which differences of opinion are effectively organised and expressed. In England, church party organisation became particularly evident in the late eighteenth century in the form of critical interest groups or societies such as the Clapham and Clapton sects. Until the late nineteenth century these parties were never more than very general opinion groupings which in turn spawned 'action' groups such as missionary societies and financial trusts designed to promote their cause.[4] These English coteries were not organised parties in the modern sense: they did not control the decision-making processes; they could only attempt to influence them. They never had direct power because the Established nature of the Church meant that the Crown, not churchmen, appointed bishops and other church leaders. Nor did the Church have an autonomous legislature: Convocation could not legislate for the Church. In this political milieu, church parties were free to influence and lobby, but they were denied the means to exercise power.[5]

These constraints of Establishment were absent in Australia.[6] There was no outside, intrusive decision-making forum like Parliament. Although the legal nexus with the Church in England was an inhibiting factor, the affairs of the Church were nevertheless determined by churchmen. Initially, the bishop was the sole decision-maker but, with the advent of synodical government, the locus of power shifted to the clergy and laity and decision-making was increasingly shared. With that development, church parties were not only able to influence and lobby, but to participate actively in the processes of power.[7]

The evolution of more definite party structures in Sydney closely parallels the development of synodical government in the Diocese. It was noted in Chapter Two that the legislative function of Sydney's synod had been undeveloped in the episcopate of Bishop Barker and the synod's principal function had been consultative rather than deliberative. The government of the Diocese had been primarily Barker's responsibility and not the concern of the clergy or laity.[8] That began to change under Barker's successors. Power began to shift from the bishop to the clergy and laity under Bishop Barry and Bishop (from 1897, Archbishop) Smith. This development was evident across a broad front — the implementation of self-determining property acts, the cultivation of parish councils and committees, and the growth in power of an effective and deliberative Standing Committee — but was best exemplified in the dramatic maturation of the legislative function of the diocesan synod.[9] Matters which had previously been unilaterally decided by the bishop, now came before the Synod for deliberation. In two decades, the volume of legislation passed by the Synod increased five fold as the Synod, not the bishop, became the centre of diocesan government.[10]

The increased intrusiveness of the Synod into the affairs of diocesan government was not restricted to financial and property matters, or to legislation which regulated Sydney's relationship with the other Australian dioceses. Synod also began to assert itself in areas which had traditionally been dominated by the bishop. The appointment of parochial clergy was one such area. Before 1869, the Bishop had sole responsibility to regulate and direct the clerical force at his disposal.[11] This considerable power was circumscribed in 1869 when a parish was given the right, subject to certain conditions, to have its minister selected by a Presentation Board consisting of representatives from both the parish and the synod.[12] That

Board nominated a clergyman to the Bishop who invariably appointed the nominee although, if he had "good and sufficient reason", he could exercise a veto.[13]

In 1895, however, the Evangelical-dominated Synod changed the structure of this Board to give the synod nominators an effective veto as well as the Bishop. The new ordinance provided for five parish representatives and four synod nominators but ruled that a majority of synod nominators had to be present before the Board could even meet: if two or more synod nominators knew or feared that a prospective meeting of the Board would go.against them, they could boycott the meeting.[14] In addition, at least one synod nominator had to support the nomination before it could be presented to the Archbishop. Thus the Synod, through its representatives, had a powerful and decisive voice in the appointment of clergymen. They were able to determine what sort of clergymen could serve in the Diocese, and which clergymen in the Diocese should be given preferment. The discretionary power which had once belonged to the Bishop alone was now shared between bishop, clergy and laity. It was a typical example of the dispersement of authority which promoted party organisation. It meant that party elders not only became concerned that the right man was elected Bishop of the Diocese but also that the four positions as synod nominators were filled by party men.

Synodsmen came to demand a say on spiritual questions as well. It was noted earlier that Mervyn Archdall unsuccessfully introduced ordinances at the 1899 and 1903 synods which would have banned the use of vestments in the Diocese.[15] Yet in 1904, the Evangelicals were more successful in passing an ordinance which gave the Synod a powerful influence in the discipline of clergymen. Previously the Bishop had determined whether a clergyman should be tried for heresy, breach of ritual laws, dereliction of duty, schism, or immoral behaviour. From 1904, this power was transferred to a Council of Reference to which the synod elected three churchmen, while the Archbishop appointed only two. Thus, in less than a decade, the Synod had assumed a powerful influence in areas which had long been dominated by the authority of the Bishop and which were crucial in determining the future character of the Diocese: the appointment and discipline of clergy.[16]

The development of this legislative power encouraged the emergence of parties and, in sharp contrast to the mere lobbying of English parties, meant that party leaders could, if their party won control of Synod, actually become the Diocese's decision-makers, exercising governmental power in much the same way as secular party leaders. Indeed, political developments in the ecclesiastical polity reflected the changes which were taking place in the Australian secular political scene. The pressure for change which was induced by the depression of the 1890s precipitated a restructuring of the political order which saw the demise of the loosely organised parliamentary factions which had hitherto dominated colonial politics. The success of the new Labor party which won 35 seats in the 1891 N.S.W. election heralded the emergence of highly organised and disciplined parties which appealed to specific sectional interests. The Australian Labor Party employed caucus methods which were more frequent, more effective and more binding than anything previously seen in the colony.[17] It was an organisational device which was soon imitated by non-Labor political groups and "by the end of the 1890s political groupings were fewer in number, more cohesive and better organised than ever before; independents were a fast, vanishing breed."[18] It was a description which was equally applicable to ecclesiastical politics in Sydney one decade later.

Before 1909, no church party in Sydney was geared to capture the Synod and thereby wield quasi-governmental power. One major reason was that just as the idea of class or sectional parties was anathema in nineteenth century secular politics the very concept of "party" and party organisation had pejorative connotations in the nineteenth century church.[19] They were considered factious organisations, a blot on the ideal of a Church whose members were enjoined to make "every effort to keep the unity of the Spirit through the bond of peace."[20] Churchmen acceded to the formation of societies with common goals and interests within the Church as "an inevitable outcome of a fundamental instinct of human nature — the gregarious instinct", but there was nevertheless a niggling, residual feeling that parties were a carnal and un-Christlike feature of their common life.[21] All churchmen deplored the existence of "the mark of the devil" — partisanship, or party spirit.[22]

The circumspection of nineteenth churchmen towards party organisations ensured that only extremists attempted to translate grass roots support into numbers in synod. Of the five party organisations in Sydney before 1909, only the Church Association and English Church Union attempted to make their societies a political force in the Synod, and only the Association recorded any success in that endeavour. The other nineteenth century party organisations in the Sydney Diocese did not resort to overtly political methods to achieve their goals, but contented themselves with the means of propaganda.[23] They preferred the pulpit, the platform and the press to "how-to-vote" tickets and the ballot box.[24]

The cautiousness of most churchmen to "party" began to disappear in the first years of the twentieth century. Although they continued to decry a factious spirit as a device of the Evil One", prominent churchmen began to concede that there was perhaps nothing wrong with parties in themselves, provided they "promoted the corporate life".[25] Indeed parties began to be regarded by some as positive blessings, necessary to the effectiveness, richness, variety and progress of the Church.[26] Some party members began to be openly proud of their membership. and while most churchmen did not join a party organisation, they nevertheless began to admit that each party stood for some important elements of the whole Truth.[27] Non-aligned churchmen considered that although the methods of extremists were often disagreeable these zealots presented neglected truths to the whole Body. One Australian bishop even suggested that the Church owed nearly all its great reforms to partisans who had "shown a valour, a self-sacrifice, a consuming love of the truth as they see it, a sustained and sustaining enthusiasm which often puts utterly to shame the coldness of more balanced minds."[28]

The new respectability of active party organisation in these first years of the twentieth century, together with the augmented legislative function of the Synod, was fertile ground for an ecclesiastical party which promised the acceptable party goals of consensus and consolidation, and rejected the exclusivist objectives of extreme partisans. That new Sydney party was the Anglican Church League.

II

The architect of this new Evangelical party was the man responsible for the election of Wright as Archbishop, Francis Bertie Boyce. Boyce was at the height of his power in the Diocese. Early in 1909, he had succeeded in persuading synodsmen to eschew extremism in their choice of Archbishop and elect a young Liberal Evangelical. On that occasion he had argued for a leader who would unite all Evangelicals and weld them into a constructive positive force in the church polity.[29]

That campaign for Wright in preference to Griffith Thomas, and Boyce's initiative in the establishment of a new party were, in fact, two sides of the one coin. Both were attempts to provide as broad a base as possible by which Evangelicals could effectively prepare for the future while not jettisoning their Reformation past.[30] But although the success of the campaign for Wright was in itself a definite catalyst in the establishment of the new Evangelical party, the character and principles of this party were once again strongly influenced by an English model, the National Church League.

The N.C.L. was the product of an amalgamation in 1906 of the National Protestant Church Union and the Church of England League.

By 1909 the N.C.L. had become "the strongest organisation that Evangelicals have ever possessed."[31] Boyce was quick to recognise the significance of that structural re-arrangement: the N.C.L. had come hot on the heels of the publication of the Report of the Royal Commission on Ecclesiastical Discipline. This Report had justified the Evangelical position on ritualism but had at the same time effectively undercut it, by concluding that the law of public worship in the Church of England was unduly restrictive for the new age, and should be reformed. The upshot of the Report — a series of moves in Convocation to make those laws less restrictive — gravely concerned all parties in the Church. The future character of their Church was at stake. Evangelicals in. England readily recognised that if they were to take any effective part in this revision and reformation of the order and liturgy of the Church, they had to organise themselves into a united front, and, if their viewpoint was to influence others, they had to avoid the appearance of an extreme lunatic fringe.[32]

Australian Evangelicals like Boyce wanted to share in that campaign. They wanted to make "common cause with their English brothers."[33] But to have that share they too needed to re-organise themselves into a new institution with a more 'reasonable' image: they too had to avoid the Church Association extremism. The evidence is sketchy but there seems little doubt that this strong sense of affinity with England was a major factor in the re-structuring of party forces in Sydney which resulted in the emergence of the A.C.L.:

...somebody got connected with the Church League in England (sic)", recalled John Bidwell, "and Archdeacon Boyce (and others) discussed it, and then they called a meeting, and decided to drop the Church of England Union (sic) and form up the Anglican Church League. Some of them objected to the name 'Anglican'. They thought it was just too much of a high churchman.

Anyhow, they accepted it. That was in 1909.... Old Archdeacon Boyce was the first President...the idea ...was so they could have link with the National Church League..(but)..they didn't really want to call it National because of the one in England.[34]

The A.C.L.'s constitution reflected these English roots: it not only affiliated itself to the National Church League and embraced all its Principles, but it also decided that its Constitution could only be altered with the express approval of the N.C.L. These Sydney Evangelicals clung determinedly to the Mother Church's apron strings. They wanted English superintendence to ensure the continuing Evangelical purity of the new party.

The emergence of this "centre-unity" Evangelical party for the new age had a telling impact on the existing Conservative Evangelical party, the Protestant Church of England Union. The Union continued to function after the formation of the League, although many of its members and sympathisers had transferred their allegiance to the A.C.L., but when Archbishop Wright banned the use of vestments at St. James' and Christ Church in 1910 and 1911 and demonstrated his determination to administer constitutionally, it spelt the end for the P.C.E.U. The Union's leaders were certainly cheered by Wright's stand, but they also recognised that the writing was on the wall for the P.C.E.U.: "With the advent of constitutional government", concluded one Union member, "the first stage of the Union's work may be said to have come to an end. The aspect of its work upon which it now enters is the educational one."[35] That shift in focus could not hide the fact that the days of the P.C.E.U. were numbered. The struggle against ritualism had been won and the Union had had little to do with the victory: it applauded but could take none of the kudos for the ritualists' defeat.[36]

The Union's attempt to educate churchmen on theologically esoteric issues was doomed to fail. By 1914, the party was experiencing problems of identity and suffering from a fall in membership. More than this, it had a leadership problem. Its founder, Mervyn Archdall, had relinquished the presidency of the Union in 1907 when he had moved from Balmain to Penrith, and his successors simply did not have the energy, passionate drive nor vision for the task of rejuvenating an enervated party. Without the firebrand Archdall as leader and without the immediate presence and threat of the ritualist enemy, the Union simply ran out of steam. It continued its modest programmes of lectures and literature, borne on more by loyalty to Archdall than by any enthusiastic sense of purpose.[37] But with Archdall's death in 1917, the Union quickly folded. The tie of loyalty had gone and with the League having demonstrated its power and Evangelical "soundness", virtually all of the Union's members transferred their allegiance to the A.C.L., where many former P.C.E.U. office bearers soon assumed positions of prominence and responsibility. The League, not the Union, was now the Inner Ring.[38]

III

In its early years the Anglican Church League was not narrowly partisan. In 1914, one of its Vice Presidents, Archdeacon (later Bishop) Gerard D'Arcy-Irvine, claimed that the A.C.L. stood for "central churchmanship, which implied spiritual, strong and scholarly churchmanship, and fought for the principles of the reformation upon which the character of future generations depended."[39] This is a significant self-perception. These Evangelicals believed that their position was truly central to the authentic character of the Church of England as Catholic, Apostolic, Protestant and Reformed. They were not about to be isolated as a lunatic fringe; nor were they about to surrender the "catholic and apostolic" attributes of the Church to their opponents. They were determined to be a party of comprehension, not narrowly exclusive.[40] From the party's inception its leaders sought to have a considerable breadth in membership, and embrace a wide range of Evangelical ideals. The result was that staunch Conservative Evangelicals stood shoulder to shoulder with men who held more Liberal Evangelical views.[41] It was a coalition which was never without a modicum of tension, but it was a tension which proved to be a creative and positive dynamic for the League in its early years.[42]

The League's real political strength was not, however, based on the attractive ideals of an Evangelical consensus which welded all sorts of Evangelicals into a happy coalition. These were certainly important features of the League's electoral appeal. But the conversion of that appeal into political success was due to the effective structural organisation of the League as a political machine in an environment which was increasingly conducive to party organisation.

The A.C.L. was never very large: Whereas the P.C.E.U.'s membership peaked at about 600, the League never had more than 163 members, and was usually no more than 100. Indeed between the years 1909 and 1939 there was a total of only 305 members in the League — 170 laymen and 131 clergy.[43] This small size was the A.C.L.'s strength. It made it possible for tensions within the coalition to be internally managed and contained; in a larger party such tensions often emasculated decision-making and action. The League's small membership also meant that it could perform as a caucus which ostensibly involved about half of the League's members in the party's decision-making processes. The Annual Meeting of the League elected a Council of 12 clergy and 12 laymen as a standing committee of the League for the year. The A.G.M. also elected the League's President, Clerical and Lay Secretaries, Treasurer, and Chairman of Committees, and these office-bearers attended and voted at Council meetings.[44] In addition, the twenty-nine councillors and office-bearers were joined at Council meetings by between 24 and 33 elected Vice Presidents.[45] The presence of these elder statesmen of the party served to protect the Evangelical "soundness" of the League, and constituted an effective check against radical or heterodox action on the part of the Council, a power that they did not hesitate to use.[46] The Vice presidents also dominated the smaller Inner Ring of the council, the twenty member Executive Council. This oligarchy, first established in 1919, was responsible for the agenda of the Council meetings, and thereby controlled and channelled the initiatives of that body, and of the League as a whole. While not theoretically denying councillors and the rank and file members of the League participation in the League's decision-making, the Executive nevertheless consolidated effective control into the hands of a few.[47]

No other ecclesiastical party in Sydney's history had been so well organised, and this organisational structure was crucial to the success of the A.C.L. Its comparatively small membership, while clearly reflecting a broad base of sympathetic support, facilitated the sort of effective political decision-making and action which often eluded parties with much larger memberships. Moreover, although the high degree of participation by the rank and file members in the League's decision-making gave the impression that the party was democratic, and mitigated unhappiness in the ranks, clear and unequivocal direction was always assured by the presence of a small inner group which behaved as a Cabinet.

This highly structured party machine was the means by which the Anglican Church League was able to formulate and implement its policy. But that implementation was not in any way spectacular. Whereas the P.C.E.U. organised lecture series and in its hey-day held "monster" public meetings, A.C.L. members remained resolutely in the back room: "We just used to work quietly, you know," recalled Bidwell.[48] That quiet organisation took many different forms. The League maintained a close watch on every aspect of life in the Diocese of Sydney; it monitored events in other Australian dioceses and occasionally took a paternalistic concern for Evangelical associations in those dioceses; it encouraged the publication of a new Evangelical newspaper; and, most important of all, it deeply involved itself in the politics of the Diocese. It was through all of these activities that the A.C.L. achieved an unrivalled political prominence.

The League's close watch of events in the Diocese was expressed in both positive and negative ways. There were successive propaganda campaigns to educate the uninstructed laity in the essentials of Evangelical Truth and the falsehoods of Modernism and Anglo-Catholicism. Numerous tracts and papers on liturgy, ritual and worship were published. Lectures were organised for the League's own membership on subjects of pressing concern: Reservation of the Elements and Prayers for the Dead in the war years; spiritualism in the immediate post-war period; Prayer Book Revision in the mid 'Twenties; and, increasingly, the question of the Nexus with England and the Constitution. The number who attended these lectures was never very» large: at most sixty League members attended them. But the small number belied their importance: these men were invariably the opinion— and decision-makers of the Diocese. These meetings served to formulate their opinions.[49]

The League also acted as a vigilance group. It initiated a successful protest in 1919 against the proposed outdoor crucifix at St. James', King Street; in 1926, it brought pressure to bear, through its members on the Standing Committee, against the proposal to hold an Anglo-Catholic conference in Sydney; in 1927, the League's attention was drawn to the alleged domination of the Lay Readers' Association by "avowed Anglo-Catholics"; in 1930, a lay member of the Council "exposed" an Anglo-Catholic cell at Moore College; and the League regularly monitored and condemned the Anglo-Catholic ceremonial at Christ Church, St. Laurence, and St. James', King Street. The field under surveillance was very broad.[50]

This watchdog vigilance was not confined to the horizons of the Diocese of Sydney. In the early 1920s the League kept a wary eye on the new Community of the Ascension in the Diocese of Goulburn. Articles were published against the "romanising tendencies" of the Community, and prominent Goulburn laymen were lobbied to stop its establishment. (51) At about the same time the League did what it could to secure the election to the bishopric of Grafton of one "who would maintain the Evangelical position."[52] These extra-diocesan interests of the League did not, however, ever become significant A.C.L. portfolios. Its leaders sensibly consolidated their strength and concentrated their energies upon their own diocesan activities. Thus, although the League always expressed hearty interest in "the idea of stimulating and encouraging Evangelicals in other Dioceses", and the establishment of A.C.L. branches, there was never any real prospect of a national Evangelical body.[53] In fact only one branch of the Sydney League was ever established elsewhere in Australia, at Port Lincoln in the Diocese of Willochra, and its formation in 1928 was more the product of a plea for help in peculiar circumstances rather than deliberate A.C.L. policy.[54] The League's ties with other Evangelical parties in Australia — the Church of England League of Tasmania (founded in 1922), the Church of England Defence Association of Queensland (1927) and the A.C.L. of Melbourne (1929) — was far more tenuous and at most took the form of occasional lecture tours by Sydney clerical members.[55]

The lack of contact between the Sydney A.C.L. and the other affiliates of the English N.C.L. was not just a matter of distance and the exigencies of time and energy. It also betrayed a crucial difference of character between the Sydney party and these other Evangelical organisations. These other Australian parties were almost exclusively lay organisations, in dioceses where Evangelicals were in the minority. The Sydney A.C.L., on the other hand, was dominated and led by clergymen. This difference had important implications for the respective directions of the parties: except for the A.C.L. in Sydney, the Evangelical organisations in Australia were stridently anti-clerical and vehemently anti-Roman in the style of the old Church Association. The very foundation of the A.C.L., on the other hand, had been a rejection of these extreme emphases of Church Associationism and the development of a moderate and positive Evangelical party with a more mature doctrinal base. Its members certainly sympathised with the lay organisations in other dioceses and were happy to encourage them in their difficult fight against Anglo-Catholicism. But closer formal ties with these crudely Conservative Evangelical lay parties was politically undesirable. They would imply that the League was embracing a form of conservative Evangelical extremism which it had specifically rejected years before. It would be a swing to the far "left" which might well have alienated Liberal Evangelical support.

The distinctively clerical character of the Sydney A.C.L. set it apart from other Evangelical organisations in Australia and was a crucial factor in the League's permanence and strength. The A.C.L.'s clerical leadership gave the party an enduring stability. It was natural for clergymen to be interested in the affairs of their profession and, as they rose through the clerical ranks, they assumed party leadership almost as a matter of course — as part of their career pattern. There was a natural method of recruitment and succession which simply did not exist for the more individualistic laymen. This clerical character of the A.C.L. was crucial to the League's survival in Sydney in marked contrast to the instability and eventual disappearance of Evangelical parties elsewhere in Australia, which were almost exclusively lay in character.

IV

The regular publication of an Evangelical newspaper to disseminate the party's message was another form of political organisation employed by the A.C.L. The *Church Record*, which was first published in 1880, had ceased publication some years before 1909 and the only Anglican papers were the Anglo-Catholic *Church Standard* and the Evangelical

Australian Churchman. The A.C.L., however, felt that they needed a more appropriate organ than the *Churchman* for their new distinctive Evangelical message. Thus, in 1912, three A.C.L. members — the Revs. S.M. Johnstone, H.G.J. Howe, and S.E. Langford Smith — attempted to resurrect the *Record* as a fortnightly paper, with Johnstone as its editor. However, the venture quickly ran into financial difficulties, and sank with little trace.[56]

When Bishop Stone-Wigg launched the Anglo-Catholic *Church Standard* in May 1912, renewed efforts were made by A.C.L. members to publish an Evangelical "counterblast". In August 1912, a group of League members met to prepare "for the promotion and flotation" of a Federal Church Paper. Over the next fifteen months, these men established a publishing company, The Church Record Ltd., with shareholders all over Australasia and a third of its Directors from Melbourne. This company took over the efforts of Howe, Johnstone, and Langford Smith, and incorporated *The Victorian Churchman* into their venture.[57] The first issue of this revamped *Church Record* appeared in January 1914 with an ambitious initial circulation of 9000. By the third issue only 2000 copies were being distributed, and its circulation never again exceeded that figure. In 1915 war shortages forced the paper to cut back publication to every fortnight, a frequency which remained unchanged in the post-war years.[58]

The *Church Record* sought to consolidate Evangelical opinion. Its founders wanted it to be "definitely and uncompromisingly Evangelical" by focussing on the final and ultimate authority of the Bible on all questions of faith and life; the death of Jesus; the work of the Holy Spirit; and the liberty of man's access to God through Jesus Christ. But, at the same time, they wanted this definitely Evangelical policy to be "followed rather from the constructive than the destructive side." Significantly, the *Record*'s first editor, the Rev. A.J.H. Priest, was not a Sydney man. He had served in parishes in Newcastle, Ballarat and Melbourne and worked for

C.M.S. in Victoria before being appointed Secretary of C.M.S. in N.S.W. in 1913.[59] Priest knew the state of Evangelicalism outside Sydney. He knew first hand that "the Church of England is a comprehensive Church, containing within its fold several different 'schools of thought' which all have their rights within the Church, provided they are loyal to its principles, as set forth in the Prayer Book and the Thirty Nine Articles of Religion."[60] He readily recognised that Evangelicals needed to promote their beliefs in a constructive fashion, and promised an editorial policy which would "try to maintain a wide outlook, so that the narrow vision which sees only one Parish, Diocese, or State, may be broadened to see the Church in Australasia as a whole."[61]

The *Record* never lived up to these high ideals of a federal, comprehensive newspaper. It came closest when Priest was editor from 1914 to 1916, and from 1926 to 1930 when it was edited in Melbourne by the Rev. Dr. A. Law of Toorak. But from 1916 to 1926, under the editorship of the Rev. Stephen Taylor, and from 1930 when the Rev. Stephen Denman headed an editorial group including Revs. S.J. Kirkby, Leo Gabbott, R.B. Robinson, John Bidwell, D.J. Knox and P.J. Dryland, the shared convictions of these men prevented such an idealistic objective ever being achieved. Without a broad spectrum of Evangelical opinion to draw upon, the *Record* developed a narrow outlook, oriented towards the one Diocese in which its circulation was greatest, and became a paper in which only the views of Sydney Conservative Evangelicals were articulated.[62]

V

The A.C.L.'s influence grew by its "prayerful interest" in other dioceses, its support of an Evangelical newspaper which had been established by prominent A.C.L. members, and by the maintenance of a watchdog vigilance on the Diocese of Sydney itself. But what made the A.C.L. the strongest and most effective party organisation that the Diocese — and Australia — had ever seen was its keen political involvement in the ecclesiastical elections of the Diocese.

The most important aspect of this political involvement was the pre-selection of candidates for elected positions in the Diocese. One cannot credit the Anglican Church League with introducing this practice into the Diocese of Sydney: the caucusing of the huddled coterie is an ancient practice, and although no documentary evidence survives, it seems certain that the Church Association and the N.S.W. branch of the E.C.U. pre-selected candidates. The sudden populating of the Synod by members of the Church Association in the late 1880s was hardly coincidental. Yet immediately prior to the formation of the A.C.L. Evangelicals had not been heavily engaged in methods of caucusing and pre-selection. The P.C.E.U. under Mervyn Archdall had been without political sophistication. The advent of the A.C.L. transformed the political landscape of the Diocese: "The A.C.L.", John Bidwell noted later, "took (this electoral work of pre-selection and putting out tickets) up in a very wonderful way." Bidwell added that the A.C.L. was not alone in this electoral work: the High Churchmen were not unfamiliar with the practice. But "they didn't get anywhere...We used to watch that (not too many High Churchmen were elected to the Standing Committee). We kept them off everything."[63] The High Churchmen simply did not have the numbers to ensure the success of any political efforts they mounted.

The general method of pre-selection by the A.C.L. involved the appointment by its Council of a sub-committee 6f four to seven men to draw up a list of nominations which the Council as a whole could ratify. Despite Bidwell's colourful recollection, this Inner Cabinet did not, up until the late 1920s, select only A.C.L. men or fellow travellers. Party loyalties weighed heavily, certainly, but personal qualities were also considered: invariably their list included well-qualified High Churchmen and Broad Churchmen. Indeed in 1921 the A.C.L. Council instructed its Nominating Sub-Committee that "save and excepting positions of strategic importance, ... as far as possible, one fourth (of the nominees) should be High Churchmen."[64] The four positions as synod nominators (five from 1926 to 1933) were obviously strategically important, and remained the distinct reserve of trusted Evangelical members of the A.C.L. The League also ensured that its majorities in the Standing Committee and the Moore College Committee were unassailable but the party was powerful and confident enough to be ostensibly magnanimous in supporting — or not opposing — the candidature of non-A.C.L. men for Standing Committee and positions on committees of less strategic importance.[65]

In the early years of the League, there was even an attempt at democracy in the pre-selection process. When the A.C.L. was considering a nomination for the vacant canonry at the Cathedral in 1919, the A.C.L. Council resolved that five names be selected and submitted to clergy "sympathetic with our objects", so that they might express their preference for any of the five, or, indeed, any other clergyman. By this consultative process the League discovered the most favoured candidate and endorsed his nomination.[66]

Both the magnanimous patronage of selected High Churchmen by "allocating" them a proportion of elected positions and the method of pre-selection by plebiscite were astute political devices. One disarmed the High Church opposition and the other dissipated possible discontent within the Evangelical ranks. But never at any stage did the ruling junta divest itself of power and control. Indeed, its very selection of some High Churchmen to positions within the Church diocesan structure demonstrated this: it was the League, and not the High Churchmen concerned, who decided what proportion of the elected positions they should hold, and the extent of the influence they were allowed. It was only when the party elders became more defensive and exclusivist and nominated fewer and fewer men who were not avowedly "true-blue" Evangelical party members to the decision-making councils of the Diocese, that discontent from both inside and outside of the Evangelical ranks began to occur and rival organisations were established to express that discontent.[67]

That ferment did not materialise until the late 1920s. Before that, the Anglican Church League was able to enlist the support of Evangelicals of different complexions, consolidate Evangelical opinion within the ranks of the party, and assume an unassailable electoral dominance in the Diocese. The process by which the party translated nominations into electoral successes before 1933 is somewhat unclear. The formal "how to vote" ticket did not appear until 1933, although informal lists were probably in circulation long before that to jog the memory of forgetful party faithfuls.[68] Certainly the annual pre-election meeting, organised by the A.C.L. from its earliest days, served the same purpose by indicating to Evangelical synodsmen those whom the party supported. It is not known whether the A.C.L. had other methods of commending its candidates to synodsmen, but what is evident is the spectacular and sustained success of the party: in the 1918 Synod election A.C.L. members won 73 of the 89 strategic positions (82%); in 1923 they won 82 of the 99 (83%); and in 1926 85 of the 104 (81%).[69] In 1918 and 1923 all of the synod nominators and General Synod representatives were A.C.L. members, and in all three survey years, the cases where a non-A.C.L. candidate was preferred by Synod to an A.C.L. candidate were rare.[70] Thus, by 1926, the A.C.L.'s influence was pervasive. In Standing Committee, nine of the ten clerical and fourteen of the nineteen lay elected members belonged to the League. Four of the five synod nominators and ten of the twelve members of the Moore College Committee were card-carrying members of the A.C.L. In fact, there were only two Synod committees in 1926 in which the League did not have absolute or substantial majorities: the Social Problem Committee and the Board of Education. The party clearly did not consider these committees of "strategic importance".[71] The League's dominance of the Diocese's synod and committees in the 1920s was unassailable: virtually all of the small number of non-A.C.L. candidates who held positions on synodal committees only did so because the Anglican Church League allowed them.

Three external factors promoted this strong electoral position. First, it has already been noted that political organisation had acquired a new respectability. Party activity, an ancient practice, was becoming more and more acceptable in the eyes of churchmen. Moreover, the forbearance and moderation with which the A.C.L. was able to practise the "very wonderful way" of pre-selection and caucusing in the first ten to twenty years of its existence helped to cement the acceptance of its means to power.[72] This moderation was only made possible by the prevailing mood of consensus. Soon after the crises at St. James' King Street and Christ Church St. Laurence in the years 1910-1911, reconciliation was the keynote for the Diocese as a whole.[73] Irenical meetings were held — with the active support and encouragement of Archbishop Wright — between A.C.L members and High Churchmen to discuss "how best to promote a little more unanimity and fellowship among ourselves, and by doing so perhaps to replace by a better understanding whatever disagreement may exist between Church parties in Sydney." By 1914 there was a growing conviction that a "spirit of concord and brotherly sympathy is abroad, silently leavening the Church."[74] The outbreak of World War One served to advance this "notable hushing of partisan strife". Churchmen were urged to sink their differences and unite in a concerted effort against the common enemy beyond the seas.[75]

This brotherly climate well served the fledgling party. If the heightened party tensions which had existed in 1910 and 1911 had continued throughout the war and immediate post-war years, the A.C.L. may well have been forced to abandon its centre-unity stance for an uncompromising Conservative Evangelical position. But the relative peacefulness of these formative years for the A.C.L. ensured that it was able to hold onto both the middle ground and the "left" Conservative Evangelical wing. In a political environment which was not polarised, and with no open party warfare, the League could exercise its political power in a manner which alienated no-one. Its caucusing and pre-selection were not so narrowly partisan as to appear arrogant and abrasive to its opponents. Nor were these methods overly obnoxious to those who sympathised doctrinally with the A.C.L., yet who were anxious that a spirit of goodwill prevail in Sydney. In that peaceful environment the Anglican Church League's political methods were all the more effective.

The second external factor assisting the A.C.L.'s strong position was the augmentation of the power of the Standing Committee, which allowed the A.C.L. to strengthen its grip on the legislature of the Diocese. It has already been noted that the Synod's legislative function had developed significantly since the episcopate of Barker, and that this development was a key factor in growth in party organisation. By World War One the sheer volume of business at the synod demanded some form of delegation. Following the passage of the 1917 Church Property Trust Act, the Synod was able to resolve this problem by delegating powers to the Standing Committee in order to allow it to handle trust and property matters. This move had been foreshadowed in 1912 and 1916 when the Synod had given its Executive the power to pass ordinances on two specific matters, but the new power gave the Standing Committee the same rights as Synod itself to sell, mortgage, exchange or lease property, and invest monies.[76] It was a delegation which freed Synod from the time-consuming consideration of ordinances which only involved sales or mortgages of land, and allowed it to spend more time on weightier subjects. But it also concentrated important financial and legislative power into the hands of a committee of thirty men far less exposed than the Synod itself to the cold breeze of public accountability.

Thus, from 1917 the Standing Committee developed from a mere "Council of Advice" to a powerful executive vested with sweeping legislative authority. Its powers were soon enlarged: in 1921 it was permitted to vary the trusts which governed church property if it deemed that it was "impossible or inexpedient" to observe such trusts. That delegated power, which had been vested in the Synod by the 1917 Church of England Trust Property Act, was greater than the power of the Equity jurisdiction itself.[77]

The Standing Committee was enlarged to cope with these greater responsibilities. Before 1915, it had consisted of six ex-officio members — the Archbishop, the Dean, the two senior Archdeacons, and the Secretaries of Synod — and five clerical and fourteen lay elected members.[78] From 1915 five more clerical and five more lay members were elected to the Committee. This increase in size (to thirty-five) reduced the proportion, and the influence, of ex-officio members and, reflecting the growth of clerical influence, increased the proportion of elected clergy from one in three to one in two.[79]

The concentration of power in the hands of that one committee meant that the decision-making processes of the Diocese could be more easily captured and held by one political organisation. A party which was able to marshal votes in the Synod was bound to reap the benefits of this concentration of power. Control of the Synod could never be taken for granted: even if a party was certain it had the support of the majority of synodsmen, it could never be certain that a majority would actually be in attendance.[80] Control of an elected executive committee was more manageable, and made consistent, stable "government" by one party possible. That party, the Anglican Church League, thereby quickly tightened its control over the Diocese.

The third factor which facilitated the League's rise to power was the Archbishop himself. It was noted earlier that even before Wright's episcopate there had been a shift of power away from the Bishop to the clergy and laity of the Diocese. Archbishop Wright did not attempt to reverse that trend. He did not attempt to aggrandise his own position. He did not perceive his role as an intrusive and autocratic "prince of the church" but as a Moderator who was the focus of unity for the Diocese, an administrator who ensured that the Church in that Diocese conformed to the existing constraints of the Anglican polity, and a Chief Pastor who had the responsibility to minister to, exhort and encourage all those in the Diocese committed to his charge.[81] That perception of his role meant that Wright did not seek to concentrate power at the top, but was willing for power to be exercised by others 'below' him in the church polity. He rarely acted unilaterally but "...as a general rule he acted on the advice of the Standing Committee."[82] Never at any time did he attempt to obstruct the activities of political groups or try to minimise their influence. In addition, Wright's aloof impartiality was exacerbated by his own ill health in the 1920s.[83] He was forced regularly to leave Sydney for many months in order to recuperate, and at other times obliged to remain bedridden at Bishopscourt.[84] He was, for example, out of action for all of the years 1924 and 1927. Wright's enforced detachment from the daily administration of the Diocese had serious repercussions. It created a vacuum in which a powerful political base, which challenged the Diocesan's own political power, could develop without hindrance. Indeed his ill health made the development of that power base a practical necessity.

VI

The A.C.L.'s exercise of power in the war and immediate postwar years was not oppressive. There were few complaints against it as obnoxiously partisan or narrowly obscurantist. Non-League churchmen did not allege that they had been excluded from the decision-making councils of the Church, as it consciously articulated a position of "central churchmanship" and actively sought to have non-Evangelicals represented in the decision-making process.[85] A peaceful detente existed between the A.C.L. and non-Evangelicals.

Yet within a few years that peace was broken and the A.C.L. was confronted by the most serious challenge ever to its dominance. The cause of this change was a fundamental shift within the A.C.L. itself. It had been founded as a party of comprehension, a coalition of Conservative and Liberal Evangelicals which sought to maintain cordial relations with legitimate non-Evangelical sections of the Church of England. That platform had been a basis of the party's electoral success and a significant factor in its rise to power. But in the mid- to late 1920s the coalition began to break apart. There began to be a steady shift away from that consciously "moderate" position to an exclusive rejection of that comprehensiveness. The Conservative Evangelical forces which had previously co-existed with Liberal Evangelical elements in the League became the dominant group from 1926 to 1933. Their influence was no longer balanced by that of the party's Liberal Evangelicals. The effect was a transformation in the character of the League as it became a narrow, monochrome and Conservative Evangelical organisation with a fiercely partisan spirit. It was an orientation which was at odds with its founding ideals.

It is a thesis of this dissertation that the triumph of the Conservative Evangelical within the League was primarily due to forces and events which were external to the Diocese, yet were perceived by many in the League as a threat to its Evangelical heritage. These external forces were manifest in two arenas: first, the experiences of English Evangelicalism in the 1910s and 1920s; and second, the debates on a new Constitution for an autonomous Church of England in Australia. Each of these matters had a telling impact upon the development of power and party in the Diocese of Sydney.

NOTES - CHAPTER FIVE

1. See Peter Bachrach (ed.), *Political Elites in a Democracy* Atherton Press New York 1971 pp.13-49.

2. J. Blondel, *Voters, Parties and Leaders* Penguin London 1966 Chapter Four.

3. C.S. Lewis, "The Inner Ring" in *Screwtape Proposes a Toast and Other Pieces* Fontana Glasgow 1978 pp.33-34.

4. Cross and Livingstone, *op. cit.*, pp.297, 308.

5. Hinchliff, *op. cit.* pp.159-160 and Ch. 5, *passim*; It was only in the twentieth-century that incremental *de facto* changes in the form of the Establishment meant that the Church in England was increasingly self-determining and, commensurately, church parties became more directly involved in the church's decision-making processes. Nevertheless, the 1928 rejection of the Deposited Book was a strong demonstration of the enduring constraints of Establishment.

6. R.A. Giles, *The Constitutional History of the Australian Church* Skeffington London 1929 pp.10-11,84; see also H. Lowther Clarke, *Constitutional Church Government*, S.P.C.K. London 1924 pp.206-258.

7. See Chapter 7 for a discussion on the legal nexus.

8. Clarke, *op. cit.*, pp.1,8 and 43 ff.; See *Proceedings* of the Synod of the Diocese of Sydney 1866-1881. Apart from ordinances which adopted Determination of the General Synod, there were only about five issues which were the subject of an ordinance — the

Cathedral (1868), the Ecclesiastical Tribunal (1868), Presentation (1869/76), Superannuation (1873/76/77), and Election of the Bishop of Sydney (1873) — under Barker.

9. See also Bollen, *op. cit.* Chapters 4 and 6.

10. Atkins, *op. cit.*, *passim*; see *Proceedings* 1866-1919. The total number of ordinances under each bishop, and the average per year in brackets, is given below:

Bishop	Years	Ordinances	Average
Barker	(1866-81)	18	(1.725)
Vacant	(1882-83)	3	(1.5)
Barry	(1884-88)	14	(2.8)
Vacant	(1889-90)	9	(4.5)
Smith	(1891-99)	48	(5.3)
"	(1900-08)	58	(6.4)
Wright	(1909-19)	98	(8.91)

11. G.P. Shaw, *op. cit.*, pp.197-198.

12. See *Proceedings* of 1869 Synod pp.74-77, 1876 Synod pp.85-88, 1887 Synod pp.189-90, 1895 Synod pp.179-182, 1912 Synod pp.246-250.

13. Wright to Davidson 15/1/1911, 1911 S.34 Davidson Papers. It was by this provision that Wright refused to appoint Dean Kite in 1910, and Saumarez Smith initially rejected William Carr Smith for St. James' in 1895.

14. Parishes could still leave it to the Archbishop to appoint a minister. By this stonewalling tactic the parish would, after three months, lose its right of nomination to the Archbishop. Canons Boyce and Vaughan cleverly used this tactic in 1911 to secure a clergyman for Christ Church St. Laurence who was acceptable to them. See *S.M.H.* 5/4/1911 p.11, 7/4/1911 p.9 and Standing Committee *Minute Book IV* 27/3/1911 p.451, 24/4/1911 p.454. S.D.A.; See also A.C.L. *Minutes* 11/7/1924, 5/9/1924, 22/7/1927 M.T.C.

15. See above, pp.89-90.

16. *Proceedings* of Synod, 1904, p.114; Broome, *op. cit.*, p.90.

17. Crowley, *op. cit.*, pp.234-236.

18. *ibid.*, p.240.

19. *ibid.*, p.234.

20. Ephesians 4:3.

21. Hinchliff, *op. cit.*, pp.140-141; *C.S.* 14/6/12 p.6, 4/10/12 p.3, 18/4/19 p.6.

22. *S.M.H.* 10/5/10 p.4.

23. Robinson, "A.C.L.",p.18, quoting 1910 Handbook of the P.C.E.U.; Teale, *op. cit.*, pp.149, 154.

24. Bidwell Transcript, pp.9-10; See also Chapter Two.

25. *C.S.*; 16/8/12 p.4.

26. *ibid.*, 18/4/19 p.6. (H.N. Baker).

27. *A.C.R.*; 18/8/16 p.13 (Kirkby).

28. *C.S.* 30/7/15 p.67. *A.C.R.* 13/8/15 p.8 (Bishop Gilbert White, Willochra); see also A.H.G. to D.A.G. 17/11/1940. Garnsey Papers.

29. Bidwell Interview Transcript p.14; Boyce, *op. cit.* p.146.

30. D.W.B. Robinson, "A.C.L.", p.26.

31. Balleine, *A History of the Evangelical Party in the Churgh of England* Church Book Room Press London 1951 ed. (Appendix by G.W. Bromiley) p.254.

32. Robinson, "A.C.L.", p.26.

33. Bidwell Interview Transcript pp.1 and 9.

34. *ibid.* Bidwell implied that the A.C.L. was established between the election of Wright and his arrival in Sydney in November, 1909. Bidwell Interview Transcript, pp.1 and 9.

35. Robinson, "A.C.L.", pp. 23-24.

36. The Union's "educational" function was expressed in lectures on, in 1914 for example, the Ornaments Rubric, the Kikuyu Controversy, and Prayer Book Revision. See 1912 and 1914 Annual *Reports* of the P.C.E.U., Corish Papers.

37. Archdall's successors as President were the Revs. C.C. Dunstan, W.H.H. Yarrington, and R. Nelson Howard; Archdall objected to

the A.C.L. on theological grounds, see Robinson, "A.C.L.", pp.30-31; *S.M.H.* 29/11/1909 p.8; 16/4/1910 p.8; 9/2/1912 p.18.

38. The following P.C.E.U. stalwarts had, by 1917, been converted to the A.C.L. cause: one-time President and Secretary, W.H.H. Yarrington, its lay secretary, Hugh A. Corish, and the Revs. Joseph Best, Stanley Howard, S.M. Johnstone, S.J. Kirkby, D.J.Knox, and R.B. Robinson, and laymen T.C.J. Foster and C.B. Smith and all assumed positions of influence in the League. The only man apart from Archdall who did not go over to the League was a former President, R. Nelson Howard; the last reference to the P.C.E.U. was to do with a lecture series from June to December 1917, see *A.C.R.* 28/5/1917 p.6; 25/5/1917 p.6; 25/6/1915 p.9. see Membership lists of the A.C.L., and W.H.H. Yarrington to Corish 19/3/17 and 24/3/17, both in Corish Papers.

39. Bidwell Interview Transcript, p.10; Robinson, "A.C.L.", p.27.

40. Robinson, "A.C.L.", pp.27-28.

41. Conservatives such as Canon Langford Smith, the Rev. S.J. Kirkby, and laymen W.J.G. Mann, and C.R. Walsh, and Liberal Evangelicals such as the Revs. Ernest Cameron, O.V. Abram, E.G. Cranswick, D.J. Davies, and Dean Talbot, and laymen such as Sir Henry Stephen and M.M. D'Arcy-Irvine. See A.C.L. Membership Lists. Corish Papers.

42. A.C.L. Membership Lists, *loc.cit.*; Robinson, "A.C.L." p.28.

43. Broome, *op. cit.*, p.87; A.C.L. Membership Lists in Corish Papers.

44. In 1917, the President was Mr. C.R. Walsh, who had just succeeded Boyce, who was now an Archdeacon. The Rev. S.J. Kirkby and Mr. T.W. Conolly were its secretaries, Mr. S. Scott-Young was its Treasurer, and Mr. W.J.G. Mann was its Chairman of Committees. A.C.L. Minutes 1916-1927, M.C.L.

45. In 1917, 16 clergymen and 17 laymen were elected Vice Presidents; in 1924, 12 clergy and 12 laity; and in 1933, 14 clergy and 12 laymen, A.C.L. Minutes 3/12/1917, 21/11/1924, 12/9/1933.

46. For the power of Vice Presidents, see Chapter Eight.

47. The first A.C.L. Executive included Archdeacon Bertie Boyce, Canons A.E. Bellingham and W.A. Charlton, Revs. Edgar Langford Smith, S.M. Johnstone, H.G.J. Howe, and S.J. Kirkby, and laymen C.R. Walsh, W.J.G. Mann, and M.M. D'Arcy-Irvine. See A.C.L. *Minutes* 20/1/1919.

48. Bidwell Interview Transcript, p.10.

49. A.C.L. *Minutes* 11/9/1923, 28/11/1916, 9/8/1921, 8/5/1924, 17/10/1924, 5/10/1923.

50. *ibid.*, 24/3/1919, 16/12/1926, 18/3/1927, 19/12/1930. The A.C.L. Minutes 1916-26 are held in Moore College Library; those after that date are in the hands of the present Secretary of the League, the Rev. R.E. Lamb.

51. *ibid.*, 15/4/1921.

52. *ibid.*, 9/8/1921. It is unclear whether John William Ashton, who was elected Bishop of Grafton in 1921, was in actual fact the A.C.L's nominee.

53. *ibid.*, 8/8/1930.

54. For further information on the Port Lincoln episode, where parishioners fought a rearguard action against an Anglo-Catholic rector, see N.W. Wright (of Port Lincoln) to Dean Talbot, 28/1/1931; Wright to Corish 29/1/1931, 31/1/1931, 14/3/1931, 27/2/1931, 16/12/1932, 21/12/1932, 27/4/1933, 28/4/1933; Wright to H.C. Leplastrier 21/12/1932, 10/2/1933. Corish Papers; *A.C.R.* 2/8/1928 p.4: 30/8/1928 p.7: 28/2/1929 p.4, 1/8/1929 p.3, 7/11/1929 p.7, 22/5/1930 p.3, 3/9/1931 p.9.

55. See Henry Caulfield (Sec. C.E.D.A. of Qld) to Hugh Corish 4/7/1932, 15/7/1932, 17/11/1932; Hugh_Corish, Memo on "The Federation of Evangelical Societies" in Corish Papers; *A.C.R.* 1/8/1929, p.5, 21/11/1929,p.3, 19/12/29 p.3, 25/9/1930, p.9, 8/5/1930,p.3, 2/1/1930, pp.8-9; J.A. Thick to H.A. Corish 6/2/1933 in Corish Papers; D.J. Davies lectured on the 39 Articles for the Melbourne party, see leaflet in Corish Papers.

56. *C.C.* 31/1/1912 p.5. The Australian Churchman ceased publication in 1914.

57. The League members involved in this venture in 1912 included the Revs W.L. Langley, S.E. Langford Smith, W.A. Charlton, D.J. Davies, Stephen Taylor, Robert Rook, S.H. Denman, H.S. Begbie, G.A. Chambers, William Martin, and Messrs. Walsh, H.L. Tress, E.E. Brooks, L. Leplastrier, and W.E. Shaw.

58. Australian Church Record *Minute Books* 9/8/1912, 24/11/1913, 24/4/1914, 5/5/1914, 30/7/1914 in M.T.C.; *A.C.R.* 13/2/1914 p.13, 14/7/1922 p.1, 20/10/1922 p.1.

59. I am indebted to Assoc. Professor K.J. Cable for the biographical information about Priest and other clergymen who served in Sydney.

60. Church Record *Minutes* 19/9/1913 (check).

61. *A.C.R.* 2/1/1914 p.1.

62. See A.C.*Record Minute Book* 9/5/1930; See e.g. A.C.L. *Minutes* 5/9/1919, 6/9/1921. Sales patterns for the A.C.R. are not available, although it would appear that the paper never had a circulation higher than 1900 and was usually between 1200 and 1500. Most sales were in Sydney, with a small number of subscribers in Melbourne, and complimentary copies distributed in Victoria and Tasmania in a bid to increase sales. See e.g. A.C.R. *Minutes* 24/11/1925.

63. Bidwell Interview Transcript, pp.9-10.

64. A.C.L. *Minutes* 6/9/1921.

65. In 1918, seven men served on the A.C.L. nominating sub-committee: Revs Langford Smith, W. Greenwood, H.J Noble, and S.J. Kirkby, and Messrs C.R. Walsh, William Beaver, and C.R. Walsh. In 1919, only Langford Smith, Boyce, Mann and Beaver were entrusted with the task. See A.C.L. *Minutes* 2/9/1918, 5/9/1919.

66. *ibid.*, 6/9/21.

67. See Chapter Eight.

68. See 1933-1939 "How to vote" tickets in Corish Papers.

69. The strategic positions are defined as those on Standing Committee, Moore College Trustees and, from 1923, Moore College Committee, Synod Nominators and representatives to General and Provincial Synod.

70. In 1918, for example, four A.C.L. members were beaten in synod elections but two of these were defeated by fellow A.C.L. members. The other two failed to gain a seat on Standing Committee although two non-A.C.L. men were successful. See 1918 *Proceedings* of the Synod of the Diocese of Sydney pp.84-87, 96-98.

71. 1927 *Year Book*, p.27; 1926 *Proceedings* of the Synod of the Diocese of Sydney pp.23-35; and A.C.L. Membership Lists, *loc.cit.*

72. Bidwell Interview Transcript, pp.9-10.

73. *S.M.H.* 5/8/1911 p.10. The Church Defence League, which was established by Anglo-Catholics after the St. James' dispute in 1910, was short-lived.

74. *C.S.*, 7/8/1914 p.12, 6/11/1914 p.10.

75. *A.C.R.* 4/9/1914 p.8.

76. Regulations re Ordinances under the Church of England Trust Property Act, 1917, passed 3/10/18, in C.R. Walsh (ed) *Ordinances of The Synod of the Diocese of Sydney 1908-1923*. Madgwick Sydney 1924.

77. • 1918 Initiation of Ordinances Ordinance in *ibid.*, pp.409-12;
    • 1921 Initiation of Ordinances Amendment Ordinance, in *ibid.*, pp.633-634;
    • 1923 Initiation of Ordinances Further Amendment, in *ibid.*, pp.743-44
    • 1926 Initiation of Ordinances Ordinance in 1927 *Year Book* of the Diocese of Sydney, pp.159-163
    • 1917 Church of England Trust Property Act, in W.G.S. Gotley (ed.), *Sydney Anglican Handbook*, Sydney Diocesan Secretariat Sydney 1976 pp.86-97.

78. 1897 Standing Committee Ordinance, in Atkins, *op. cit.*, pp.218-222.

79. 1915 Standing Committee Amendment Ordinance, in Walsh, *op. cit.*. p.202.

80. Synod may have been developing along the lines of the Westminster parliamentary system, but Government Whips had not yet been introduced.

81. *S.D.M.* March 1933 p.5; *S.M.H.* 25/2/33 p.14.
82. J.A.I. Perry to Abp. Cosmo Lang 30/1/32, Sir Philip Game to Lang 26/9/33. 1932 S.7. Lang Papers.
83. Wright never fully recovered from pneumonic influenza in 1919, and he suffered regular and persistent respiratory problems until his death in 1933. He suffered the added afflictions of phlebitis and ulcers which restricted his mobility from 1924. See e.g. *S.D.M.* April 1920 p.3, November 1921 p.3, January 1922 p.4.
84. *ibid.*, February 1924 p.2, March 1924 p.2, April 1924 p.2, May 1924 p.2, June 1924 p.2, July 1924 p.2, September 1924 p.2, October 1924 pp.2-3, November 1924 pp.2-3, February 1927 p.2, March 1927 p.2, April 1929 p.2, December 1929 p.3, March 1930 p.20, December 1931 p.2, April 1932 p.5, May 1932 p.2.
85. A.C.L. *Minutes* 6/9/21.

CHAPTER SIX -

THE ENGLISH EXPERIENCE

I

At the beginning of the twentieth century, the Evangelicals appeared to be a significant force in the Church of England in England.[1] Evangelical clergymen occupied the pulpits of 4,000 churches, and the Evangelical flagship, the Church Missionary Society, was experiencing an unprecedented level of support from the Church as a whole.[2] In the last quarter of the nineteenth century, the fight against ritualism, led by the aggressive and energetic Church Association, had been ostensibly successful in the law courts, where ritualists had been consistently defeated and five clergymen had been inhibited and imprisoned for offences of ritual under the Public Worship Regulation Act of 1874.[3]

This appearance was deceptive. Evangelicals were pre-eminent on the Northern Bench but there were few Evangelical bishops in the Province of Canterbury and successive governments overlooked Evangelicals for preferment. In addition, the Anglo-Catholics had made steady, significant advances all over the country in the last quarter of the nineteenth century despite the Church Association's campaign against them. That campaign had in fact damaged the Evangelical cause. The imprisonment of ritualists defeated the purpose of the Evangelical plaintiffs: indeed, a surer way of enlisting public support for the accused could not have been devised.[4] The spectacle of one group of churchmen taking another group into a secular court upon matters of spiritual significance prompted widespread sympathy and support for the harried ritualists, a sympathy which Anglo-Catholics assiduously cultivated. When Bishop King of Lincoln was practically acquitted by Archbishop Benson of Canterbury of ritualist illegality in 1890 the legal campaign against ritualism foundered, and it was the Evangelicals, not the ritualists, who had been discredited.[5]

The Evangelicals' poor public image was not improved by the Kensitite disturbances in London between 1897 and 1902. John Kensit, the secretary of the Protestant Truth Society, organised "noisy and offensive" disruptions of ritualist services in selected London churches.[6] Feelings ran high as groups of men were counter-organised to protect these ritualist centres from the Protestant assailants.[7] By 1902 there seemed no prospect of peace within the church. The inquisitors who had sought to curb ritualism by prosecution or direct agitation had "run too wild a race" and lost the support of public opinion.[8] They were, ironically, on the defensive, seeking to hold the pass from the forces of Anglo-Catholicism which grew steadily in strength each day.

The Church Associationists blamed the bishops for the spread of ritualism. The Association alleged that the bishops as a group failed to maintain discipline and encouraged the spread of ritualism by not prosecuting ritualists. Although some bishops did their best to maintain discipline, English bishops did veto 33 prosecutions between 1874 and 1906, and many other actions failed to get off the ground because the diocesan bishop's antagonism to prosecution had become well-known.[9] But the development and spread of ritual was not just due to episcopal appeasement. The taste of the Victorian age for the elaborate, the colourful and the ornamental pervaded all avenues of life.[10] Second, there was the belief that ritual was an effective tool for the evangelism of the poor.[11] There were shining examples of thriving centres of ritual in the slums of London, though their success was probably more due to the high calibre of the priests than the ritual they practised.[12] Finally, the growth of the English towns and cities had contributed to the disintegration of the parish as a geographical unit and replaced it with an emphasis on the church as a congregation. This shift encouraged specialisation: individual churches developed customs and traditions which appealed to worshippers far beyond the parochial boundaries.[13] The spread of ritual — and of other special usages and traditions — was greatly facilitated by this development of associational congregationalism.

In 1902, the Evangelical campaign to steer the Church of England back to the safe anchorage of Reformation principles switched from the law court to the Parliament when the Church Association published a pamphlet, *Contemporary Ritualism*, and sent a copy to every Member of Parliament. The pamphlet's effect was explosive.[14] The Protestant vote was still an undeniably powerful element in English politics, particularly in the North, and parliamentarians were fearful lest they bore the brunt of a surge of anti-ritualist feeling. Many churchmen may have felt that the methods of Kensit and his allies were deplorable, but it was still an era when the cry "No Popery" raised passionate emotions, and the questions of Irish home rule and the place of the Established Church in education were controversial and divisive issues.[15] M.P.s demanded action from Prime Minister Balfour. If the bishops would not curb ritualistic excesses, then the Parliament indicated that it would. Faced with the threat of his own party voting against him and bringing down the Government, Balfour appointed a Commons' Select Committee to investigate Ecclesiastical Discipline. However, after intense lobbying by Archbishop Davidson of Canterbury, Balfour reconsidered that decision and announced in March 1904 that a Royal Commission would enquire into the matter instead.[16] The functions_and membership of the two instruments were significantly different: a Select Committee judges; a Royal Commission merely enquires and, whereas a Commons' committee would have only comprised laymen, the Commission was composed of bishops and clergymen as well as laymen.[17]

Two years, 118 sittings, and 164 witnesses later, the Royal Commission produced a unanimous report. It substantiated many of the Evangelical claims that illegal ritualism was ubiquitous and should be "promptly made to cease" by episcopal action. But, at the same time, the Commissioners concluded that "the law of public worship....is too narrow for the religious life of the present generation. It needlessly condemns much which a great section of Church people...value."[18] The Commissioners therefore recommended that a new Ornaments Rubric be formulated, which would "tend to secure the greater elasticity which a reasonable recognition of the comprehensiveness of the Church of England and of its present needs seem to demand."[19] While the Commission's other recommendations were never acted upon, these findings that the existing law required broadening and that a new Ornaments Rubric should be drafted became the catalyst for a series of moves in the assemblies of the Church which culminated in a complete revision of the 1662 Book of Common Prayer.[20]

The findings and proposals of the 1906 Royal Commission presented Evangelicals with a great opportunity. The Commission had categorically condemned ritual which involved doctrinal change and, at the same time, had suggested many changes to the Prayer Book which were unquestionably required. But the Evangelical school of thought was then dominated by Conservatives who failed to exploit that advantageous position. Instead of taking the initiative with a positive propagation of their own position and devising a realistic programme of reform, these Conservative Evangelical leaders were negative and defensive, obsessed with preventing the aberrations of others. Evangelical laymen were not enthusiastically mobilised for Evangelical truth, but warned against the errors of fellow Churchmen. The Conservative Evangelicals were suspicious that the basic thrust of the Report was to legitimate what the Commission had declared illegal, and to hand over matters of doctrine over from the Parliament to the Bishops.[21] The Conservative Evangelicals had a deep-seated mistrust of the bishops as a group and, if doctrinal issues were decided by them "there would be danger", Dean Wace declared, "of Evangelicals permanently losing out in any dispute over doctrine."[22] To Conservative Evangelicals the risk of change was too great. They dug their heels in, professed satisfaction with the existing Book, and demanded adherence to the *status quo*.

The eminent "reasonableness" of the Commission's *Report* did, however, appeal to many other churchmen who saw it as a positive step towards resolution of tensions in the Church. Anglo-Catholics, on the other hand, began a strong campaign to legitimate their own position and practices. Within a year of the *Report's* publication the Upper House of the Convocation of Canterbury adopted a report which asserted that the Eucharistic vestments were legal, and in the following year the Upper House of York, despite its ostensibly Evangelical majority, passed a compromise resolution to the effect that a white vestment could be worn on the understanding that its use in no way assimilated the service of Holy Communion to the pre-Reformation Missal, and that those who wore it should guarantee that they did not intend to alter the doctrine of the Church of England.[23]

This resolution was naive. The Northern bishops had merely played into the hands of the Anglo-Catholics, who dismissed the idea of a "safeguard":

> "Is there any difference at all between the post-Reformation
> Communion or Lord's Supper and the pre-Reformation Mass?" The
> Anglo-Catholics asked. "Upon any other hypothesis than that of
> identity, our boast of continuity is a pure myth. We are sincere in
> our assertion of the principles of continuity and we cannot honestly
> divest these ornaments of the associations which have gathered

round them through their use in the ministrations of the Mass... We venture to think it a childish proceeding to insist, in any case, that vestments, if they are tolerated, must only be white."[24]

The ritualists clearly believed that Holy Communion was "neither more nor less than the Mass in English" and were determined to have their view legitimated in the Church of England.[25] They were not about to be appeased by half measures.

Nevertheless, despite the opposition of both Conservative Evangelicals and Anglo-Catholics, to whom colour was irrelevant and the use of vestments was a matter of principle, the concept of a white vestment became popular. It was the talisman of peace. By mid-1909 all four Houses of Convocation in England had endorsed the use "with safeguards" of a plain, distinctive vestment, and notice was given of further ritual reforms. Conservative Evangelicals were despondent at these decisions. To them, it was the not-so-thin end of the wedge. They believed that soon only churches held by Evangelical trustees would be safe from the ritualist threat; the Mass would be revived in English churches and, because an inherently Protestant Parliament would find a "Romanized Establishment" repugnant, disestablishment of the Church of England would be an inevitable consequence.[26]

It was that general direction which deeply concerned Conservative Evangelicals. The issue of vestments and, later, Reservation of the Sacrament, were the specific bones of contention. But it was the fear of a widespread "Romanising" of the Church by extreme Anglo-Catholics — with their auricular confessions, the invocation of saints, Mariolatry, Crucifixes, crosses, candles, altar screens, services of Benediction and Mass of the Prae-sanctified, celebrations without communicants, the veneration of images, and other accoutrements — which alarmed Conservative Evangelicals and actuated their energetic involvement in bitter controversies. Their defence of their faith was taken on particular issues: vestments in 1907-1909, prayers for the dead during the war, and Reservation after 1918. These different battles were part of the same conflict against the steady Anglo-Catholic advance within the Church of England, a struggle which Bishop Straton of Newcastle called "the war which would not cease."[27]

The campaign for liturgical change accelerated after all Houses of Convocation had agreed to a policy of liberalisation of the vestiarian laws. Between 1909 and 1914 Anglo-Catholics seized the initiative and pressed for a more "ancient" service of Holy Communion, Reservation of the Sacrament, and Prayers and Services for the Dead. Their efforts were largely successful: first, the Upper House of Canterbury endorsed a proposal to restore the 1549 Order of Holy Communion, a service which the English Reformers had deliberately superseded in 1552. This was a liturgical change which clearly brought back pre-Reformation practices, and reinforced in practice the doctrine of the Eucharistic Sacrifice. Then, in 1914, the Upper Houses of both Provinces passed resolutions which permitted the Perpetual Reservation of the Sacraments, purportedly for the sick only.[28]

These measures deeply offended most Evangelicals, particularly Conservatives. The proposal to re-institute the 1549 Order of Communion meant that the Lord's Supper now more closely resembled the Mass, while Reservation seemingly negated the belief in God's omnipresence. Moderate Anglo-Catholic apologists claimed that Reservation — putting aside some consecrated bread and wine, instead of consuming it all at the Communion — was necessary to enable the sick to communicate. But both Conservative and Liberal Evangelicals believed that the practice localised God's presence and suggested that Christ was physically present in the Elements, which then became the subject of idolatrous adoration. They maintained that it was ludicrous to suggest that the practice was only for the sick, and cited as proof the claim by Anglo-Catholics that all people had a right to have access to the reserved sacrament because

"Where our Lord is, there He is to be worshipped, is a principle that lies at the root of Christianity."[29]

Conservative Evangelicals were convinced that there was a concerted campaign by Anglo-Catholics against the Reformed character of the Church of England, a campaign which owed much of its success to the Episcopal Bench. The bishops, concluded one Conservative Evangelical,

> "...appear to have had only one idea of the means of abating law-lessness, and that is to alter the law in a sense favourable to those who have been breaking or straining it. The sole aim of those who have conducted revision seems to have been to make such concession both to the Ritualistic and the Rationalistic clergy as will enable the Bishop to say, like the Bishop of London, that the law is obeyed in their dioceses, because disobedience to law is treated as lawful."[30]

The few Evangelical bishops were an ageing minority, confined to the Northern Province. Most bishops, including Archbishop Davidson of Canterbury, were motivated by a desire for peaceful compromise, and believed that the Anglo-Catholics could be satisfactorily appeased. Indeed, some were staunch Anglo-Catholics themselves. Archbishop Lang of York, for example, displayed considerable satisfaction that he had introduced Anglo-Catholic practices into the strongly Evangelical Northern Province: "...quietly and without any fuss, first at an Ordination in the Minster, I wore cope and mitre, certainly the first to do so either there or in the whole Province since the Reformation. The custom was gradually extended and indeed welcomed...I lived to see vestments in ordinary use in the Minster..."[31] Conservative Evangelicals came to regard the Episcopal Bench as dominated by compromisers and Anglo-Catholic patrons, from whom they could expect little sympathy, and in whom they had little faith. When in 1915 the Upper

House of Canterbury approved 150 changes to the Prayer Book in one day, the outlook for the Conservative Evangelical cause looked bleak. Their leaders openly discussed the prospect of Disestablishment and an Evangelical exodus from the Church of England. A parting of the ways appeared inevitable.[32]

The seemingly unstoppable advance towards a Prayer Book Revision which restored pre-Reformation practices was, however, checked by the "awful hurricane" of war.[33] A moratorium on Prayer Book Revision was declared for the duration of the war: the disputes and discussions were temporarily swept aside. But although formal proposals for change were shelved, war conditions provided a conducive environment for *de facto* changes. The practice of Reservation became more widespread because wounded men in hospitals and in the field desired Communion at all hours of the day and night, and, as the shocking casualties mounted, Prayers for the Dead were introduced into more and more parish churches where pressured priests sought to console their grieving congregations.[34] Thus, with the stimulus of war, the Sacrament came to be openly reserved and worshipped, Prayers for the Dead became more common, and the concept of a Eucharistic Sacrifice was increasingly taught.[35] The pressure for Revision intensified: in 1918 the Canterbury Convocation agreed to a restructuring of the Canon of Holy Communion which gave that service a far more sacrificial character. The Convocation made the decision on the expeditious ground that the restructuring had become so common in the previous three years that it could not now condemn the practice.[36] Conservative Evangelicals were alarmed:

> "It is not exaggeration to say these decisions do establish a coun-
> ter-reformation in the Church of England," said Bishop Knox.
> "They affirm that all our divines and saints, from Cranmer to
> the middle of last century, were in error, and that all Evangelical
> Churchmen to-day are in error. From this point of view

Evangelicals may be tolerated as imperfect Churchmen, but they are Churchmen whose faith is defective. It is idle to pretend that the steps which the Convocation of Canterbury has taken are not of the gravest importance to Evangelical Churchmen. They do, in fact, challenge their right to call themselves Churchmen."[37]

The moratorium on Revision was lifted after the War, and the push towards a new Prayer Book became relentless. Formal proposals for revision passed through all four Houses of Convocation in 1920; and in 1922 the newly-created National Assembly passed the Revised Prayer Book (Permissive Use) Measure. But a number of church parties, unhappy with the compromising character of this Measure, published their own idealistic "Prayer Books" for public debate and discussion. There was a flood of pamphlets on the Revision issue, and petitions were circulated which attracted hundreds of thousands of signatures.[38]

The struggle over Revision was by no means polarised between Evangelicals and Anglo-Catholics. First, Evangelicals were not united in their opposition to the Revision proposals while extreme Anglo-Catholics, led by Dr. Darwell Stone, the principal of Pusey House Oxford, *opposed* the proposals for Revision because they believed that whereas the ambiguities in the existing formularies afforded them great practical latitude, the proposed Revised Book would be more definitive and restrictive. Second, although extremists saw it as a two-party dogfight, most churchmen occupied the middle ground. The majority favoured a revision which would merely modernise the language and style of the Prayer Book without substantive changes to its principles. However, in the interests of peace and unity, they were willing to compromise and support attempts to devise a settlement which would not create schism in the Church. If vestments were cleansed of all doctrinal significance, if Reservation was only for the sick, and if there were assurances that changes to the Holy Communion service were merely stylistic and without doctrinal import, then they would concede them all. It was the belief of these men in the necessity of Revision and their enduring willingness to compromise for the sake of peace which kept the process of Revision alive in the 1920s.

After years of debate and masses of propaganda, the Revised Book was submitted to Parliament for legal sanction in December 1927. It still contained the crucial changes to the structure of the service of Holy Communion, included Prayers for the Dead, allowed Reservation, and legitimated the use of vestments. These were all things which Conservative Evangelicals had steadfastly opposed throughout the years of debate on Revision. Thus, when the Ecclesiastical Committee of Parliament declared that the proposed new Prayer Book did not prejudicially affect the constitutional rights of the English people, and the House of Lords passed the Measure in December 1927, there were few Conservative Evangelicals who did not resign themselves to a Revision which was antagonistic to their doctrinal standpoint. Few thought that the Commons would reject the Measure: indeed, many churchmen believed that the members of the Commons, of whom only about one in fifteen were communicant members of the Established Church, would pass the Measure without debate.[39]

Yet when the Commons decided to debate the issue, the opponents of the Bill were well prepared to defeat it. While those who spoke in support of the Measure were pedestrian, long-winded and uninspiring, the opponents of the Measure captured the attention and the support of the House with inspired and powerful speeches. They quickly centred the debate on the question of doctrine and were able to convince the House that the Measure constituted a real doctrinal reversion to pre-Reformation beliefs. One extremely effective opponent of the Measure "inflamed all the latent Protestant prejudices in the House", and linked the secret colloquies between the Roman Catholic Archbishop of Malines and the Anglo-Catholic Lord Halifax with what he perceived were the Romeward propensities of the Prayer Book Measure.[40] Another speaker against the

Measure gave the House "a rhetorical presentment of 'no-Popery' phrases and arguments...a simply ultra-Protestant harangue", which was, in Archbishop Davidson's view, "the most effective speech of all as regards votes."[41] These opponents of the Measure were successful: when the vote was taken, the Measure was defeated by 238 votes to 205. After two decades of Prayer Book Revision debate, the Conservative Evangelicals had at last achieved a significant victory.[42]

The Measure's defeat seriously jeopardised the Established relationship of Church and State. Some churchmen were angered that Members of Parliament who were neither Anglican nor English should presume to reject a Measure which had been passed by the Church's own decision-making processes. If, as this vote implied, national Establishment meant that the nation's representatives had a veto power over the Church, they preferred a severance of that nexus — disestablishment — and an assertion of the spiritual independence of the Church.[43] Archbishop Davidson, however, with "his unconquerable yearning for compromise", attempted to avert that possibility by securing changes to the Measure which would appease the Commons.[44] But the watered-down version of the Bill failed to satisfy Members of Parliament, who again rejected it even more decisively in June 1928.[45] The Commons plainly believed the Measure did involve a change in doctrine which would not bring peace and harmony to the life of the Church in England, nor restore discipline.

The ancient fear of Rome was at the basis of Parliament's rejection of the Prayer Book Measure. The successive defeats in the Commons convinced Archbishop Davidson that "there is no force on earth so determined and uncompromising as the force of the No-Popery cry in England...We suffered so much from Rome that everything which can be depicted, however unfairly, as having a Romeward trend, is condemned *ipso facto* without need of argument".[46] Archbishop Lang concurred, and thought that the militance of the Anglo-Catholics was largely responsible for the Measure's defeat. The nineteenth century public sympathy for the persecuted ritualist had been replaced with bitter resentment towards the aggressiveness of Anglo-Catholicism:

> "...one cause of the temper of the House, at least certainly among a large number of quiet English members — especially from the country — was the long-accumulating resentment against too many Anglo-Catholics who have thrust their way upon quiet country folk entirely unprepared for them. This resentment has now, so to say, exploded. When some of their stalwarts say 'All we have gained has been gained by fighting', this strong resentment on the part of multitudes of quiet folk is the price that has been paid. It is extremely difficult for the Archbishops and Bishops to continue to do their utmost to give a generous place within the Church to the ideals of the Anglo-Catholic movement when many of its leaders, and not least its organ The *Church Times*, are perpetually sneering at their authority, treating their efforts almost with contempt, and enormously increasing the difficulties with which they are faced."[47]

The irony is that the extreme Anglo-Catholics opposed the Measure as strongly as the Conservative Evangelicals, but because the Measures did not go far enough.[48] Even those Anglo-Catholics who did support the Measure did so without enthusiasm, out of loyalty to the bishops. To a large extent this Anglo-Catholic opposition only confirmed Conservative Evangelical fears that the Measure was a step in the Romeward direction.[49]

The Parliament's rejection of the Prayer Book Measure left the Bishops with three courses of action. They could submit to Parliament, the course desired by Conservative Evangelicals, but an option which gravely affected the spiritual integrity of Anglicanism; they could assert their spiritual independence by seeking disestablishment; or they could navigate a middle course which avoided disestablishment but nevertheless asserted the Church's right to self-determination of its doctrine and worship. The Bishops elected to pursue this last course. They circumvented the verdicts of the Commons, and facilitated a *de facto* introduction of the 1928 Prayer Book into the pews of England, by declaring that they would not treat as disloyal the use of any part of the rejected Prayer Book, provided its use received the consent of the respective parishioners.[50] The Bishops' action was a bald-faced authorisation of the 1928 Book and a cynical disregard of the obligations of Establishment. Conservative Evangelicals felt cheated, and their contempt for the Episcopal Bench grew. But, as Walmsley points out, the Bishops' decision to disregard Parliament's rejection of the Book and allow its use, saved the Church, for good or ill, from disestablishment and open schism:

"Had the Book been accepted, it is difficult to see how Conservative Evangelicals could have remained within the Anglican Church. It is also doubtful whether Nonconformists would have been prepared to accept the new doctrinal basis of the Anglican Church as the Established Church of the Realm. On the other hand, had the bishops accepted the decision of Parliament and adhered to the ruling, then many Anglo-Catholics could well have found themselves in an impossible situation. In the event, the bishops were able to salvage some credibility, the Commons had asserted its authority over the Established Church, the Evangelicals had had their long campaign vindicated by the highest authority in the land, and the Anglo-Catholics were now able to adopt many of the practices for which they had fought so hard and which they sincerely believed to be of the 'bene esse' of the true Church of God.

"It was these several factors", concludes Walmsley, "which allowed the Liberal wings of both Evangelicalism and Catholicism to come closely together and, over a period of 30 years, prepare the ground for.... a new Book acceptable to the majority and bringing once more uniformity to the Church of England."[51]

Yet it was a "uniformity" of formulary which could not disguise the inherent tensions within Anglicanism, tensions which were most immediately expressed in Evangelicalism itself.

II

It was over the issue of Prayer Book Revision that serious splits within English Evangelicalism first developed. The fundamental reasons behind the final schism will be examined in detail in Chapter Eight but the first clear signs of division appeared in 1906. At that time many Conservative Evangelicals were concerned that some of their Liberal Evangelical brothers lacked sufficient resolve in the face of aggressive demands by Anglo-Catholics. Conservative Evangelical Bishops Chavasse, Straton and Knox were dismayed by the timidity of Bishop Handley Moule of Durham, the compromising accommodation of Bishop Drury of Ripon and the vacillation of Bishop Jayne of Chester: "These good bishops," concluded Bishop Knox, "were like men trying to turn tigers into tame cats by feeding them on buns."[52] Did these men not see, asked Conservative Evangelicals, that white vestments and the Anglo-Catholic "Six Points" shopping list were mere stepping stones to more radical Romanising changes?[53] In the eyes of conservative Evangelicals, their brothers who caved in on the issue of vestments refused to see

"that (their) surrender implied that the use of vestments could be regarded by Protestants as a matter of secondary importance and, if it was to them a matter of secondary importance while to the Anglo-Catholics it was of vital importance, the predominant interests of peace and uniformity must, in the end, lead to the general or universal adoption of vestments in the Church of England."[54]

For their part, Liberal, often younger Evangelicals, found themselves out of sympathy with "older Evangelicals", whom they believed were unresponsive to the demands of the new age. The Rev. H.C. Beeching, a Liberal Evangelical Canon of Westminster, argued that the permissive use of vestments should be tolerated by Evangelicals purely on the grounds of expediency:

> "…The use is desired by large numbers of faithful and loyal Churchmen. If the Evangelical party cannot agree to allow the policy of a maximum and minimum use, have they an alternative policy for getting back to a condition of law and order in the Church? Do they expect to convince the High Churchmen. or do they propose to prosecute them?"[55]

Beeching believed that vestments should be tolerated because law and order could only be happily and peacefully restored in the Church by an alteration of the law. Other Liberal Evangelicals sought to demonstrate that there was "no necessary antagonism between Evangelicalism and Ritualism". They recognised that the Prayer Book services of the Church of England were lacking in symbolism, colour, even reverence and dignity, and their solution to this deficiency was to develop an "Evangelical Ritual" which included artistic presentations of the Living Christ, musical accompaniments to Communion, and the Westward position for the celebrant. These suggestions were, of course, anathema to many Conservative Evangelicals who believed that any symbolism or ceremonial detracted from the centrality of "The Word". But the suggestions were an acknowledgement on the part of men raised in the

Evangelical tradition of the need in the new age for a new expression of the Gospel in corporate worship.[56]

The fact that Liberal Evangelicals were willing to accommodate radical liturgical revision and believed that it was better for the sake of peace to change the law in order to curb lawlessness greatly facilitated progress towards the formulation of concrete proposals by which "the greater elasticity" advocated by the 1906 Royal Commission might be effectively implemented.[57] It was an accommodation that struck a weighty blow against the Conservative Evangelicals. Liberal Evangelical opinions were more and more perceived by other churchmen as representative of the "Evangelical" viewpoint and, concomitantly, Conservative Evangelical views were increasingly consigned to a distant isolated fringe of the "comprehensive" spectrum of the Church of England. It was a position which only served to exacerbate the negative defensiveness of the Conservative Evangelicals.

The great ideal of Liberal Evangelicals was for peaceful unity in the fellowship of Christ. They shunned the extremism of both sides and pleaded with their more partisan brothers for moderation. They urged that a spirit of Christian love over-rule the process of Prayer Book Revision so that it would be an edifying, and not a schismatic, experience for the Church of England. But in promoting that ideal, Liberal Evangelicals often only succeeded in presenting themselves as naive, vacillating and decidedly unhappy men, who gave in to concerted pressure, compromised cherished principles in the sincere but vain hope that their conciliatory attitude would promote peace, and cut the ground from under the feet of the Conservative Evangelicals.

This is well illustrated by two private conferences on Prayer Book Revision between Liberal Evangelical leaders and Archbishop Davidson in 1915. These Liberal Evangelicals told Davidson that they were "profoundly anxious about the Romanist extreme wing" which, in their view, threatened "the comprehensive character of the Church of

England", and, while they approved of a moderate revision, they were "seriously *opposed*" to any change in the Canon of Holy Communion, to Reservation, and to the legalization of vestments. They were, therefore, ostensibly, in accord with their more conservative brothers.[58] But their position was not uncompromising: in one breath they opposed the legalisation of vestments, but in the next breath they phlegmatically submitted a request that if vestments were legalised, there should be three conditions placed upon their use: first, the congregation should consent to their use; second, those who used vestments should be obliged to declare that no counter-Reformation doctrine was asserted by their use; and, third, the surplice should also be permitted. These conditions made it quite clear to Davidson that, with pressure, Liberal Evangelicals would resile from their opposition to these changes, and would then, as they themselves admitted, "...loyally abide by them, and would use their influence to win such loyal assent from other Evangelicals: they valued Church principles too much to break away because they were not themselves satisfied."[59]

The Liberal Evangelicals' accommodation of the demands of the ritualists bitterly disappointed Conservative Evangelicals. They felt that Liberal Evangelicals had sold out fundamental Evangelical truths for the illusion of peace. These differences between Liberal and Conservative Evangelicals became clearer in 1922 with the split in the Church Missionary Society, which resulted in the formation of the Bible Churchman's Missionary Society, and was further institutionalised in 1923 when the Group Brotherhood, to which many Liberal Evangelicals belonged, decided to come out into the open as a public party, the Anglican Evangelical Group Movement.[60] Thus by 1923, the Conservative-Liberal Evangelical divisions had solidified and been publicly aired: the Prayer Book Revision had convinced Conservative Evangelicals that they were "no longer wanted in the Church of England", while Liberal Evangelicals, ever-hopeful of making their mark on Revision by negotiation and compromise, were "prepared to stretch the traditional comprehensiveness of the Church of England to the utmost possible limits" to reach a settlement.[61]

By the mid-1920s it was too late for the Conservative Evangelicals. They only realised then that the Liberal Evangelicals had acted for the past two decades as a fifth column in the Evangelical ranks, augmenting their own influence at the expense of the Conservative Evangelicals, whose position they had consistently undermined. The Conservative Evangelicals had been steadily supplanted in the councils of the Church: their leaders had grown older and their places had not been taken by younger Conservative Evangelicals, but by Liberal Evangelicals who, by staying for so long under the over-arching and monolithic umbrella of the Evangelical party, had captured positions of great influence and authority within that party without the Conservatives being able to do much about it. By the mid-1920s Conservative Evangelicals could not attempt to minimise the influence of Liberal Evangelicals: they were already too strong. The Conservative Evangelicals could. only look on and protest as these younger men, who appeared "so plastic that they did not mind what happened", regularly and expediently buckled under to the pressures to compromise.[62] It became quite plain that a divided Evangelicalism was no match for a determined Anglo-Catholicism.[63]

III

The long, slow process towards Prayer Book Revision in England was closely watched by Australian churchmen. Many of them, particularly those in positions of authority within the Australian Church, were English born, and had a natural interest in events in the Mother Country; many more had a strong sense of their English heritage by which they felt bound to imitate developments in England. Before 1911, many Australian Liberal Evangelicals were quite eager for a local revision of the Prayer Book. They realised that the 250 year old Book of Common Prayer was in need of amendment, if only to make it more suitable for the Australian context. For example, at Archbishop Wright's first Sydney Synod in December 1909, Canon Boyce and John Lingen tried unsuccessfully to convince their more Conservative fellow synodsmen "that it is expedient that the Church in this State should have power to abbreviate the Morning Service without waiting for changes in England."[64] The next year, the Liberal Evangelical Archbishop of Melbourne, Lowther Clarke, argued for an Australian initiative in the task of Revision.[65] It was, ironically, the Anglo-Catholics and the conservative High churchmen who opposed these suggestions of local revision: the Anglo-Catholics believed that a local revision would restrict them more than before, while High churchmen believed it "would be a profound misfortune" if the Australian Church undertook the task of Revision independently of the rest of the Anglican Communion.[66]

The supporters of local revision in Australia received a setback in 1911 when the English legal opinion on the question of the nature of the relationship between the Church of England in Australia and the Church in England was made public. The three English lawyers concluded that the Dioceses in Australia were not merely "in communion with" or "in connection with" the Church of England, but were actual parts of that Church of England. Australian churchmen were subject to the same laws as were binding in England, except with regard to political circumstances peculiar to Australia. They were bound to adhere to the faith, doctrine and discipline of the Church of England, and conform to the Book of Common Prayer in the same way as members of the Church in England. If they did not, they risked forfeiture of their property. Local revision was, therefore, out of the question: the Australian authorities were not competent to alter or diverge from the Book of Common Prayer. The only relief was the English 1872 Act of Uniformity Amendment Act which gave power to the bishop to approve special services which were not provided for in the Prayer Book.[67]

The impact of this legal opinion was profound. Australian churchmen were not as autonomous as they had thought. The Church in Australia was in an anomalous situation: it enjoyed complete autonomy in matters of government, but its formularies and doctrine were legally tied to England through the Civil Courts of the Realm. A minority of churchmen believed this was an intolerable inhibition, and they began to press for a reconstituted, autonomous Australian Church.[68] But most churchmen were less perturbed. England was still the fount of all wisdom and its Church could be well trusted to revise the Prayer Book satisfactorily.[69] Moreover, they were comforted by the opinion of one of the most prominent ecclesiastical lawyers in Australia, Harold Minton Taylor, who maintained that while Australian churchmen could not participate in the revision of the Prayer Book, there was no risk of unwelcome changes being thrust upon them because "whilst we are precluded from making any alterations except in conformity with such as may be made in England, yet we obviously are empowered to decide whether or not we will adopt such alterations."[70] This was legally accurate, but of course any English Revised Prayer Book would have brought with it a weight and prestige which few Australian dioceses could have confidently withstood.

The prospect of a new English Prayer Book was still far off in 1912, and although Australian churchmen were obliged to continue to use the English Common Prayer Book, they nevertheless enjoyed a practical autonomy in matters of finance and organisation. The moves before World War One towards a complete autonomy, by which they could determine their own formularies and discipline were, therefore, temperate and cautious. It will be shown in the next chapter that inter-diocesan discussions on a new Constitution proceeded slowly as individual dioceses prepared for the long interval before its introduction. For its part, Sydney's Synod passed an ordinance in 1912 which embraced parts of the 1872 English Act of Uniformity Amendment Act, which meant that no English law automatically became law in the Diocese of Sydney and no Prayer Book revision in England would necessarily become law in Sydney unless the Synod specifically accepted it (except if the British Parliament expressly made an alteration apply to the Church in the Sydney Diocese). It also meant that the Synod of the Diocese could make additions, omissions or changes to the Prayer Book which were in conformity with alterations made in England.[71]

Just as in England, the interest in Prayer Book Revision in Australia was revived by the experiences of war. The exigencies of war highlighted the limitations of the Book of Common Prayer, and resulted in the Bishops in each Diocese authorising additional special services in connection with the war and its effects, which were not catered for in the Prayer Book. The result was that after the war Australian interest in Revision in England was greater than ever before, and there was a more urgent demand for a new Constitution which would enable Australians to have a Prayer Book which was "more workable in modern conditions."[72] Some churchmen rightly believed that the national self-consciousness which the War had fostered was responsible for this demand for a new Constitution by which Australians could become more self-determining in matters of faith and doctrine.[73] But, for both Conservative and Liberal Evangelicals, there was another, stronger reason for their more urgent post-war interest in autonomy: the trend of events in England seriously disturbed them. They had monitored developments in the Mother Church during and immediately after the war and concluded that, on the whole, the proposals for Revision ratified by the English Convocations would "...weaken the authority of the Scriptures, impair the Reformation Settlement, and are not calculated to promote the unity of the Church."[74]

Evangelicals throughout Australia, but particularly in Sydney, began to question the value of the Nexus. They had previously considered that the Nexus prevented the Church in the Colonies from going off the rails and embracing anti-Evangelical formularies, doctrinal standards, and articles of faith. The Mother Church had been trusted to adhere conservatively to the Reformation Settlement, and uphold the authority of the Scriptures. But now Australian Evangelicals were no longer so sure that the Church in England could be trusted. The English Revision proposals were not just a matter of grave concern for men such as Mervyn Archdall and Digges La Touche, those fervent Irish Conservative Evangelicals who had perceived early in the war the "insidious influence" of German liberal theologians and philosophers in the campaign for Revision in England.[75] After the war, a far broader cross-section of Evangelicals began to view Revision in England askance. Even the temperate Archbishop Wright was deeply troubled by some of the decisions on the Revision issue: "...recent developments in England", Wright declared in 1921, "(have) made some of us doubt whether the fountain of all wisdom was to be found exclusively in the old Mother Church."[76] He was forced to re-assess his earlier contentment with the Nexus. The Old Church in England seemed to be slipping, giving into the demands of Anglo-Catholic militants. Wright was no longer certain that the Australian Church could rely upon the English Church to uphold the cause of Reformation truth: it therefore seemed to be in the interests of Evangelical Australians to secure those Reformation principles for themselves.

Both Conservative and Liberal Evangelicals in Sydney gave their undivided attention throughout the 1920s to the developments in Prayer Book Revision. They had a voracious appetite for English news and publications on the subject. Canon Langford Smith, a Conservative Evangelical party leader, and Archdeacon D.J. Davies, a Liberal Evangelical scholar, became the local authorities on the subject, and those Evangelical leaders who visited England were soon in demand to speak on the Revision question upon their return.[77] For example Dean Talbot, the Liberal Evangelical President of the A.C.L., announced after a holiday in England in 1924 that the Revision proposals were entirely unsatisfactory and "are accepted merely in the spirit of compromise, and not a few anticipate that their effect will be to widen the divisions in the Church."[78]

Under the leadership of these men the prevailing opinion of Sydney Evangelicals in the 1920s developed from a willingness to accept liturgical abbreviation and dictional changes, to an outright opposition to the 1926 Deposited Book. Davies was particularly critical of the concept of alternative uses which was propounded in England. He believed they would accentuate rather than heal the unhappy divisions within the Church, and perpetuate within it two quite distinct parties because, although the days of rigid uniformity in details were over, there was a big distinction between "...a diversity which merely means adaptation to local circumstances and does not involve serious doctrinal or disciplinary issues, and a diversity which is due to fundamental differences, and an incompatible presentation of the faith."[79] It was not a question of preference but of doctrine. Davies concluded that the failure to insist that no doctrinal changes be included in the revision had given "..the ecclesiastical anarchists their glorious opportunity to legitimise their ceremonial eccentricities" and produced a reactionary reconstruction, not a revision of the Prayer Book.[80] He and other Evangelicals therefore protested against the "undue tampering with the ancient landmarks" on the part of weak-kneed bishops who submitted to the demands of persistent "revolutionists."[81]

Evangelicals in Sydney could not influence events in England, but they were united in their determination to awaken Australians, and particularly Sydney churchmen, to the enervating developments which threatened the Mother Church. They urged vigilance lest these poisonous propensities irreparably infected their Church life in Australia. In fact, vigilant Conservative Evangelicals were already becoming aware of a kind of fifth column activity in Australia. They noted with alarm that Archbishop Lees and Dean Aicken of Melbourne, two Liberal Evangelicals, supported the Deposited Book and proposed that it be used in Melbourne if it became law in England.[82] In their support of the Deposited Book, these Melbourne Liberal Evangelicals identified closely with Liberal Evangelicals in England. It is important to note that their counterparts in Sydney, on the other hand, were united with Conservative Evangelicals in their firm conviction that the Revised Book introduced unacceptable doctrinal changes. Conservative Evangelicals were at a loss to understand the attitude of Melbourne Liberal Evangelicals and perplexed by what seemed to be the unity of interests between Liberal Evangelicals and Anglo-Catholics in Melbourne in their support for the introduction of the Revised Book. They could not understand why their brothers "... ignored the history of the past or the conditions of the Church in the present..." and played into the hands of the Anglo-Catholics, gladly giving them a Book which was demonstrably contrary to cherished Reformation truths? They were at a loss to understand it: but they were determined to defend their coveted heritage.[83] It was a naivety which heightened Conservative Evangelical suspicions of Liberal Evangelicalism as a whole.

The news of the defeat of the Prayer Book Measure was received with much thankfulness by Sydney Evangelicals. Bishop D'Arcy-Irvine naively asserted that the Commons vote would lead to a tightening of discipline; the *Record* believed that the "splendid NO!" was the vote of the people against the doctrine of Transubstantiation, and a great Evangelical victory.[84] Dean Talbot sympathised with Randall Davidson, but agreed with the Commons' decision and with its right to reject the Measure. The Establishment, he maintained, was a contract which could not be repudiated without the assent of both parties.[85] Other Sydney Evangelical leaders sadly reflected that the prospect of "a revision that would have adapted the Prayer Book to modern needs without destroying its essential characteristics" had been lost because unacceptable concessions had been given to lawless extremists. But, as a whole, Sydney Evangelicals were united in their thankfulness that the proposed Revised Prayer Book had been defeated. It indicated to them that, "...to put the matter bluntly, the main body of Churchmen did not want the Mass, but preferred to retain the Holy Communion. They could not rid themselves of the impression that the alternative new order at least suggested such a change, and voted accordingly."[86]

IV

The attempt at Prayer Book Revision in England confirmed Conservative Evangelical suspicions in Australia that there was a concerted campaign by Anglo-Catholics, with the connivance of the bishops, to overthrow the Reformed character of the Church of England. It made Conservative Evangelicals vigilant lest similar moves were attempted in Australia. Any suggestion for reform, revision or amendment of the formularies was viewed with suspicion. The Anglo-Catholic attack had been defeated in England; Australian Conservative Evangelicals were determined that the Anglo-Catholics would not succeed here.

Yet there were developments in Australia which worried them, and, with their Protestant sensibilities now highly attenuated by the English experience, they suspected that such a campaign was, in fact, already underway. Before the defeat of the Prayer Book Measure they had considered a new Constitution and an Australian revision "on conservative lines without additions of doubtful and controversial matters" as matters of urgency.[87] "A great responsibility rests upon Evangelical clergy and laity at this juncture to stand four square for an Australian revision," the *Church Record* declared.[88] A new Australian Constitution and a subsequent Australian Revision was their only hope. But after the Revision Proposals were rejected, Conservative Evangelicals suddenly made *volte face*. Their earlier support for the Constitution movement had been based upon the expectation that they would do better out of a Prayer Book in which Conservative Evangelical churchmen from Sydney had considerable say in drafting (and on which the Sydney diocese had a veto), than by rejecting the 1928 Revised Prayer Book which would come with all the weight and prestige of the Established Church of England behind it. But Conservative Evangelicals lost all enthusiasm for an Australian revision after the Commons' defeat of the Deposited Book in 1927-1928. Their reason for a local revision had disappeared. The Book of Common Prayer, a book which was steeped in Reformation principles, had been saved, and the Evangelical position vindicated. They were happy enough, now that the crisis had passed, with the *status quo*. But, concomitantly, the defeat of the Prayer Book Measure in England resulted in the demands by the proponents of autonomy for a new Constitution being intensified. Bishop Long of Bathurst, a High Churchman, angrily exclaimed that the Measure had been defeated by "..the fatuous blindness of rancorous fanatics of the ultra-Protestant faction", and he looked forward to the consummation of the new Constitution so that Australians could draft their own Revision free of that Erastian obstructionism.[89] Archbishop Harrington Lees, a Liberal Evangelical member of the A.E.G.M., also consoled his disappointment at the Commons' vote with the heartening prospect of a new Australian Prayer Book under the new Constitution.[90]

Conservative Evangelicals were startled: was the defeated 1928 Prayer Book to be introduced into Australia under a different cover — as the Australian revision? Was the campaign for a new Constitution, which would give the Church in Australia a completely independent polity, merely a device to get an Australian Prayer Book tailored to Anglo-Catholic requirements? Conservative Evangelicals began to suspect as much. They were determined to be cautious, for once the painter had been cut, and the Church in Australia made independent, that new heroic bulwark of Conservative Evangelicalism, the British Parliament, could not come to their rescue, if they were swamped by a wave of Anglo-Catholicism. Conservative Evangelicals were determined not to barter with their sacred heritage. They resolved that Sydney, the citadel of Australian Evangelicalism, would ensure that the cause of Evangelical truth in Australia was not put in the least jeopardy.

NOTES - CHAPTER SIX

1. J.W. Walmsley, "The History of the Evangelical Party in the Church of England between 1906 and 1928." Unpublished Ph.D Thesis, University of Hull, England, 1980 page v.
2. *ibid.*
3. See James Bentley, *Ritualism and Politics in Victorian Britain: The Attempt to Legislate for Belief*, Oxford U.P. 1978. Chapter Five, pp.97ff. and pp.115-116.
4. *ibid.*, p.115.
5. *ibid.*, pp.117,119; Chadwick, *op. cit.*,II, p.354.
6. Louise Creighton, *Life and Letters of Mandell Creighton* Longmans Green and Co. London 1913 v.2, pp.284-315.
7. Chadwick, *op. cit.*, pp.312,317-318.
8. Bentley, *op. cit.*, p.112.
9. Chadwick, *op. cit.*, II, pp.347-350.
10. *ibid.*, II, p.310.
11. *ibid.*, pp.310-311.
12. *ibid.*, p.313.
13. *ibid.*, pp.313-315.
14. *ibid.*, p.324; G.K.A. Bell, *Randall Davidson* Oxford Uni. Press London 1935 v.1 pp.456-457; Roger Lloyd, A *The Church of England in the Twentieth Century* Longmans London 1946 v.1 p.144
15. *ibid.*, p.457; Chadwick, gp.cit., II, pp.3l9-320. 4
16. Bell, *op. cit.*, I, pp.457-461; Lloyd, *op. cit.*, I,p.145.

17. Lloyd, *op. cit.*, p.145. Bell, *op.cit.*, I, p.462. The Commissioners were Archbishop Davidson, the Bishops of Oxford and Gloucester, Sir Lewis Dibdin, Sir Edward Clarke, Sir Samuel Hoare, Sir Michael Hicks-Beach, Sir John Kennaway, Lord Alverstone, the Marquess of Northampton, the Rev. T.W. Drury, and Messrs. G. Harwood, J.G. Talbot and George Prothero.

18. *Report* of the Royal Commission on Ecclesiastical Discipline. Wyman London. 1906. pp.72.

19. *ibid.*, p75-77.

20. Bell. *op. cit.*, I. pp.470-473.

21. *Church Intelligencer* August 1906 pp.114-117. Walmsley, *op.cit.*, pp.16,20.

22. *The Gazette*, August 1906 p.174.

23. *Church Intelligencer* July 1908. p.98; Walmsley, *op. cit.*, pp.28-30

24. *Church Times* 29/5/1908 pp.6-7.

25. Lord Halifax, quoted in *The Churchman*, April 1905, p.196.

26. William Joynson-Hicks, *The Prayer Book Crisis*, Putnam London 1928 pp.153-155.

27. *Chronicles of Convocation.* 18/2/1909. p.33. quoted in Walmsley, *op. cit.* p.33.

28. See *Church Intelligencer*, December 1911, p.178, Knox, *op. cit.*, p.311; Dyson Hague, *The Story of the English Prayer Book* Longmans London 1930 pp.144-45; The resolution for Reservation passed 4 votes to 3 through the Upper House of York when three bishops were absent.

29. *Church Times* 22/9/1916, quoted in *Church Intelligencer*, November 1916, p.137.

30. *The Record*, 13/10/1911, p.258.

31. quoted in J.G. Lockhart, *Cosmo Gordon Lang* Hodder and Stougton London 1949 p.145. Although the cope and mitre have no doctrinal significance in themselves, their *usage* denotes an exalted view of the episcopate which is based upon doctrinal assumptions.

32. See Knox, *op. cit.*, pp.307,310; Henry Wace, *Prayer Book Revision: Proposals of the Canterbury Convocation* London 1915 p.6.

33. Knox, *op. cit.*, p.313.

34. *The Intelligencer* April 1917 p.43.

35. Bishop Watts-Ditchfield to Knox n.d., quoted in Knox, *op. cit.*, p.314; Alan Wilkinson, *The Church of England and the First World War* S.P.C.K. London 1978 pp.174-9; Walmsley, *op. cit.*, p.66.

36. Walmsley, *op. cit.*, p.66. The restructuring concerned the relocation of the Prayer of Oblation, which asks God to "accept this our sacrifice of praise and thanksgiving." In the 1662 Order this was after the Communion and constituted part of a post-Communion act of praise which was clearly spiritual. When it was relocated between the Consecration and Administration of the Elements it reinforced the idea of a Eucharistic Sacrifice.

37. *The Record* 18/7/1919 p.81.

38. Walmsley, *op. cit.*, pp.67-68. In 1923, the English Church Union produced the "Green Book", which resembled the Roman Missal, the Alcuin Club published a less extreme Anglo-Catholic "Orange Book", while a group of anonymous Liberal Evangelicals published the "Grey Book". The Conservative Evangelicals, of course, did not need to produce a prototype Prayer Book. Their Book had already been in print for over 260 years — the Book of Common Prayer.

39. Sidney Dark, *op. cit.*, pp.204-6, 220-30; Knox, *op. cit.*, p.322; *The Intelligencer* April 1927, pp-41 and 44; *S.M.H.* 18/11/1927 p.12; Lockhart, *op. cit.*, p.304; Bell, *op. cit.*, II, pp.1325-1344; see Hensley Henson *Bishoprick Papers* Oxford Uni. Press. London 1946 p.95 re: estimate of Anglicans in the Commons and the number of communicant members. See also The Archbishops' Committee on Church and State, *Report*, S.P.C.K. London 1916 pp.28-29.

40. Lang to Wilfred Parker, quoted in Lockhart, *op.cit.*, p.305-306; The principal speakers against the Bill in the Commons were Sir William Joynson-Hicks, Colonel Applin, and Sir Thomas Inskip, while Lord Hugh Cecil proposed its acceptance; Bell, *op.cit.*, II, p.1346.

41. Lockhart, *op.cit.*, p.306; Bell, *op.cit.*, II, p.1345.
42. *ibid.*
43. Bell, *op.cit.*, II, pp.1352-1353; *S.M.H.* 9/1/1928 p.6, 10/1/1928 p.6, 12/4/1928 p.10; Dark, *op.cit.*, p.231; Lockhart, *op.cit.*, p.306.
44. Dark, *op.cit.*, p.232.
45. Bell, *op.cit.*, II, pp.1350-1351; Lockhart, *op.cit.*, pp.307-308. The second vote in the Commons was 266 against the Measure, 220 votes for.
46. Bell, *op.cit.*, II, p.1354. See also Joynson-Hicks, *op.cit.*, pp.145-147.
47. Lockhart, *op.cit.*, pp.308-309. See also Canon A.J. Worlledge to A.C. Headlam 27/2/1916, and Headlam to Bishop of Southwark, Hubert Murray Burge n.d. July 1916., Headlam to Davidson 15/3/1916. 1916.9. Headlam. Davidson Papers.
48. Lockhart, *op.cit.*, p.308; Dark, *op.cit.*, pp.207-208.
49. *ibid.*
50. Lockhart, *op.cit.*, p.309.
51. J.W. Walmsley, *op.cit.*, pp.119-120.
52. Knox, *op.cit.*, pp.311-312.
53. The "Six Points" were Eastward Position, Mixed Chalice, Eucharistic vestments, Altar Lights, Unleavened Bread and Incense, See Cross and Livingstone, *op.cit.*, p.1281. A Further Six Points were campaigned for soon after these had been won.
54. *Churchman*, April 1925, p.111.
55. H.C. Beeching, "The Permissive Use of vestments" in *Churchman*, April 1925 p.111. See also *ibid.*, 1911, p.173.
56. B. Herklots, "Evangelicals and the Problem of Ritualism" in *Churchman* 1913, pp.357, 387-89; E.C. Dewick, "Evangelicals and the Problem of Ritualism", in *Churchman* January 1913, p.16.
57. 1906 Royal Commission on Ecclesiastical Discipline, *Report* p.76.
58. The Revs F.S. Guy Warman, Lisle Carr (Liverpool), H.L.C. de Candole (Clifton), Stanton Jones (Middleton), Arthur Tait (Ridley Hall, Cambridge), E.N. Sharpe (Marylebone), and Drs. Carlyle (Oxford) and Dawson Walker (Durham) were the Liberal Evangelical leaders who interviewed Davidson. See "Record

of Conference: Davidson with 'Certain Evangelical Clergy'"
16/7/1915. "Prayer Book Revision" Box Three 1915-20 Special
Subject Series. Davidson Papers; 1906 Royal Commission *Report*
pp.75-77.

59. *ibid.*, Warman to Davidson 28/6/1915, 21/7/1915; Arthur J. Tait to
Davidson 23/7/1915. *loc.cit.*

60. Eugene Stock, "The Recent Controversy in the C.M.S.", in *Church
Missionary Society* 1923 pp.29-37; Joan Bayldon, *Cyril Bardsley,
Evangelist*, S.P.C.K London 1942; Leonard Hickin, "The Origins
and Early Years of the Anglican Evangelical Group Movement",
"Liberal Evangelicals in the Church of England", Unpublished
Articles in the A.E.G.M. Papers DEM 7/24 *loc.cit.*

61. Knox, *op. cit.*, p.313; Memo, A.E.G.M. to Bishop of Bristol n.d.
1927. in "Prayer Book Revision" Box 9 in Special Subject Series.
Davidson Papers.

62. *ibid.*

63. Walmsley, *op. cit.*, pp.310-312.

64. *Proceedings* of the Synod of the Diocese of Sydney 6/12/1909. p.47.

65. *S.M.H.* 11/10/1910 p.10.

66. *Church Commonwealth* 31/10/1910 p.13, 31/3/1909 p.870.

67. Australia Ex-Parte the Archbishops of Melbourne and Brisbane and
Bishop of Perth. Case for the Opinion of Counsel n.d; *Opinion* of
Arthur Cohen, Hugh Cecil and A.B. Kempe 20/6/1911. "Australia".
Special Subject Series. Davidson Papers; see also W.S. Smith to
Davidson 2/6/1909; Wright to Davidson 23/6/1910, 20/12/1910,
26/3/1911; Davidson to Wright 30/9/1910, 14/7/1911, 24/2/1911,
4/8/1911; Donaldson to Davidson 20/6/1910; *Church Standard*
14/6/1912 p.10.

68. *C.C.*, 29/6/1912 pp.13-14; *C.S.*, 28/6/1912 p.1.

69. *C.S.*, 5/7/1912 p.5.

70. *ibid.*, 4/10/1912 p.3.

71. *S.M.H.* 9/10/1912 p.13, 22/9/1913 p.8; Standing Committee *Minute
Book No.V* 24/7/1918 pp.393-4, 27/5/1918 p.379, 1/7/1918 p.386.

72. *A.C.R.* 11/6/1915 p.8.

73. e.g. *A.C.R.* 29/7/1921 p.7; *S.D.M.* January 1921 pp.4-5.

74. *Proceedings* of the Synod of the Diocese of Sydney 21/10/1914 pp.65-66, 10/9/1915 pp.88-89, 13/9/1915; *Church Standard* 9/10/1914 p.10.

75. e.g. *C.S.* 9/10/1914 p.10; *Proceedings* of the Synod of of the Diocese of Sydney 1/10/1914 pp.65-66.

76. *A.C.R.* 7/10/1921 p.7; See also 29/7/1921 p.7.

77. Langford Smith had many of the National Assembly drafts, the partisan "suggested" Prayer Books, and many publications of parties and individuals from England. See Langford Smith collection.

78. *S.D.M.* April 1924 pp.11-13, July p.12.

79. *S.D.M.* July 1924 p.12; *A.C.R.* 9/6/1927 p.5.

80. *S.D.M.* August 1924 p.12, December 1924 p.6.

81. *A.C.R.* 3/2/1927 p.6, 9/6/1927 p.5.

82. *A.C.R.* 21/12/1927 p.1, 27/10/1927 pp.4-5, 24/11/1924 p.3.

83. *ibid.*, 10/11/1927 pp.3 and 6, 10/11/1927 p.3.

84. *S.M.H.* 20/12/1927 p-11; *A.C.R.* 21/12/1927 p.7.

85. *A.C.R.* 25/10/1928 p.4; *S.M.H.* 6/1/1928 p.14.

86. *S.D.M.* September 1928 pp.14-15

87. *A.C.R.* 7/7/1924 p.4.

88. *ibid.*, 13/10/1927 pp.6-7.

89. *S.M.H.* 4/1/1928 p.14.

90. *ibid.* 20/12/1927 p.11.

CHAPTER SEVEN -

DEFENDING THE CITADEL

I

Always at the heart of the constitutional issue in Australia were the different conceptions of the nature and function of the Church held by Evangelicals and Anglo-Catholics. As outlined in Chapter One, these two schools had irreconciliable orientations. The Evangelicals' focus was upon the individual, although they recognised the diocese as an efficacious nexus between scattered, isolated congregations and a pragmatic unit of administration. Anglo-Catholics, on the other hand, focussed on the universality of the One Holy Catholic and Apostolic Church visible on earth. It was not simply the aggregation of local congregations, but the visible society and divinely constituted home of the great salvation. For Anglo-Catholics, the institutional was not mere human accretion, but the very body of Christ militant on earth. While Evangelicals were content in the knowledge that believers were united in their allegiance to the same Lord, the Anglo-Catholic ideal was a *visible* unity of the Body of Christ.[1]

The Anglo-Catholic believed the purpose and function of the Church was the redemption of human society and the ushering in of the reconsecration of the whole of creation to God. This vocation of the Church meant that her officers must seek to bridge the gulf between the sacred and the secular, including the political and social order. They had to identify with it: the Anglo-Catholic call in the 1920s for "a new Church in a new nation" was, therefore, motivated as much for doctrinal as nationalistic reasons. Their Evangelical brethren, on the other hand, believed the Church achieved its purpose in the very act of meeting together for the common worship of God and for mutual edification. It was no grander than that. While Anglo-Catholics sought "to bring in the Kingdom", Evangelicals were content to proclaim it as a present fact, and witness to it in their individual lives.[2]

The Anglo-Catholic conception of authority within that ecclesiastical structure was neither democratic nor diffused. All authority came from Christ, and his human agents were divinely called to rule, and received their commission and power from these above them. Bishops, the highest officers in the Church, had an authority which was therefore *essential* to the spiritual welfare of the whole church; the episcopate was critical to the proper and true functioning of the Body of Christ here on earth. The Evangelical, however, had a far more democratic view. They believed that authority from Christ came to the whole Church — all believers — and not through any corporation of officials, the Episcopal Bench. Authority was therefore diffused and democratic.

The tension created by these conflicting Anglo-Catholic and Evangelical propensities was a critical underlying factor in the debates on the question of a new Constitution for the Australian Church. But the fact that the development of the Australian colonial Church had been characterised by a strongly independent diocesanism was also a crucial determining factor in the constitutional issue.[3] Just as geographical circumstance caused the different Australian Colonies to develop independently, without necessary reference to each other, so Anglican colonial organisations developed in separate ways. Co-operation between the colonial bishops was negligible, and they journeyed to England to consult the Home authorities rather than seek the advice of their fellow bishops in Australia.[4]

The 1850 Conference had been the catalyst for the Church in each Colony to organise itself either by "legislative enactment", whereby the colonial legislature gave its imprimatur for the establishment of legislative synods by the Church in that Colony, or "consensual compact" alone, whereby the Church constituted itself like any other voluntary association, without reference to a secular legislature. The dioceses in New South Wales proceeded by legislative enactment; the Diocese of Adelaide was constituted by consensual compact.[5] The 1866 N.S.W. Act gave legal effect to the way the Church in that Colony wanted to organise itself but restrained the Church from delegating legislative authority to any outside body. It therefore inhibited the Church in N.S.W. from later granting plenary powers to the General Synod of Australia. It did not look beyond colonial boundaries but merely provided for diocesan government and the management of Church property within the Colony.[6] Above all it upheld the supremacy of diocesanism: although the Provincial Synod was empowered to make ordinances, these only had force within a diocese whose synod ratified them. There was, therefore, effective diocesan veto over corporate provincial action, as "...the provincial synod was left to glean in the fields of diocesan autonomy."[7]

The impetus for co-operation and consultation between the various parts of the Church in Australia increased as the ties with the Church at Home weakened. In October 1872 ten bishops, together with an average of three clerical and three lay representatives from each diocese, attended a conference in Sydney at which they settled upon a Constitution for the General Synod in Australia, and subsequently formed themselves into its first session.[8] This Constitution, with amendments, bound the General Synod until 1961. It not only regulated the functioning of the General Synod, determined its basis of representation and, in its original form, directed that the Bishop of Sydney would be Australia's Primate, but also gave the General Synod power to make Determinations on a wide range of subjects including the formation of new dioceses and

Provinces, the confirmation of bishops and the election of future Primates, the promotion and regulation of intercommunion with other Reformed Episcopal Churches, and the promotion of Home and Foreign Missions. In fact the General Synod was able to discuss any subject which affected the well-being of the Australian Church.[9]

The General Synod's power was in fact quite illusory. Real power remained with the dioceses because no Determination of the General Synod was binding upon a diocese until it was accepted by the diocese's synod. General Synod was in fact merely a consultative and co-operative body.[10] Effective legislative action remained with the dioceses: "We can never get over the fact," Archbishop Wright later remarked, "that we started ... with large Diocesan independence."[11]

The 1872 Constitution's bias against the establishment of any centralised plenary power was one which most Australian Evangelicals heartily endorsed. They opposed the relegation of plenary power to a higher, more remote decision-making council, and preferred the locus of power to be the diocesan synods:

> Supersession of diocesan by provincial (or national) action
> involves the danger of forcing the will of some upon others
> without securing the true advantage of all..." It was preferable
> "..that those who think that they have a vision can so commend
> it by argument that others, if not all, will voluntarily adopt it...[12]

High churchmen and Anglo-Catholics, however, argued that the continuity, indeed the very catholicity, of the Church was at risk if its unity and uniformity was lost by the separate and independent actions and decisions of its atomised parts, which was little more than a "system of chartered anarchy".[13] A central decision-making authority was essential. The impotence of the General synod, and the supremacy of the dioceses frustrated such men. They pressed for change, maintaining that diocesanism produced unequal results because human, physical and financial resources were unevenly distributed.[14]

II

The division of power between the General and Diocesan Synods remained a matter of contention in the Australian Church well into the twentieth century. Successive sessions of General Synod were pre-occupied with the Synod's Constitution, a tedious self-consciousness which betrayed the Synod's impotence.[15] But in the 1890s this concern was eclipsed by the related question of the relationship of the Church in the Colonies to the Church in England. The issue rose to prominence in 1891 when the General Synod resolved that an Australian Metropolitan (the senior bishop in a Province) was not required to promise if "all due reverence and obedience" to the Archbishop of Canterbury.[16] Archbishop Benson of Canterbury strongly contested the decision. He believed that the object of the oath was

> beyond question to preserve the constitutional NEXUS...
> (between the Church in the Colony and the Mother Church.) If a
> Metropolitan were consecrated without (the oath) and if he con-
> secrated Bishops who took no oath except to him, the NEXUS
> contemplated by our statute law would be at an end." Benson
> was fearful that such an eventuality would rend the Anglican
> Communion: it would mean, for example, that clergy coming
> from that colony "would not have taken an oath to any prelate
> within the NEXUS.[17]

Australian churchmen were in a cleft stick. Whereas they had long exercised powers of self-government, Benson now contended that they were *not* autonomous. This conundrum became even more complex in 1897 when the Australian Primate, Saumarez Smith, acquired the title of "Archbishop", thereby assuming the same canonical status as Canterbury, something which Benson believed was counter to "the Nexus contemplated by (English) statute law."[18] What exactly was the relationship of the Church in Australia to the Church in England? Did that relationship impinge upon the institutionalised relationships which had already developed between the Australian dioceses? Was the power which had been arrogated to various synods illegitimate?

The legal opinion on these matters which was obtained in 1905 and 1911 from both Australian and English lawyers indicated that the law of the Church of England in England determined the purposes of the Church of England in Australia. The Australian dioceses were

> all organised upon the basis that they are not merely Churches 'in communion with' or 'in connection with' the Church of England, but are actual parts of that Church. In most of the States this status is recognised by Statute and we think that in all it must be taken that this is their actual status.

> Therefore," the English lawyers concluded, "if they (Australian churchmen) want to use and enjoy property settled for the purposes of the Church of England they are bound to adhere to the faith doctrine and discipline of the Church of England. They must conform to the Book of Common Prayer to the same extent as members of the Church of England in England conform. They would not be using their churches for the purposes of the Church of England otherwise.[19]

Any ordinance of an Australian synod which ignored these constraints "necessarily affected the right of members of the Church of England to have use of churches." If such an ordinance was supported unanimously, dissolution of the Church of England in that diocese could result. But even if a small minority opposed it (and thereby implicitly upheld the *status quo*) they, and not the majority, would be entitled to use the churches and other property. Only the State legislatures could authorise dioceses to make changes to these formularies including the Book of Common Prayer without prejudicing their right to the use and enjoyment of churches or other property. That legislation would effectively break the nexus with England.[20]

These legal opinions deeply disappointed the proponents of autonomy, who were predominantly Anglo-Catholic. They realised that their ideal of a healthy freedom to make changes as they thought best was "very far off, and we appear to be bound so tight ....that we cannot make any alteration whatever in the Prayer Book without risking the loss of our property."[21] Their disappointment stemmed from their belief that the Church in Australia needed to be independent if it was to be a powerful force in the new nation and "give the lead to Australia."[22] But they also objected to the legal nature of the nexus. They believed that the Civil Courts had no business intruding into the affairs of the Church, and that this "Erastianism" was an unnecessary and dangerous encumbrance upon the liberty of the Church as a living organism.[23]

Most Evangelicals in Sydney, on the other hand, were "... glad that the legal difficulties in the way of constitutional alteration are so great" because it meant that change would be slow: "Australia stands to lose much by the hasty and ill-conceived grasp at quasi-independence of the Church as regards freedom to enact ..."[24] Sydney Evangelicals simply saw no necessity for any change in the existing relationship. In what did the Constitution fail them? Where did the shackles gall? They demanded that the proponents of autonomy declare what the changes were for. They were not convinced that change should occur purely because it was theoretically ideal: "It is hardly wise to enter upon revolutionary legislation merely for the sake of a theory, except it be a theory that is a new and true revelation."[25]

Sydney Evangelicals were very conscious that the pressure for autonomy was not coming from the settled ecclesiastical environment of Sydney, but from the less developed, less institutionalised areas of Australia — Queensland, South Australia, and Western Australia. The Provinces of Queensland and Victoria had only been created in 1905 and Western Australia was established in 1914. The too rapid division into an excessive number of Provinces was "a matter of considerable anxiety" for the Primate, Archbishop Wright. He believed that the provincial organisation of these youthful, thinly populated, inadequately ministered and generally undeveloped parts of Australia was a recipe for disaster. Events were moving too fast.[26] Wright could not prevent three dioceses devolving into a Province, but at least the legal nexus meant that absolute self-determination was forestalled. Wright was not being reactionary. Rather, he was firmly convinced that this was a formative stage in the history of the Church in Australia and that

carelessness (now) would breed trouble later...Our difficulty is that we are ignorant how population will come — and what will be the future of the States. We need every care against precipitate action. We are making history.[27]

The Church in Australia at that time was in a state of flux. The ecclesiastical map of Australia had been transformed by the creation of nine dioceses between 1900 and 1915.[28] There were too many unknown variables for the churchmen in Sydney to feel at ease with the concept of autonomy from England. Moreover, that unease was exacerbated by the churchmanship of these new dioceses. In 1872 four of the eleven dioceses in the Australian Colonies were "Evangelical".[29] In 1912, only forty years later, the number of dioceses had doubled yet a radical shift in churchmanship away from

Evangelicalism had occurred.[30] This meant that Evangelicalism was a strong influence in only five of the twenty-five Australian dioceses.[31] Only two of the new dioceses could be called "Evangelical" (Bendigo and Gippsland) while Tractarian developments in the older dioceses of Goulburn and Bathurst were accentuating the trend towards Anglo-Catholicism which was firmly rooted in the new dioceses. The new non-Evangelical dioceses were at the very forefront of the demand for constitutional change. Archbishop Wright was thus moved to remark that

> The drive for independence is voiced by the Young Guard, who are possessed by a wish for ritual liberty at any cost, and who are apt to let their prepossession blind them the factors which make (for? — two words unclear) the influence of the Church in this Commonwealth.

> It could be pitiful, when an age of soberness sets in," he concluded, "to (discover?) that we had bartered our heritage in exchange for the temporary satisfaction of certain hot-heads.[32]

Sydney Evangelicals suspected that Anglo-Catholics were conspiring to use the push to break the nexus with England as the means whereby they could "collar Australia for the High Church."[33] That fear was confirmed by the fact that whereas Australian laymen were not "dizzy for independence" and, before the War, strongly supported the nexus as an expression of their British Protestant heritage, the foremost advocates of autonomy were, with two exceptions, clergymen who had been born and trained in England.[34] English clergymen had been principally responsible for the spread of Anglo-catholic practices in Australia, particularly in the new young dioceses which had been created since the 1880s. Now they supported the breaking of the nexus and the assertion of self-determination for the Church in Australia. Sydney Evangelicals, already "fearing the growth of romanizing tendencies" were cautious, lest this push for autonomy was the means whereby a counter-Reformation in Australia was effected.[35]

III

Just as the First World War promoted the cause of Prayer Book Revision in England, it also stimulated the autonomy movement in the Australian Church. In an atmosphere of national consciousness, the limitations of the 1662 Prayer Book were made palpable. An Australian revision, however, could only be achieved after constitutional change.[36] Both Conservative and Liberal Evangelicals became more willing to consider constitutional reform after the War. Before 1914, Evangelicals, particularly Conservatives, had opposed precipitate action lest Reformation truths be endangered. They had presumed that those Evangelical truths were secured by the nexus to a trustworthy and wise Mother Church. Now, as we noted in the previous chapter, Evangelicals watched solicitously as those very truths were under attack within the Church at Home. Australian Evangelicals began to question whether they wanted to be tied to the Church in England after all.[37]

That did not mean they were less cautious of constitutional change. But, by 1921, Bishop Gilbert White of Willochra, an eager supporter of autonomy, noticed a distinct change in their attitude:

> A considerable change has come over many of the (Evangelical) opposition. At first they said that no action was necessary at all. Now they are prepared to approve the report (supporting auton-omy by a committee appointed by General Synod to report on the Nexus) provided that the safeguards are sufficient to secure that the majority does not over-ride the minority...[38]

This change in attitude was exemplified by Archbishop Wright who, by the time of the 1921 General Synod, had "made a remarkable advance in his attitude towards autonomy."[39] He was no less determined that Evangelical principles should be neither threatened nor compromised, but he was now willing to endorse "something which serves larger corporate action whilst yet preserving the reasonable independence of individual dioceses." The war experiences had convinced him that the Australian Church should accept the "full measure of self-government", while his concerned monitoring of Revision in England made him question the intrinsic value of the Nexus.[40]

The Evangelical contingent at the 1921 General Synod was nevertheless determined to drive a hard bargain. They were not about to swallow any autonomy proposal that was served up to them. First, they demanded a fairer basis of representation in the General Synod. They quite legitimately declared that the existing basis of representation was disproportionate and "undemocratic". The Evangelical strongholds of Sydney and Melbourne had 35.7% of all clergy in Australia and 37.2% of the "C of E" laity, but only 12.6% of the General Synod representatives. By contrast, the predominantly Anglo-Catholic country representatives in the General Synod were adamant that dioceses were clearly over-represented. Sydney's there could be "no alteration without representation." The representation issue had to be resolved before the nexus question could be tackled.[41]

Non-Evangelicals came half-way on this issue. They would not agree to a completely proportional scheme of representation, but an accord was reached whereby the representation of Sydney and Melbourne was increased by 100% and 67% respectively, mainly at the expense of the middle-sized dioceses. This was a marked improvement on the existing position but the two most populous and Evangelical dioceses were still clearly under-represented. Despite considerable discontent in Sydney that the Determination did not go far enough, Sydney's Diocesan Synod was induced to accept the change, swayed by Archdeacon Boyce's plea that "half a loaf is better than no bread at all."[42]

Sydney Evangelicals were less successful in influencing the terms of the 1921 General Synod Determination on "The Extension of the Powers of Management and Government" of the Australian Church. This Determination broke the nexus with the Church in England and gave plenary powers to the General Synod. The General Synod accepted the Majority Report from its Nexus Committee which maintained that the existing legal position was unsatisfactory and that changes to the formularies of faith and order should occur with the assent of three-fifths of all three orders of General synod, three-fifths of all diocesan synodsmen and two-thirds of the Diocesan Synods. The Synod rejected a Minority Report, prepared by the Sydney representatives on that Committee, which opposed any proposals for a new Constitution which did not provide an unalterable basis of "fundamental" doctrines and beliefs.[43] The Sydney representatives rightly pointed out that it was unrealistic to suggest that they could simply change their standards and formularies by mere, even overwhelming, majorities in Australian synods: "Of course any religious body can alter its doctrines, ritual, and formularies of worship...", one Sydney representative remarked. "But it cannot alter the trusts of property, and this is the point many zealous churchmen have failed to grasp. All property held in trust must be used for the purposes defined in such trust..."[44] The Church in Australia was constrained by property rights in the same way as any other voluntary association. It was, therefore, highly

> unlikely, practically impossible, that the State would allow the Church, or any other corporate body, to play ducks and drakes with its trust property...The Church consists of men and women who have rights as citizens...which the State will always recognise and reinforce.

If a minority was ignored, the Church risked disenfranchisement of its property.[45] Nevertheless the General Synod ignored this sound legal argument and resoundingly carried the Nexus Determination. Apart from a handful of men from other dioceses, the Sydney representatives were alone in opposing its passage.[46]

The normal process after this strong vote for the second reading of the Nexus Determination would have been a third reading, submission to the diocesan synods for adoption and, if accepted by two-thirds of them and ratified at the 1926 session of General Synod, submission to the State Parliaments for approval. If these legislatures passed the Bill, it would mean that the Nexus with England was broken and the Australian Church was autonomous. However, the Determination's sponsors decided not to proceed this way, but to gain wider support for the Measure by referring it to the dioceses after only two readings so that they could discuss the Bill and make suggestions which could be incorporated into a new document. It was an astute move designed to disarm the opposition to the Bill and secure its more general acceptance. The Bill could probably have secured the requisite acceptance of two-thirds of the dioceses in Australia, but it was clear that Sydney was not about to be steam-rollered, and Melbourne, Bendigo, Gippsland and Tasmania were adamant that Sydney could not be ignored or left out of any new constitutional arrangement. More than this, the New South Wales Parliament would certainly have refused to give its assent to an Act which Sydney, with more than half the clergy and laity in the State, opposed. The circuitous procedure was eminently expeditious if, by appeasing its opponents beforehand, it pre-empted a rejection of the Bill by Parliament.[47]

The attempt at consensus came unstuck when a number of diocesan synods rejected the Determination. First, Sydney's Synod refused to accept the Determination, and indicated its antipathy to any proposed Constitution which did not have a basis of fundamental standards of faith:

Do the nexus breakers really think that Church-people in Australia are going to give them a blank cheque to fill in as they please?" D.J. ('Ben') Davies asked rhetorically, summing up the attitude of most Sydney Evangelicals. "We know where we stand just now. But we should be extremely foolish to give up our present prayer book and other standards of worship and doc-trine, however desirable certain changes may be, until we know what sort of prayer book we are likely to get instead of it. The nexus breakers are full of destructive propaganda, but they have not put forth one single constructive proposal.[48]

Although the primatial see showed a preparedness."to stand out in splendid isolation", its stand was soon supported by the diocesan synods of Tasmania, Melbourne, Ballarat, Gippsland and, surprisingly, Brisbane, where the laity showed an unwillingness "to throw over the historic basis of their church position in order to get they know not what."[49]

The movement for autonomy was about to stall. Sydney Evangelicals were adamant that they would not be a party to any Constitution which did not safeguard the existing doctrinal foundations of their Reformed Church. They insisted that the 39 Articles of Religion be scheduled in the new Constitution as unalterable except by the consent of *every* diocese: "It must be a change to which we all agree."[50] Archbishop Wright had no doubt that such an uncompromising stance on the standards of faith would be unpopular with Anglo-Catholics who , he said, "wish to alter the Articles not because of obscurity of diction, but because of the plainness of the content." A Liberal Evangelical scholar, he nevertheless shared the concern of his Conservative Evangelical brothers that there were "forces" at work within the Church which aimed to "disintegrate the Reformation structure of our Church, and fling us back into pre-Reformation darkness and uncertainty." Thus, whatever their attitude to the Nexus question, Evangelicals of all complexions were united in their determination that the new Constitution should not be the means whereby these Anglo-Catholic "forces" imposed upon them "...opinions destructive of the very foundations of Church doctrine and order under which we have been brought up..."[51]

The failure of the Nexus Determination to secure substantial agreement in the dioceses dimmed the prospects of a settlement by 1926. Nevertheless, the General Synod's Committee on Autonomy continued working towards a solution and, in a bid to revive hopes of an early consensus, changed tack. The 1921 Determination was discarded and a five-man committee appointed to draft a Constitutional Bill which would be presented to a special Constitutional Convention in 1926 for discussion and amendment.[52] This Committee quickly recognised that the 1921 Determination had foundered because it broke the nexus without making clear what would be put in its place. Evangelicals were not the only ones who had rejected this "blank cheque" proposal. The supporters of autonomy now sought to allay those fears by presenting a proposed new Constitution. They hoped that autonomy could be achieved if agreement was secured on what was to come after they had cut the painter with England.[53]

The publication of the Constitutional Committee's Draft in February 1926 did not come too soon for Australian Evangelicals. They had not minded when the Autonomy question had been consigned to the committee room in 1923, but two and a half years later the progress towards Prayer Book Revision in England meant that they felt an urgent need to resolve the Constitutional issue and press on with an Australian revision of the Prayer Book.[54] That did not mean they would be bull-dozed into accepting *any* Draft Constitution: "Evangelicals cannot forget or ignore the fact," said Canon Langford Smith, "that in England a very deliberate, determined and partially successful attempt has recently been made to re-introduce in the Book of Common Prayer doctrines and practices.. (expunged at the Reformation)."[55] In fact, the Draft Constitution did not satisfy Sydney's Evangelicals. Once again their two grounds of complaint were the basis of representation to General Synod and the absence of adequate safeguards against doctrinal changes. First, they protested that the Draft only gave Sydney and Melbourne one-quarter of the seats in General Synod even though they had nearly 40% of the Anglican population. Second, and more dangerous in Evangelical eyes, the proposed Declarations of doctrine were not unalterable. The Draft gave General Synod the power to alter the Prayer Book and the Articles of Religion with the assent of two-thirds of its members and of the diocesan synods.[56] Even though such changes would have no effect in any diocese which did not assent to them, Sydney Evangelicals were united in fearing that the Australian Church would face a very real danger of being divided by the use of different Prayer Books which represented different standards of faith and doctrine.[57] That possibility could only be eliminated by securing existing doctrinal standards and making them inviolate:

> In any New Constitution," concluded Dean Talbot of Sydney, "..though provision should be made for such alterations in the Prayer Book as are necessary for adapting it to our local and modern needs, the Doctrine of the Church of England as set forth in its formularies, should be *inviolate*. Unless the Proposed Bill is drastically altered in this regard it cannot hope to preserve the unity of the Church...[58]

Sydney's Diocesan Synod rejected the Draft Constitution in August 1926, before the Constitution Convention had even met, on the ground that the proposed Bill facilitated methods by which the Church's Reformed and Protestant character could be changed, gave the smaller dioceses powers quite out of proportion to their Church membership and, last, gave unnecessary powers to the General Synod which unduly derogated from the sovereign rights of the dioceses.[59] The Evangelical majority in Sydney's Synod would not overlook these potential dangers for the sake of unity: "Why must we take the risk?" asked Canon Langford Smith, a Conservative Evangelical. "Why should we be called upon to surrender our heritage, or sell our birthright, with no corresponding gain to ourselves or to the church of God?"[60]

Yet Sydney's Evangelicals were not completely negative. They held out an olive branch to the proponents of autonomy in the form of an Alternative Draft. The able ecclesiastical lawyers in their number drafted a positive statement of their position which demonstrated that the Mother Diocese was willing to countenance a new Constitution, but not at any price.[61]

IV

The Constitutional Convention of General Synodsmen commenced on the 12th October 1926 with an air of caution. Archbishop Wright attempted to ease tensions by calling on the Convention "to approach the whole issue with an absolutely open mind, untrammelled (by previous controversy and debate)... with mutual respect for each other and goodwill."[62] But the lack of mutual trust remained all too evident. The mood of the Convention was captured by one sceptic in this limerick:

> The work of a famous Convention
> Was held in a state of suspension,
> For some were suspicious,
> That somebody vicious,
> Would some day do things we won't mention.[63]

Nevertheless, incremental progress was made as the Convention tackled the time-consuming task of debating each clause of the Draft Bill. Sydney's Alternative Bill was on hand for reference. Many changes were made, and the Draft soon took on "a form that its very parents would hardly recognise."[64] The Convention quickly removed one of Sydney's objections to the Draft by acceding to the demand for proportional representation in the General Synod. Then the Convention further accommodated Sydney Evangelicals on the issue of the doctrinal Declarations. First, the Declaration on the authority of the Church was deleted, the sacraments were defined as Baptism and Holy Communion, and the Scriptures became not simply inspired by God, but "the ultimate rule and standard of faith." Second, these statements were made unalterable.[65] To most Evangelicals, this was a cautious covering of all contingencies. But for many non-Evangelicals it negated the whole concept of the corporate responsibility of the Church for its own definition of faith, and restricted the work of the Holy Spirit in the development of the Church:

> Who are we that we should fetter in advance the mind of the Church of the future?..." Asked Bishop Radford of Goulburn. "The Church in stating its position in its constitution, must take over from its past at some point or other. It is claiming for itself authority, subject to due safeguards, to deal with such things as the articles and canons.

That Radford and others wanted to "take over" from the past confirmed Evangelical suspicions that the truths of their Reformation Fathers were in danger. They remained adamant that the Declarations had to be unalterable and their intransigence finally prevailed.[66]

Two other issues brought into sharp relief the determination of Evangelicals to preserve diocesan autonomy. First, the Draft Bill had given plenary powers to General Synod in specified areas and the power to make canons on any matter, although these latter required the assent of two-thirds of the dioceses. Anglo-Catholics supported this arrangement, arguing that "in the last resort the Church must rule and the diocese must submit." But Evangelicals maintained that General Synod only had those powers which were willingly relegated to it by the dioceses, and the sovereignty of the dioceses should not be violated. The Evangelicals prevailed once again: General Synod's plenary powers were considerably circumscribed, and no diocese was bound to accept its provisional canons: if the canon was inconsistent with an ordinance of the diocese, even one made after the canon, the canon did not apply to that diocese. The Diocese remained the sovereign church unit in Australia.[67]

The second issue revolved around the issue of tribunals. Tribunals were ecclesiastical courts convened to hear and determine charges against any clergyman for breaches of faith, discipline or ceremonial. They were empowered to admonish, suspend or expel from office, deprive of rights and emoluments, or degrade from holy orders. The Draft Bill provided for appeals to be made to a supreme tribunal from the judgments of diocesan and provincial tribunals. Evangelicals believed that this arrangement would seriously impair the autonomy of the Diocese. The Diocesan Tribunal could, for example, convict a priest of breaches of ceremonial only to have that man exonerated by the Supreme Tribunal. The Diocese would be then obliged to accept the decision of that Appeal Court. High Churchmen and Anglo-Catholics, on the other hand, asserted that while the diocese had the right to judge conduct and character, the church as a whole, not the diocese, had to decide on broad questions of faith and ceremonial.[68]

The Draft had also left the composition of the Supreme Tribunal up to the General Synod. This was totally unsatisfactory for the Sydney representatives who were quite unwilling to accept a blind date. They had to know how the Supreme Tribunal would be constituted before they could even consider acceptance. Canon Langford Smith and his fellow Sydney Evangelical leaders frankly admitted that they were afraid of the Tribunal, and they were unwilling to leap into the dark, only to find out later that the Bishops were not only to administer the law, but also to adjudicate upon it as well. They argued that this judicial function should be performed by men well removed from the legislative and administrative arms of the Church. The Tribunal's independence was vital to the integrity of the appeal. In their view the question was one of law: therefore, lawyers should constitute a significant, if not predominant, element on the Tribunal.[69]

This argument horrified Anglo-Catholics who believed that it was the responsibility of the bishops, the official guardians of the faith, to decide matters of faith doctrine and ceremonial. The Tribunal should be episcopal in character. Nevertheless, the Evangelicals persuaded the majority of Convention members to accede to their demand by a compromise move whereby the pre-eminence of the Supreme Tribunal was upheld, yet it was composed of a bishop as president and six other members — three bishops or priests, and three lawyers.[70]

The final form of the Bill was strongly influenced by the Sydney representatives. Their convinced and resolute — and at times objectionably persistent — tenacity held the Convention to a full and reasoned discussion of the Bill, and it was a contribution which was generously acknowledged by their adversaries at the close of the Convention. Sydney Evangelicals were particularly influential in the four crucial areas of representation, the powers of General Synod, the composition and authority of the tribunal and the Declarations.[71]

These vital concessions were made because the majority of Convention members were convinced that the time had come for concerted action. They wanted a new Constitution, and were willing to make sacrifices for it.[72] Nor did this spirit of earnest co-operation leave the Sydney delegation unmoved: many Sydney Evangelicals were also anxious, with the ominous dark cloud of English Prayer Book Revision in the background, for a new Australian Constitution. Men such as Boyce, Minton Taylor, Dean Talbot and Archdeacon Davies were eager to co-operate, to the extent that their beliefs and principles would allow, in order that juxtaposed opinions could be reconciled.

The proposed Constitution was passed by the Convention on the 21st October 1926, and was immediately commended to the Dioceses for acceptance by Bishop Long of Bathurst, and the veteran Evangelical leader, Archdeacon Boyce. To many Convention members, it was "a thrilling moment". The whole Convention stood "and with loud and unanimous voice sang the Te Deum as an act of thanksgiving for the completion of its labour, with a spirit of goodwill and brotherliness that no one could have anticipated who had listened to the first day's debate."[73]

No-one joined in singing the Te Deum with greater fervour than Archbishop Wright. At the start of the Convention he had been unhappy with the Draft, and pessimistic about the Convention's outcome. Now he was convinced that they had settled upon "a constitution more directly conservative than the constitution of any other branch of our Anglican Communion."[74] He acknowledged that no-one had achieved their every desire, and many had made sacrifices for the common good. But he believed that they now had

> reached an harmonious and concerted agreement along the lines of which our beloved Church can advance as a united whole for the greater good of our children's children, and for the continual building up of the Kingdom of God in our Australian continent." He believed that "the document must be considered in its fulness, and not in isolated sections, if its real value is to be discovered. Its balance depends upon its unity, and this unity must be interpreted by the principles that inspired it. These principles are the preservation of the basis of doctrine that has been the foundation of our life since the Reformation, and secondly, the adaptation of our activities to the new needs and ideals of a new age. But the greatest gain has been a full realisation of the underlying brotherliness which exists in Christ Jesus amongst

the members of His flock, by Whom the vision comes coloured differently by individual traditions and idiosyncrasies.[75]

V

Not everyone joined in the singing of the "Te Deum". Canon S.E. Langford Smith and W.J.G. Mann, two Sydney Conservative Evangelicals, left the Convention before the final resolution. They did not stay to praise God: they felt "there was policy in the singing of it." Instead, they preferred to retreat — and fight another day.[76]

They had the job ahead of them. The Archbishop, his Assistant Bishop, Gerard D'Arcy-Irvine, the Principal of Moore College, D.J. Davies, Archdeacon Boyce, the founder of the A.C.L., Dean Talbot, its President, Harold Minton Taylor and many other Sydney church leaders supported the 1926 Constitution. They believed that the "best genius of the Church" had produced a Bill that was "wonderfully good, and its few imperfections should not make us stand aloof from our people in the other parts."[77]

Even many Conservative Evangelicals who were not completely happy with the settlement believed that "it would be useless for a minority to stand out against the new Constitution" and concluded that acceptance of it was "the best to do under all the circumstances."[78] Canon Langford Smith and Mann were undaunted by this pessimism and began a vigorous rearguard action against the Bill. Mann leapt into print at every opportunity with the claim that the Constitution really established a new Church in Australia. He asserted that the "character" of this Church could be altered by simple amendment of the Prayer Book, the Constitution and a biased judgment by the Supreme Tribunal. He further contended that the proposed Constitution gave the laymen no recourse if this happened. They would have to watch an alien Church use their property.[79]

This unsophisticated argument was highly effective. It aroused Conservative Evangelical suspicions that the rug was about to be pulled from under their feet. The spectre of the South African experience, the Anglo-Catholic threat, and the fear of the loss of property were powerfully persuasive, particularly to laymen. While Mann carried the burden of public propaganda, Langford Smith organised a series of small meetings for about twenty Conservative Evangelical clergy, "who take a prominent part in maintaining the Evangelical character of our Diocese", to discuss the proposed Constitution. The first of these took place in December 1926. Later, he took the issue to Anglican Church League meetings. Langford Smith impressed upon all these meetings his belief that "We are face to face with the greatest crisis in the history of the Church in Australia, and the future of Evangelicalism is in the balance. A wrong step taken at this juncture must have very far-reaching results, and would perhaps be quite irretraceable."[80]

Like Mann, Langford Smith did not object to the Constitution Bill as it stood. His objection was that it could be *changed*. He claimed that the name and doctrine of the Church could be changed, and that two-thirds of the whole Constitution could be altered by canon of General Synod alone without approval of any diocese. He argued that Provisional Canons of General Synod should be inoperative in a diocese until *after* the passing of a confirming ordinance, rather than operative until invalidated by a diocesan ordinance. Lastly, he was particularly disturbed with the prospect of a Supreme Tribunal which could, in his view, "re-interpret the Prayer Book in an Anglo-Catholic direction making things now unlawful not only lawful but compulsory."[81]

Langford Smith's claims appalled Archdeacon Boyce:

Are we to be like the old Medes and Persians whose laws altered not?" asked old Boyce. "...Is Sydney to refuse to join this federation? Is it to play a lonely hand and isolate itself from the rest of the Church in Australia? Is it to be charged with schism by our being called separationists?[82]

Yet Conservative Evangelical members of the A.C.L. were not prepared to take the risk that Langford Smith was wrong. Despite "spirited" opposition from Liberal Evangelical members of the League, Langford Smith and Mann soon won over a majority of the League's members.[83] In 1927, the League publicly backed Langford Smith and published a booklet which detailed his objections to the Constitution and by early 1928, the Conservative Evangelical opposition to the Bill had swelled.[84] The despondent, unspoken resignation of Conservative Evangelicals had been transformed into an arrogant obstinacy. Langford Smith's booklet was acclaimed as a "clear-sighted statement. The 'log-rolling' methods of the Anglo-Catholics have bluffed quite a number into thinking that we must follow what they have already done."[85] He had convinced many Conservative Evangelicals of the "very real and irremediable...dangers to which we would expose our Church in this diocese, by accepting the Constitution in its present form."[86]

With Conservative Evangelical suspicions excited, those Evangelicals who did support the Constitution were accused by the Conservative Evangelicals of naivety, negligence and even treasonous expedience. Even that veteran party boss, Archdeacon Boyce, was not spared:

It is pathetic to see Archdeacon Boyce, after his great services in many departments of our life," exclaimed the pugilistic Mann, "now offer a lead to Church of England people in reversal of, or at least jeopardising, the reformation settlement.[87]

Would he (Boyce) advise a teetotal friend", asked the Rev. (later Bishop) S.J. Kirkby in mock horror, "to marry someone known to

have occasional sprees in the chance of effecting a post-matrimo-
nial conversion to total abstinence?

We are not going to be afraid," Kirkby concluded defiantly, "even
though the archdeacon himself forsake us.[88]

The ageing Boyce could not understand their vitriolic suspicion.
Under the new constitution the General Synod would be a truly representative body: representatives from Sydney and Melbourne would constitute
nearly 40% of the Synod. "Why should we refuse power when we can
have it?" asked Boyce plaintively.[89] Yet the Conservative Evangelicals
remained suspicious and unmoved. They posited a powerful, but false
antithesis: adopt the constitution and have Anglo-Catholic services
legalised, or reject the constitution and remain secure in Protestant
truth. Many were the voices which protested that this was not true, but
the Conservative Evangelicals exulted in their severe, lonely position:
indeed, its very loneliness was a sign of virtuous rightousness.[90]

The key to the Conservative Evangelicals' fears for the future of the
Australian Church was Melbourne. Although Charles Perry had established
Melbourne as a distinctly "Evangelical" diocese, his successor, James
Moorhouse (1876-1886), had succeeded, in stark contrast to Bishop Barry
in Sydney, in eroding the Conservatism of that Perry tradition. Then, after
the lacklustre episcopate of Field Flowers Goe (1887-1901), the Diocese
of Melbourne began to develop a tradition of Liberal Evangelicalism. There
was a deliberate cultivation of the comprehensive in Melbourne which did
not occur in Sydney. Trinity College catered for the theological training
of the High Churchman; Ridley College for the Evangelical; Canons H.T.
Langley of Caulfield and E.S. Hughes of Eastern Hill represented the
extremities of an ecclesiastical spectrum in which men from all schools
of thought were found. Successive Archbishops of Melbourne were
members of the Anglican Evangelical Group Movement.[91] The Diocese of

Melbourne began to approximate the style of a Northern English diocese: an Evangelical past, a comprehensive present, and an abhorrence of the controversial. Melbourne's encouragement of variety and plurality was clearly reflected in Melbourne's representatives to General Synod.

Melbourne's shift in ethos had permeated throughout the Victorian countryside. At the turn of the century, many Victorian country centres had looked to Sydney for clergy. Then, after the Langley tradition ended in Bendigo in 1919, and Bishop Pain retired from Gippsland in 1917, the Victorian dioceses increasingly recruited from within the State.[92] The Sydney Evangelical influence diminished and the Victorian country dioceses, with the exception of Anglo-Catholic Wangaratta, began to align themselves with the Melbourne ethos and eschew the sharply defined Catholic-Evangelical dichotomy.

These developments left Sydney more and more isolated. While ever the Melbourne-Sydney Evangelical axis had remained firm, there was no chance of constitutional reform without the approval of both large metropolitan dioceses. The gradual shift in Melbourne and the fact that the Victorian country diocese identified with Melbourne rather than Sydney meant that the Mother Diocese of Australia was without reliable allies. Sydney's representatives to General Synod in the 1920s found that they could not rely upon definite, consistent support from Victorian representatives on constitutional issues, and Conservative Evangelicals in Sydney began to fear that Melbourne would shift further away from Sydney in the future and permit "anti-Evangelical" changes to the Constitution. They became convinced that they were on their own in defence of Evangelical truth.

VI

Sydney's Synod finally met in March, 1928 to consider the proposed Constitution, and it was clear that deep, and in some cases bitter, differences of opinion existed between Conservative and Liberal Evangelicals on the issue. Archbishop Wright, who admitted that he usually "carried reticence to a fault", came out strongly for acceptance of the Bill. Harold Minton Taylor introduced the assenting ordinance and drew strong support from Dean Talbot, Bishop D'Arcy-Irvine and Archdeacons Boyce, Martin and Davies, and J.A.I. Perry, a prominent lawyer. Their leading Conservative Evangelical opponents were W.J.G. Mann, Canon Langford Smith and the Revs. W.G. Hilliard, Leo Gabbott and D.J. Knox. It was a clash of Evangelicals.[93]

The debate lasted five days and resulted in a victory for the Conservative Evangelicals. The sponsors of the assenting ordinance were out-manoeuvred on the floor of the House by their Conservative Evangelical adversaries. From the very first day, when the Conservative Evangelicals accused the Liberal Evangelicals of trying to stampede the synod and stifle discussion, the Liberal Evangelicals found themselves on the defensive. Fearful that their Conservative Evangelical brothers might convince Synod to throw the whole Constitution out, the Liberal Evangelicals were conciliatory throughout the debate and willing to make concessions if they thought it advanced the Bill's prospect of success.[94]

Thus, although the Conservative Evangelicals failed to hamstring General Synod by making its provincial ordinances inoperable without diocesan sanction, and were unsuccessful in pushing through an amendment to the basis of General Synod representation (which would have increased the representation of Sydney and Melbourne still further), they were able to score significant victories in other areas. Sydney's Synod agreed that modifications should be incorporated into the proposed Enabling Bill to be presented to the State Legislatures which defined the "character" of the Church as including the 39 Articles; substantially increased the numbers of clauses in the Constitution which could only be altered with the consent of all dioceses; re-affirmed that General Synod could not alter the constitution of a diocese without that diocese's consent;

and allowed the Diocese of Sydney to exclude any question of faith, ritual, ceremonial or discipline from appeal to the Supreme Tribunal.[95]

The Conservative Evangelical leaders succeeded in exacting these changes by creating "an atmosphere of suspicion" in the Synod. Ordinary synodsmen had to decide on issues about which their Evangelical leaders were divided.[96] Harold Minton Taylor, Archbishop Wright and Dean Talbot said that the Declarations of Faith included the 39 Articles and were unalterable; Canon Langford Smith, William Mann and the Rev. W.G. Hilliard violently disagreed. The same men clashed over the composition of the Supreme Tribunal, the alterability or otherwise of particular clauses, and specific points of law. Ordinary Evangelical synodsmen were confused. Usually, if the majority of synodsmen did not understand a complex issue, they trusted the judgment of their Evangelical leaders. But on this occasion the President of the A.C.L. was at loggerheads with the party's Chairman of Committees, and Vice President refuted Vice President.[97] How could synodsmen decide? W.S. Mowle, the lay representative for Campbelltown and one-time Clerk of the N.S.W. Legislative Assembly, voiced the feelings of many ordinary synodsmen:

> A great many of us are in the dark and we cannot get too much enlightenment ... If there is any doubt or likelihood of any loophole being placed in the Constitution, I say by all means do not vote for it. Do not take the risk. Once we take the risk we are done for.[98]

The Conservative Evangelical victory was based on that anxious fear. Indeed one leading Conservative Evangelical frankly said it was impossible for him to approach the question of the Supreme Tribunal without suspicion or fear. He had seen that the bishops in England had been unable to maintain discipline and had legalised illegality and that the Anglican Church world-wide had been white-anted by the

Anglo-Catholic movement. He therefore believed that Evangelicals would be delivered into the hands of the Anglo-Catholics if they submitted to a Tribunal which had a majority of bishops as members. He proudly admitted that, having been raised on Fox's Book of martyrs, his mind was prejudiced. But, he declared, "it enables me … to view what is before us in the light of the past."[99] Conservative Evangelicals were convinced that Anglo-Catholics were conspiring to overturn the Reformation Settlement, drive Evangelicals from the Church, and use every device available to spread their practices and beliefs. They were determined to frustrate this campaign by ensuring that fundamental doctrines were inviolate and every loophole was closed. Liberal Evangelicals, on the other hand, while not careless of the possible abuses of constitutional power, were persuaded that the probability of unreasonable or partisan abuse of the Constitution was outweighed by the advantages of their participation in an Australian federation. They preferred the exciting possibilities of a federation, in which they believed Evangelical truth would have a wholesome influence, to the dour certainties of separation by the Diocese of Sydney from the rest of the Church in Australia.[100]

The passage of the Bill, with its four important modifications, was hailed unanimously as a remarkable result after such a protracted, unhappy debate. But the rhetoric could not hide the fact that any semblance of, Evangelical unity in Sydney had been smashed. Conservative and Liberal Evangelical speakers had bitterly wounded each other in gladiatorial debate. Archbishop Wright had snubbed W.J.G. Mann; Mann, the A.C.L. Chairman, had accused Dean Talbot, the A.C.L.'s President, of dishonesty and a "jazz disposition … you do not know which foot to stand on because in jazz you must keep moving."; Bishop D'Arcy-Irvine had warmly charged Mann with "unworthy" suggestions; and Canon Langford smith had sprung to Mann's defence by asserting that D'Arcy-Irvine was using his official position for political ends.[100] The inflammatory exchanges widened the breaches within the Evangelical camp and introduced an acrimonious, personal element to the divisions which lingered on well after the Synod had ended. The final settlement papered over these divisions, but it did not heal them. Instead, they rankled for years.

VII

Sydney's modifications were reluctantly agreed to by the other Australian dioceses who, although unhappy with the special treatment Sydney demanded, were at that time unwilling to jeopardise the 1926 accord over the issue. Thus, by late 1928, only the parliamentary legislation remained for the Church in Australia to receive a new Constitution.[102] But in a matter of months, the uneasy settlement had collapsed. First, an unforeseen difficulty arose over the question of an Australian Prayer Book when it was realised that the proposed Constitution did not provide for the possibility of a litigious person challenging the orthodoxy of a Prayer Book Revision. The matter would have had to be decided in the Civil Courts. The Australian Bishops met in November 1928 and resolved to cover this contingency by a Constitutional amendment which meant that no Revision could be made without two-thirds of the Australian bishops, including all the Metropolitans, certifying that the Revision was doctrinally consistent with the Solemn Declarations.[103] However, the Bishops dropped this proposal when they were advised that representatives of the Diocese of Sydney would never accept "this drastic change".[104] Sydney Conservative Evangelicals maintained that questions of faith should be in the hands of the whole body of the Church and not the bishops alone.

The obstinacy of Conservative Evangelicals was not, however, based solely on doctrinal grounds: first, after June 1928 the impetus for Australian Conservative Evangelicals to break the nexus with England

and co-operate in the formation of an autonomous Australian Church had gone. In that month, the English Parliament had thrown out the Deposited Book for the second time. The 1662 Book of Common Prayer remained the common use and standard of doctrine. The danger of an authorised "anti-Evangelical" Prayer Book had been removed and with it went any inclination on the part of Australian Conservative Evangelicals to make sacrifices for the sake of a new Constitution.[105] Second, the unwillingness of Conservative Evangelicals to entrust their own Archbishop with a veto power on matters of faith was not only based upon their belief that matters of doctrine should be decided by the whole church and not just a group of officials, but also reflected the general uneasiness of Conservative Evangelicals with the Liberal Evangelicalism of Archbishop Wright. Wright had supported the Constitution before the Conservative Evangelicals had, in their opinion, definitely secured Evangelical fundamentals. He was not quite as "solid" as they would have liked and they had no guarantee that his successor would be any different. Their only security was the conservatism of the Sydney Synod.[106]

The immediate opportunity for a new Constitution was lost. "The old happy unanimity", which had never been more than an uneasy accord, disintegrated amid angry accusations from churchmen in other dioceses that "Sydney has banged and bolted every door through which agreement might be found".[107] Bishop Feetham of North Queensland, an Anglo-Catholic, suggested that it was time for the other dioceses to go it alone and leave Sydney, "to stew in its own juice".[108] Yet with a resolution of the issue no longer possible before 1930, the Australian Bishops postponed formal discussion of the matter until after the 1930 Lambeth Conference. Moreover, Sydney Conservative Evangelicals were not the only one for whom this adjournment was agreeable. Many bishops had realised after the 1926 Convention "that the 1926 Draft was far more rigid than they had first thought..(and)..they themselves became anxious for reconsideration, and many of their legal advisers concurred."[109] Although Sydney Conservative Evangelicals received much of the blame for the delay, many Anglo-Catholics and High Churchmen were only too glad that the stalling of the Constitutional movement afforded an opportunity for re-assessment.

The Australian Bishops met in London prior to the Lambeth Conference in 1930 and decided that another Convention should be called in 1931 to discuss the Constitution, although the economic depression precluded this from being held until October 1932. The movement for autonomy suffered another severe setback when Bishop Long of Newcastle died during the Lambeth Conference.[110] Bishop Long had been the leading light of the move towards a new Australian Constitution. He had drafted the 1926 Constitution with Sir John Peden; he had been responsible for guiding it through the 1926 Convention; and had elevated the whole Constitutional issue above mere questions of churchmanship and prejudice, and inspired churchmen of all schools with a breadth of vision for the prospect of an Australian Church.[111] His death was a tragic loss for the autonomy movement, a loss which was exacerbated by his role being taken over by Bishop Hart of Wangaratta, a staunch Anglo-Catholic. Hart's sponsorship and guidance of constitutional reform made it even more difficult to allay Conservative Evangelical suspicions. Nevertheless, the Constitution Committee "thrashed out points in dispute" throughout 1932 and succeeded in submitting a revised draft to the second Constitutional Convention in October 1932.[112]

The settlement concluded at this Convention differed significantly from the 1926 Bill. First, the Constitution was less rigid. No section was unalterable. Some crucial clauses, such as those concerned with the Appellate Tribunal, the faith ritual and ceremonial of the Church, and the restriction on the General Synod from interfering in diocesan affairs, could only be changed with the consent of all dioceses.[113] The Prayer Book and the 39 Articles could be revised by a canon which required a two-thirds' majority of General Synod, as long as the bishops and the

Appellate Tribunal declared that the changes were consistent with the Declarations of faith. Even then, each diocese could reject the changes within its boundaries, or preclude its use in a parish if the parishioners opposed it. Diocesan autonomy was thereby preserved.[114]

The second significant feature of this 1932 Constitution was the function and composition of the Appellate (formerly called Supreme) Tribunal. The new Bill enlarged the powers of the Tribunal so that it not only heard appeals from subordinate tribunals but also adjudged validity of canons or ordinances and decided whether new doctrinal statements or Prayer Book revisions were constitutional.[115] It was to be the High Court of the Australian Church. But Sydney Conservative Evangelicals only agreed to this enlargement of the Tribunal's powers when its proposed composition was also changed. Instead of a bishop as its president, they demanded that the Tribunal be chaired by a laymen, a change which gave laymen a 4-3 majority on the Tribunal.[16] From the Conservative Evangelicals' point of view, this established the Tribunal more as a dispassionate court of appeal which, although it was obliged to consult the Bishops on any question of doctrine, would make judgments based on legal principles, not unpredictable sentiment.

The success of the 1932 Convention produced an atmosphere of supreme confidence that at last the Church in Australia would succeed in re-constituting itself. A "dead tired" Archbishop Wright believed that the Enabling Acts would be passed in a matter of months. The movement for a new Constitution which had occupied the mind of the Australian Church throughout his twenty-three years as Primate would be over. Now, the seventy-one year old prelate said, "I can sing my Nunc Dimittis."[117] His song was answered and, four months later, he was dead.

Wright's confidence was premature. Although all Sydney Evangelicals welcomed the 1932 Bill and the Sydney Synod, together with those of Melbourne, Perth and ten other dioceses readily assented to it, a strong propaganda campaign against the Bill was launched soon after the Convention.[118] This time it was not Conservative Evangelicals who opposed the proposed Constitution but Anglo-Catholics. They maintained that the bishops were the Church's guardians of the faith and, since all appeals to the Appellate Tribunal would turn upon questions of doctrine, the bishops alone had the authority and power to determine those questions. That responsibility should not be entrusted to lawyers.[119] Within three years, the predominantly Anglo-Catholic dioceses of Rockhampton, North Queensland, New Guinea, Willochra, Bunbury and Brisbane refused assent to the Bill until the Tribunal was constituted differently, while Adelaide and Kalgoorlie proposed substantive amendments.[120] The Anglo-Catholics were adamant that there could be "no compromise", and therefore no prospect of a new Constitution, unless the Tribunal was constituted so that bishops had the final decision on any matter of doctrine.[121]

The dispute over the respective authority of the bishops and the Appellate Tribunal to decide doctrinal questions, highlighted the deep doctrinal divisions within the Australian Church. But it was a doctrinal division which was reinforced by the increasing polarisation of the administrative economies of the Australian dioceses. By the 1930s the majority of Australian dioceses were small country dioceses served by fewer than forty clergy. The clergy worked in scattered, isolated centres and the bishop was not just the single unifying factor in the diocese but had absolute control as well. By contrast, the metropolitan dioceses were becoming very large organisations and their decision-making processes were becoming more complex. Power within these large diocesan units was not exercised by the bishop alone, but shared by bishop, clergy and laity. The decision-making processes of the metropolitan and country dioceses were becoming increasingly alien from each other. The synods of Anglo-Catholic dioceses such as North Queensland, New Guinea, Willochra and Bunbury supported demands that bishops alone should decide matters of doctrine as much because that mode of decision-making was consonant with their experience of power and authority as because it was consistent with their doctrinal position. The synods of Melbourne and Sydney supported the proposal for the independent Appellate Tribunal to decide doctrinal questions for exactly the same reasons. *Their* experience of power and decision-making and their traditional doctrinal position were completely different.[122]

By 1935, some Conservative Evangelicals concluded that the Anglo-Catholics were determined to frustrate the Constitutional settlement. They believed that the Anglo-Catholics no longer wanted a Constitution which conceded any of their cherished ideals for the sake of federation, but preferred to hold out until the document was substantially Anglo-Catholic in character: "Some of their (Anglo-Catholic) leaders have expressed to me", one Melbourne Conservative Evangelical wrote, "the hope that nothing will be done for a generation — Obviously they think that time is on their side..."[123]

Time may well have been on the side of the Anglo-Catholics, but the Diocese of Sydney refused to be bullied. In 1935, Sydney was wounded by the loss of the Primacy when the Australian bishops snubbed Sydney's new Archbishop, Howard Mowll, and chose Archbishop Le Fanu of Perth as Primate. Soon after, Sydney's Synodsmen reacted angrily to the Anglo-Catholic pressure for amendments by rescinding their earlier acceptance of the 1932 Bill by a 2 to 1 majority.[124] Although committee meetings and conferences continued into the 1940s, it was the end of any real possibility of a new Constitution for a generation.[125]

VIII

The Constitution saga had critical importance for the development of power and party in the Diocese of Sydney in the 1920s and 19303. First, the Constitutional issue thrust all Australian dioceses into a greater degree of negotiation with each other than ever before. Their differences were highlighted: their different perceptions of "the Church", of its organisation and purpose, and the locus of authority within it, became clearly evident as Australian churchmen sought to settle upon a satisfactory document by which they would reconstitute themselves. The distinctiveness of Sydney in the Australian context became more clearly pronounced during these years than ever before. It was a distinctiveness which was increasingly characterised by loneliness. The Melbourne-Sydney axis which had dominated General Synod in the nineteenth century had broken down. Sydney's representatives found less and less support from churchmen in other Australian dioceses and Melbourne was no longer a certain ally. It was an isolation which bred a defiant defensiveness amongst Sydney's Conservative Evangelicals.

The Constitutional issue also influenced the internal politics of Sydney Diocese. Before 1926 Evangelicals in Sydney had been largely united on the Constitution 'question, and "Sydney's position" had been expressed by Liberal Evangelicals such as Boyce, Davies and Talbot. It was a policy which sought to secure the independence of the Diocese and ensure that Evangelical truths were not jeopardised, but, at the same time, sought to augment the influence of Evangelicalism in the whole of the Australian church. They were cautious of the terms of federation but, equally, they were eager that Evangelicalism leaven the whole lump, and not be confined to one diocese. It was the ideal which had first inspired,the formation of the Anglican Church League in 1909.

From 1928, however, the influence of these Liberal Evangelicals was eclipsed by the Conservative Evangelical faction. There were two reasons for this. First, the lonely isolation of Sydney Diocese in the Constitutional debates generated within the Diocese a suspicious and fearful ghetto mentality which was fundamentally anti-liberal. Conservative Evangelical leaders fanned this defensiveness and, at the same time, gained in political influence and power because of it. The views of Canon Langford smith and William Mann on the Constitution became increasingly authoritative, and pushed the opinions of Boyce, Talbot and Davies into the background. But the eclipse of the Liberal Evangelicals was not just because of differences of opinion on the Constitution issue. The Constitutional debates certainly created an atmosphere in which Liberal Evangelicalism struggled to survive. But a second and concomitant reason was that a re-alignment of forces was taking place within the Diocese of Sydney which was characterised by increasing Conservative Evangelical distrust of their Liberal Evangelical brothers, a suspicion which had its roots in the schism in Evangelicalism in England in the 1920s. Conservative Evangelicals had witnessed from the secure distance of Sydney the defeat of Conservative Evangelicalism in England. They had perceived that in England Liberal Evangelicals had undermined Conservative Evangelical power, influence and authority and then, having rendered Conservative Evangelicals impotent, promptly surrendered to the pressures of a militant Anglo-Catholicism in the ecclesiastical politicking over Prayer Book Revision. Conservative Evangelicals in Sydney were determined that the same enervating developments should not occur there. The Constitutional debates provided them with clear evidence of the enemy outside the gates of the Sydney citadel; but the Liberal-Conservative schism in England, and their own break with Liberal Evangelicals on the Constitution issue, alerted them to the enemy within. Forewarned, they were fore-armed.

NOTES - CHAPTER SEVEN

1. *C.S.* 29/5/1914 p.5. (Rev. J.S. Hart, later Bishop of Wangaratta.)
2. *C.S.* 16/11/1917 p.6: *A.C.R.* 25/11/1925 p.6, 30/8/1918 p.8; Stephen Sykes, "Authority" p.ll.
3. Wright to Davidson 20/12/1910. "Australia" in Special Subject Series, Davidson Papers.
4. R.A. Giles, *A Constitutional History of the Australian Church* Skeffington and Son. London 1929 pp.75-82; G.P.Shaw, *op. cit.*, pp. 254ff.
5. Lowther Clarke, *Constitutional Church Government*, S.P.C.K. London 1924 pp.84, 87-89;
6. The Church was similarly constituted in Victoria and Tasmania. The 1866 Act was repealed at the instance of the N.S.W. Provincial Synod and replaced with the "Church of England Constitutions Act Amendment Act of 1902". The Church of England in N.S.W. continues to be governed and managed within the provisions of that Act; H.L. Clarke, *op. cit.*, pp.88, 130-136; Giles, *op. cit.*, p.111; the 1866 and 1902 Constitutions were only registered at the Supreme Court, and were not dependent upon Legislative sanction.
7. *A.C.R.* 13/2/1920 p.13.
8. 8. Giles, *op. cit.*, pp.150.
9. Section 8 of the 1872 Constitution. Adopted by Conference 23/10/1872. Document T in Giles, *op. cit.*, pp.271-275.
10. *ibid.*, pp.273-74.

11. Wright to Davidson 20/12/1910, "Australia" in Special Subject Series, Davidson Papers.
12. Archbishop Wright at Prov. Synod 1915, *A.C.R.* 17/8/1917 p.6.
13. *C.C.* 30/9/1910 p.8; Canon Stephen, quoted in Giles, *op. cit.*, p.154.
14. Montgomery to Davidson 5/10/1891 v.33. ff.1-19 T.1 Tasmania; see also *Verbatim Minutes* of the 1897 Lambeth Conference v.38 ff.27-33.
15. Giles, *op. cit.*, p.155; Smith to Benson 14/2/1394. v.133. ff.47-54. Benson Papers.
16. Smith to Benson 14/2/1894. v.133. ff.47-54; Clarke, *op. cit.*, pp.239-241.
17. Benson to Smith 28/8/1894 ff.55-59. Benson Papers.
18. Benson to Smith 28/8/1894 v.133, ff.55-59, Smith to Benson 8/10/1894 ff.60-61. Benson Papers. Benson's attitude was despite the fact that the British Government had supported such moves in the 1850s.
19. *Opinion* of Arthur Cohen, Robert Cecil and A.B. Kempe 20/6/1911, *loc.cit.*; The Australian opinion came from Adrian Knox (later Chief Justice of Australia) and John Musgrave Harvey (later Chief Justice in Equity in N.S.W.). See Giles, *op. cit.*, pp-161-167- 8
20. *ibid.*
21. Donaldson to Davidson 29/10/1917. 1917.2. Brisbane, Abp. of. Davidson Papers.
22. Donaldson to Davidson 20/6/1910, 11/10/1905 in "Australia". Special Subject Series. Davidson Papers.
23. *C.C.*31/5/1912 p.9, 29/6/1912 pp.13-14; *C.S.* 23/10/1914 p.3.
24. Wright to Davidson 12/9/1911 in "Australia". Special Subject Series. Davidson Papers.
25. *C.S.* 16/8/1912 p.5.
26. Wright to Davidson 1/1/1912. 1913. A.20 Australia. Davidson Papers.
27. Wright to Davidson 1/5/1911 *loc.cit.*

28. The nine new dioceses were Carpentaria (1900), Bendigo, Wangaratta, Gippsland (1902), Bunbury (1904) N.W. Australia (1909), Kalgoorlie (1913), Grafton (1914), and Willochra (1915).
29. Sydney, Melbourne, Goulburn and Bathurst.
30. In addition to the nine dioceses mentioned in footnote 28, five dioceses were established between 1872 and 1900: Ballarat (1875), North Queensland (1878), Riverina (1884), Rockhampton (1892) and British New Guinea (1898).
31. Sydney, Melbourne, Gippsland, Armidale and Bendigo. The rest were predominantly High Church or Anglo-Catholic.
32. Wright to Davidson 12/9/1911 *loc.cit.*
33. Donaldson to Davidson 10/6/1912. 1912. A.11 Australia, 29/10/1917. 1917.2. Brisbane, Archbishop of, 11/10/1905 "Australia" Special Subject Series.
34. Canon Hart (later Bishop of Wangaratta) and Bishop Long of Bathurst were the only prominent Australian-born advocates of autonomy before 1914. Wright to Davidson 23/1/1912. 1912. S.43. Sydney, Archbishop of. Davidson Papers.
35. *A.C.R.* 25/5/1923 pp.2-3, 27/4/1923 p.2; see also *S.M.H.* 22/9/1913 p.8; 9121 29/6/1912 p.1; 9151 4/10/1912 pp.2-3.
36. That the limitations of the 1662 Prayer Book were plain to English as well as Australian Evangelical chaplains, see Selwyn Gummer, *The Chavasse Twins* Hodder and Stoughton London 1963 p.58; *C.S.* 4/10/1912 pp.2-3, 11/10/1912 p.3.
37. *A.C.R.* 29/7/1921 p.7 (D.J. Davies) 7/10/1921 p.7 (Wright).
38. White to Davidson 19/3/1921, 3/10/1921. 1921. 21. Willochra, Bishop of. Davidson Papers.
39. White to Davidson 7/10/1921. *loc.cit.*
40. *S.D.M.* January 1921 pp.4-5, May 1921 p.4, November 1921 pp.1,4.
41. *A.C.R.* 29/7/1921 p.14, 9/9/1921 p.6, 18/11/1921 p.1; 1921 *Official Report* of Proceedings of the General Synod of the Dioceses in Australia and Tasmania pp. 142, 177-78, Table of Dioceses p.142; The Majority report of the Committee appointed by *Sydney*

Synod on the Nexus question is more detailed on representation question — see *A.C.R.* 3/11/1922 p.14.

42. *A.C.R.*.2/12/1921 p.9.
43. Canons F.B. Boyce and D.J. Davies, Sir Albert Gould and W.J.G. Mann and Harold Minton Taylor were the Sydney representatives on the Nexus Committee; *A.C.R.* 1/12/1922 pp.6-7.
44. *C.S.* 5/7/1912 (H. Minton Taylor).
45. *A.C.R.* 1/12/1922 pp.6-7.
46. White to Davidson 8/10/1921, *loc.cit.*; The Nexus Determination was passed unanimously by the bishops, 55-17 by the clergy, and 48-13 by the laity. Thus if all 24 Sydney representatives opposed it, they were only supported by 6 men from other dioceses.
47. White to Davidson 7/10/1921, *loc.cit.*; *S.D.M.* November 1921 p.4; 1921 *Official Report*, p.45. 285 of the 563 (50.6 per cent) of the clergy, and 371,131 of the 731,532 (50.7 per cent) Church of England laity in N.S.W. were in the Diocese of Sydney; *A.C.R.* 2/12/1921 pp.9,11.
48. *A.C.R.* 1/12/1922 p.8;
49. *A.C.R.* 20/12/1922 p.1, 27/1/1922 p.14, 27/4/1923 pp.2 and 9, 25/5/1923 pp.2-3, 22/6/1923 p.1, 6/7/1923 pp.1,6 and 11, 20/7/1923 p.9.
50. *A.C.R.* 20/10/1922 p.6;
51. *ibid.*
52. Dr. Wright, Bishops White of Willochra, Long of Bathurst, and Radford of Goulburn, and the Hon. Littleton Groom M.L.A. were the members of this Constitution sub-committee; White to Davidson 27/11/1923. 1925. W.6. Willochra, Bishop of. Davidson Papers.
53. White to Davidson 27/11/1923 *loc.cit.*
54. *A.C.R.* 13/5/1916 pp.1,5,10; 16/9/1926 p.4; 14/10/1926 p.6.
55. See *A.C.R.* 30/9/1926 p.5.
56. *S.M.H.* 17/4/1926 p.9; See Table Annexed to Schedule One. *The Constitution of the Church of England in Australia. Draft Bill for Consideration* 1926. p.22. Langford Smith Papers; See Chapter 1: Clauses 2-7 (Declarations), Ch. VIII: (Alteration of Constitution) 84-87.

57. *A.C.R.* 4/3/1926 p.6, 18/3/1926 p.6 (Langford Smith).

58. *A.C.R.* 16/9/1926 p.4 (Talbot).

59. *ibid.*, 2/9/1926 p.8.

60. *ibid.*, 18/3/1926 p.6.

61. See *The Constitution of the Church of England in Australia. Alternative Draft Bill for Consideration.* Langford Smith Papers.

62. *S.M.H.* 14/10/1926 p.9; *Official Report* of the Constitutional Convention of the Dioceses in Australia and Tasmania. 12-25 October 1926. Wm Andrews Sydney 1927 p.16.

63. *A.C.R.* 25/11/1926 p.1.

64. *A.C.R.* 30/9/1926 p.7.

65. Declarations, Clauses 1-6 in *Official Report*, pp.15, 86; The new Basis of Representation provided for one clerical and one lay seat on General Synod for every fifteen clergymen in each diocese, to a maximum of 300 clergymen after which the quota was halved, *Official Report...* First Table to Schedule One p.104.

66. *S.M.H.* 13/10/926 p.15.

67. The Draft Bill permitted the General Synod to make canons with respect to the function and rights of the primate and other bishops; the oaths declarations and assents required of bishops, priests deacons and licensed lay officers; the educational standards of clergy; superannuation, insurance and property matters; and the establishment jurisdiction powers and procedures of the tribunals of the church; Clause 30, 31. *Draft Bill; A.C.R.* 26/10/1926 pp.4 and 6. (Radford and Mann), 2/9/1926 p.8; *Alternative Bill*, Clause 16 and 17.

68. *S.M.H.* 20/10/1926 p.16.

69. *ibid.; A.C.R.* 28/10/1926 p.4.

70. Clause 48 of Bill as Passed, *Official Report...* p.97; The laymen on the Tribunal had to be judges, or barristers or solicitors of ten years' standing.

71. *A.C.R.* 28/10/1926 pp.3,7; The "splendid efforts" of Harold Minton Taylor were especially singled out for congratulation by Bishop Long, Archbishop Lees and Dean Hart.

72. *A.C.R.* 25/ll/1926 p.7.

73. *S.M.H.* 23/10/1926 p.14, 26/10/1926 p.12; *A.C.R.* 25/11/1926 p.7.

74. *S.D.M.* December 1926 p.3.

75. *S.D.M.* November 1926 p.2.

76. *S.M.H.* 1/11/1926 p.10; *A.C.R.* 9/12/1926 p.5.

77. *A.C.R.* 28/4/1927 pp.11-12.

78. Charles Hughesdon (Rector, Wahroonga) to Langford Smith 19/7/1927; Andrew Colvin (Rector, Eastwood) 20/7/1927, in Langford Smith Papers.

79. *A.C.R.* 9/12/1926 pp.4-5; A.C.L. *Minutes* 28/1/1927, 25/2/1927, 18/3/1927, 13/4/1927.

80. Circular from S.E. Langford Smith 25/11/1926; Note on Whole Day Conference 7/12/1926 at Summer Hill. Langford Smith Papers.

81. Sections 6, 21, 56, 58, 65 and Table One in Bill; "Sydney's Objections", Memo in Langford Smith Papers.

82. *S.M.H.* 26/4/1927 p.8 (Boyce), 27/4/1927 p.8; *A.C.R.* 28/4/1927 pp.11-12 (Boyce). See Mann's reply *S.M.H.* 27/4/1927 p.8.

83. R.A. Pollard (Rector, Lithgow) to Langford Smith 9/1/1928, P.J. Evans (Rector, Enmore) to Langford Smith 9/1/1928.

84. S.E. Langford Smith, *The Sydney Diocese and Proposed New Constitution of the Church of England in Australia*, A.C.L. Sydney 1927, Langford Smith Papers.

85. R.A. Pollard to Langford Smith 9/1/1928 *loc.cit.*

86. P.J. Evans to Langford Smith 9/1/1928 *loc.cit.*

87. *A.C.R.* 13/3/1926 p.6; *S.M.H.* 27/4/1927 p.8.

88. *S.M.H.* 14/1/1928 p.12, 18/1/1928 p.10. (Boyce was the founder of the N.S.W. Temperance Alliance).

89. *S.M.H.* 23/1/1928 p.7.

90. *A.C.R.* 6/1/1927 p.11 (H.G.J. Howe), 3/2/1927 p.11 ("Sigma"), 23/6/1927 p.10; *S.M.H.* 21/1/1928 p.21.

91. The three successive Archbishops of Melbourne who were members of the A.E.G.M. were Henry Lowther Clarke 1902-1920, Harrington Clare Lees 1921-1929 and Frederick Waldegrave Head 1929-1941.

92. Bishops H.A. Langley (1902-1906) and J.D. Langley (1907-1919) of Bendigo were brothers.

93. *Proceedings* of the Special Session of the Synod of the Diocese of Sydney March 1928 pp.14-15.

94. *ibid.*, pp.51, 53, 70-71.

95. *ibid.*, pp.126-7, 161, 241 *passim*.

96. *ibid.*, p.110 (Rev. A.G. Perkins).

97. *ibid.*, pp.87-94.

98. *ibid.* 97.

99. *ibid.*, pp.182-84 (D.J. Knox).

100. *S.M.H.* 14/3/1928 p.16 (Wright), 22/3/1928 p.12, 23/3/1928 p.13.

101. 1928 Proceedings, pp.61, 124, 149-53, 157-8.

102. Archdeacon Jose, Motion in Adelaide Synod 4/9/1928, from Adelaide Year Book 1928-29. Copy in Langford Smith Papers.

103. *A.C.R.* 20/6/1929 pp.4-5; *C.S.* 14/5/1929 pp.672-673.

104. *ibid.*; *A.C.R.* 9/12/1937 p.15.

105. *A.C.R.* 20/6/1929 pp.4-5, 20/10/1932 p.6, 9/12/1937 p.15; *C.S.* 14/6/1929 pp.672-3; *S.M.H.* 22/3/1928 p.12 A (Hilliard), 14/6/1929 p.15; *Official Report* of the Constitutional Convention of the Dioceses in Australia and Tasmania 11-24 October 1932. William Andrews Sydney 1933 pp.12-13.

106. See *S.M.H.* 19/1/1928 p.16, 22/3/1928 p.11, 14/6/1929 p.15.

107. Archbishop Sharp of Brisbane in *A.C.R.*; 20/6/1929 pp.4-5; Bishop Feetham of North Queensland quoted in *S.D.M.* September 1929 p.8.

108. *ibid.*

109. 1932 *Official Report* pp.12-13.

110. W.H. Johnson, *George Merrick Long*, St. John's College Press Morpeth N.S.W. 1930 p.46.

111. *ibid.*, pp.35-36.

112. Wright to Archbishop Lang 26/10/1932. 1932 A.2. Australia, Constitution of Church of England in. Lang Papers. L.P.L.

113. The clauses which could only be changed by universal consent were 1-6, 35, 52, 56(i) 61-2, 64-72, 77-8 and Table One.

114. J.S. Hart, *A Commentary on the Draft Constitution for the Church of England in Australia* William Andrews Sydney 1933 pp. 3-4, 12-15; A diocese could make a revisory canon ineffectual within the diocese if it passed an exclusionary ordinance within one year; A.H. Garnsey to D.A. Garnsey 7/9/1932 and 23/10/1932.

115. See Section 48 of 1926 Bill; Sections 56 and 62 of 1932 Bill; Hart, *op.cit.*, pp.9-10.

116. Copy of Bishop of Kalgoorlie's Letter to Diocese after '32 Convention n.d. in Langford Smith Papers.

117. Wright to Lang 26/10/1932, Lang Papers. The Song of Simeon (Nunc Dimittis):

   "Lord, now lettest thou thy servant

   depart in peace: according to thy word.

   For mine eyes have seen thy salvation,

   which thou hast prepared before the face of all people....."

118. *1935 Year Book of the Diocese of Sydney* pp.287-88; A.C.R. 20/9/1934 p.11.

119. A.C.R. 25/7/1935 pp.2-3, 28/9/1935 p.12, C.S. 26/5/1933 p.1, 21/6/1935 p.4.

120. A.C.R. 4/4/1935 p.7, 25/7/1935 pp.2-3.

121. A.C.R. 9/12/1937 p.16; A.H. Garnsey to D.A. Garnsey 25/3/1935 Garnsey Papers; *S.M.H.* 12/9/1934 p.9; Notebook No.2 in Langford Smith Papers. The other amendments demanded by the Anglo-Catholic militants were that the universal assent section be made less rigid; that General Synod representatives be elected by orders; and the representation quota be reconsidered.

122. There were exceptions, of course. Brisbane and Adelaide were Metropolitan Sees and predominantly Anglo-Catholic, and refused assent to the Bill until the Tribunal was reconstituted. But both Brisbane and Adelaide were still more like country towns than cities, and their diocesan organisations reflected that. Perth was predominantly Anglo-Catholic, but it was also the new Primatial See after 1935, and Archbishop Le Fanu was anxious for the 1932 settlement to succeed.

123. H.T. Langley to Langford Smith (St. Mary's Caulfield) 28/3/1935, in Langford Smith Papers.
124. *A.C.R.* 26/9/1935 p.8, 10/10/1935 pp.1,6, 9/12/1937 p.16; *S.M.H.* 25/9/1935 pp.5,10, 27/9/1935 p.11; *S.D.M.* October 1935 p.233 (Mowll Synod Charge); Howard Mowll to Langford Smith 26/3/1935, in Langford Smith Papers.
125. For documents on 1940s, see Langford Smith Papers. Of especial interest are letters by T.C.Hammond, one of which (5/9/1945) suggests that if a majority of Australian dioceses went it alone and left Sydney out of the federation, two Churches would be established, similar to South Africa. The Church of England in Australia would be Sydney with "branches" in other states: "We could supply the Ministry from Sydney and ultimately, if the movement spread, consecrate Bishops in other Dioceses".

CHAPTER EIGHT -

A SPECTACLE TO ANGELS AND TO MEN

I

The schism in the Evangelical camp in Sydney was to have an enduring impact upon the political scene of the Diocese. Before 1926, Evangelicals had been ostensibly united, with the Anglican Church League as the political expression of that unity. Such opposition as existed to the A.C.L. was scattered, un-organised and without leadership. But the bloody split between Conservative and Liberal Evangelicals wrecked the accord which had been the founding bias of the A.C.L. Two rival Evangelical organisations emerged in the Diocese to give political expression to viewpoints which had hitherto come under the one umbrella organisation, the Anglican Church League. This Conservative-Liberal Evangelical split not only reflected developments in Evangelicalism in England but was also a crucial factor in determining the character of the Diocese for the rest of the twentieth century.

The differences between Liberal and Conservative Evangelicals in England initially appeared to be those of temperament and emphasis. Liberal Evangelicals believed that the Conservative Evangelicals' message was too negative and geared to the refutation of error. Instead, they sought to give a more positive and modern expression of the Evangel, and in this endeavour they were willing to accommodate the tools and findings of modern scholarship. To them, reverent biblical criticism did not impugn the integrity of Scripture, but facilitated a better understanding of it.[1] As long as there seemed to be only differences of emphasis, both Conservative and Liberal Evangelicals could confidently attest to "an underlying unity which binds all sections together", and "a unanimity on the great verities of the faith." But after World War One a more serious rift occurred on the crucial question of authority. Conservative Evangelicals asserted that the supreme authority for all belief and conduct was the Bible: "The cardinal fact for Evangelical Protestantism," said Dean Wace in 1917, "is that in the Bible, from the beginning to the end, but particularly in the Gospels and in the New Testament, you have the voice of God speaking to men."[2] The Bible was authoritative because it was inspired by God. Some Conservative Evangelicals maintained that the Scriptures were *verbatim* the words of God written by men; others believed that any imperfections were the product of the human amanuenses. But central to the Conservative Evangelical position was the inspired nature of the Bible and its consequent supreme authority. This Conservative Evangelical position came under attack from the Higher Critics whose study of the literary methods and sources used by the authors of the books of the Bible became increasingly popular in the late nineteenth century.[3] The Higher Critics' challenge to traditional belief, and especially its questioning of the inspired nature of the Bible shattered the "underlying unity" of the Evangelical party. Conservative Evangelicals shunned the newer scholarship.[4] Others, usually younger men, valued the modern research and came to accept at least some of its conclusions. The result was that these "Liberal" Evangelicals began to depart from the traditional position on the inspiration of the Bible. Instead they maintained that ultimate authority should be vested not in a book but in its one Divine Fact, Jesus Christ: "Liberal Evangelicalism finds its ultimate ground of authority in the Mind and Spirit of Christ."[5]

One prominent Liberal Evangelical wrote that "...the real essence of Christianity is conformity with the mind of Christ."[6]

The Liberal Evangelical position seemed eminently reasonable and mature. But there was a problem with it. By undermining the authority of the one *common* revelation of Jesus Christ, the Bible, the authority of the "Mind of Christ" became essentially subjective. The Liberal Evangelical was forced to rely on his own personal and imperfect experience and understanding of that Mind; and the danger was that he became the authority, not the Mind of Christ. A certain freedom was gained. Liberal Evangelicals felt at liberty to re-examine the formularies and Articles of faith of their forefathers and develop new ones. But the cost of this freedom was an indefiniteness in their own position and an uncertainty as to where they stood with others.[7]

The locus of authority is at the heart of a theology, and a disagreement about religious authority could not have been more fundamental. Yet, while the Conservative-Liberal Evangelical differences were openly discernible by 1915, there was no formal fissure in the English Evangelical ranks for another seven years. Liberal Evangelicals stayed within the pale of Evangelicalism, and thereby subtly undermined the Conservative Evangelicals. They portrayed the Conservative Evangelicals as cranky, old anti-Papists from a past age, who were now being superseded by younger, more virile Liberal Evangelicals. The wealth of young, gifted intellectuals in the Liberal Evangelical ranks reinforced the contention that the New Age belonged to this new attractive expression of the Evangel. The Conservative Evangelicals were led by ageing Victorians who struggled to find younger successors, while most Evangelical theological colleges became centres of Liberal Evangelicalism, and were staffed by men who gave leadership to the Movement. Bishop Watts-Ditchfield of Chelmsford, prominent parish clergymen such as Guy Rogers of West Ham and Lisle Carr of Liverpool, and academics from university and theological colleges

...combined to give such a powerful lead to the emerging Liberal Evangelicals that the Conservatives, bereft of leadership, particularly after 1920, were totally powerless to contain. These men had not caused a spirit of Liberalism to spread throughout the party. What they did was to unite these Liberal tendencies and mould them into a cohesive force which had a powerful appeal... and, by 1923, a robust identity.[8]

The forum in which the differences between the Conservative and Liberal Evangelicals finally erupted into open schism was the flagship of the Evangelical party, the Church Missionary Society. After World War One, Conservative Evangelicals became afraid that their Society was slipping from its evangelical moorings. The increased co-operation of the C.M.S. with non-Evangelical missionary bodies, the growth of support for the Society from non-Evangelical churches, and the manifest presence within the Society of men who did not believe that the Bible was verbatim the words of God, convinced Conservative Evangelicals that the Society's Evangelical character was endangered. Liberal Evangelicals, on the other hand, were just as anxious that the Society continued to co-operate with other missionary organisations and avoid becoming narrowly "verbal inspirationist".[9]

The uneasy peace between the two factions was broken in 1922 when a number of Conservative Evangelicals brought the matter to a head by seeking to bind the Society to a policy which upheld that the Bible was *verbatim* the words of God.[10] Conservative Evangelical Bishops Chavasse and Knox and Liberal Evangelical Bishops Warman and Watts-Ditchfield worked out a compromise which satisfied the vast majority of the Society's members. But a small minority of Conservative Evangelicals — mostly members of the new Fellowship of Evangelical Churchmen — rejected the accord, resigned from the C.M.S., and established the Bible Churchman's Missionary Society.[11] Although only a handful of

Conservative Evangelicals defected to the B.C.M.S., the split meant that any semblance of unity within the Evangelical camp in England had disintegrated. Conservative Evangelicals were separating themselves not only from Liberal Evangelicals, but from fellow Conservatives.[12] More than this, these divisions were being institutionalised. Bishop Knox concluded that these divisions enervated the Evangelical witness:

> "No doubt all these divergences had all found room for some years previously among Evangelicals. The tragedy was that at a most critical moment open divisions came to light, new parties were called into being, each with its own society and its own organ in the Press, and oppositions became so sharp that the word 'vendetta' was hardly too strong to characterise some of them. This destruction of a brotherhood, the strength of which had been conspicuous in my younger days, I count to have been one of the greatest sorrows in my experiences of public life."[13]

Between a militant and energetic Anglo-Catholicism and the Christian Platonism of the Modernist movement stood a pathetic Evangelicalism, its divisions apparent to all.

II

The Liberal Evangelicals decided in 1923 that it was time to act. For the past sixteen years the Group Brotherhood had served them well in influencing opinion within an Evangelical party which had embraced a wide range of opinion. But now that the divisions within Evangelicalism were clearly defined, and the Church as a whole was showing alarming signs of polarisation, Liberal Evangelicals faced the prospect of a contraction of their sphere of influence if they did not separate themselves from the Conservative Evangelicals. They had to come out into the open if the Liberal Evangelical spirit was to survive. It was the only way a belligerent Anglo-Catholicism and an uncompromising, defensive Conservative Evangelicalism could be effectively counteracted.[14] Thus, in 1923, the private and loosely-organised Group Brotherhood became the Anglican Evangelical Group Movement, open to all clergy.[15] The A.E.G.M.'s Basis of Membership illustrated its reaction to Conservative Evangelical extremism. It contained no mention of specific doctrines, but rather spoke of the need for evangelism, modern Biblical scholarship, Christian unity and a spirit of brotherhood and fellowship.[16] In a period pockmarked with the factious fights of churchmen, it was an attractive prospectus. By the end of 1926 the Movement had a membership of 850 clergy, and doubled that figure by 1936. The Movement also opened its ranks to laymen in 1926.[17]

The Liberal Evangelicals recognised that they would not secure the middle ground by the mere establishment of a public association. They had to demonstrate the *distinctiveness* of their position, something they had assiduously eschewed during the life of the Group Brotherhood. A collection of essays, *Liberal Evangelicalism*, by leading lights in the Movement, was the result.[18] Its publication in 1923 had a telling impact upon the whole Church. It was a rally cry to Liberal Evangelicals, and a confirmation to Conservative Evangelicals that these Liberal Evangelicals had travelled a considerable distance from the traditional tenets of Evangelicalism. It also indicated to other churchmen that a new brand of Evangelicalism had arrived, with leaders worthy of the respect of the whole Church.[19]

The success of this Liberal Evangelical movement grieved Conservative Evangelicals, but they were powerless to check its advance. The fact that their best spokesmen were old men merely lent credence to the Liberal Evangelicals' contention that Conservative Evangelicalism was a thing of the past:

"The Conservatives were without anyone with the position or the learning to refute them (the Liberals) in a meaningful way. They simply did not have the organisation or the personnel to fight back. What strength they did have was expended against the Anglo-Catholics and in the parliamentary battles over the Prayer Book in 1927 and 1928. They were only concerned to stay the rot and to maintain the old traditions. The speed of the growth of the Liberal Evangelical movement after 1923 coupled with the success in large measure, in spite of the defeat of the Revised Prayer Book, of the Anglo-Catholic movement left the Conservatives in disarray and caused them to retreat into intro-spection and, ecclesiastically, irrelevance."[20]

III

Conservative Evangelicals in Sydney quickly perceived that the same Liberal Evangelical forces which had undermined Conservative power, influence and authority in England were also present in their Diocese. Indeed the Liberal Evangelicals were already in positions of authority. Their Archbishop, the first chairman of the Group Brotherhood, was sympathetic to Liberal Evangelical scholarship, and had many friends in the A.E.G.M.[21] His assistant, Bishop Gerard D'Arcy-Irvine, shared his Liberal Evangelical outlook.[22] The Principal of Moore Theological College, Archdeacon D.J. Davies, was a Liberal Evangelical scholar who believed that modern research did not undermine, but rather vindicated, the authority of the Bible.[23] As incumbent of the central church of the Diocese, Dean A.E. Talbot had for many years exercised considerable public influence and had become a figurehead for sound yet Liberal Evangelical churchmanship and, as President of the Anglican Church

League from 1924, tried to moderate the influence of the more extreme partisans in the Diocese.[24] These powerful *individual* Liberal Evangelical influences were soon complemented by the establishment of a study group of about twenty clergy which was chaired by Davies, encouraged by Archbishop Wright, and affiliated with the A.E.G.M.[25]

The basis for a significant and permanent Liberal Evangelical presence in Sydney was clearly there. The Archbishop and his co-adjutor were sympathetic; popular Dean Talbot, as A.C.L. President, was in the position to provide Liberal Evangelical leadership; Archdeacon Davies influence upon ordinands at Moore College could provide the rank-and-file support for a Liberal Evangelical movement, and the A.E.G.M. group could easily have developed into the vehicle by which Liberal Evangelicals changed the character of the Diocese. Why then was Liberal Evangelicalism a spent force by 1936? Why did these Liberal Evangelical influences not make a lasting impression upon the Evangelicalism of the Diocese?

Two important reasons have already been mentioned. First, the debates over the Constitution polarised opinion in the Australian Church. They served to articulate the deep divisions between the Conservative Evangelical and Anglo-Catholic wings of the Anglican Church. It made plain the militancy of the Anglo-Catholic movement outside Sydney and demonstrated, not least to the Conservative Evangelicals, the distinctiveness of the Sydney Diocese, which they were determined to preserve. That determination fostered a defensive extremism rather than an open liberalism, and that mood enervated moderate, Liberal Evangelical influences. The second external factor was the experience of Conservative Evangelicals in England. The conclusion that Liberal Evangelicalism in England had been a fifth column movement which had served to undermine the Evangelical witness in that country and thereby allow an aggressive Anglo-Catholicism to triumph, had a reactive but, in their eyes, prophylactic impact upon Sydney Conservative Evangelicals.[26] They became determined that local Liberal Evangelicals should receive no succour nor opportunity to cultivate the same debilitating influences. They would be vigilantly watched and vigorously opposed.

The campaign to keep Sydney distinctively Conservative Evangelical and prevent a duplication of the English experience in Sydney was also greatly assisted by two local factors. First, the Liberal Evangelicals in Sydney suffered a crippling crisis of leadership in the early 1930s. In rapid succession Bishop D'Arcy-Irvine (1932), Archbishop Wright (1933), D.J. Davies (1935) and Dean Talbot (1936) died. Their positions in the Diocese were taken by Conservative Evangelicals, while the leadership of Liberal Evangelicalism was thrust upon men who were unable to breathe inspiration and direction into the movement.[27] Second, the whole mood of the age in the late 'Twenties and early 'Thirties was against the cultivation of a liberal spirit. On the gloomy economic scene unemployment rose from 12% in 1928 to 33% in 1932; politically, the stormy term of the Lang Government polarised the State. Even the normally tranquil cricket field was not spared the bitter illiberalism of the age: the 'Bodyline' Test series of 1932-33 still stands as the most controversial and unhappy chapter in Australian cricketing history. Further, in these depressing times, parish clergymen were increasingly seeking answers to the palpable fact that people who had once attended church had now been seduced by tennis, golf and the motor-car.[28]

The Conservative Evangelical response to the new social context which was symbolised by the empty pew was not a radical "contextualisation" of the old evangel, but rather a call to closer attention to the ministry of the Word. The pews, they concluded, were sparsely populated not because of dull services and dour preaching, or even because of man's innate sinfulness, but because "the authority of Holy Scripture is being undermined and destroyed in many minds by what is called Modernist teaching."[29] Why, after all, should people bother with church if there was no certainty that any revelation existed? "These teachers (of Modernism)", one Conservative Evangelical spokesman announced, "are sometimes known as Liberal Evangelicals. Like many people in ordinary life, they are liberal with what does not belong to them...(namely, Holy Scripture and its teaching)".[30]

Sydney's Liberal Evangelicals were concerned to preserve the comprehensive character of the Church of England. They believed that the formularies of the Church permitted a measure of variation in practice and belief which was salutary: people differed in mind, temperament and character, and in a living church these differences had to be expressed. The Church's unity was not found in uniformity, but in a common Father, a common discipleship of the one Lord, and a common Faith in his saving grace. Their own convictions were Evangelical, but they perceived that other intellectual or psychological dispositions preferred a "High Church" or "Broad Church" position which was nevertheless within the ambit of the Church's formularies. The health of the Church did not, they believed, depend upon an Evangelical uniformity but upon brotherly and harmonious interaction and friendly co-operation between these different types of Anglicans.

The Conservative Evangelicals were more exclusive. They believed that arguments for friendly co-operation between different types of Anglicans were specious. Indeed, by 1928, they had concluded that the comprehensiveness of the Anglican Church was "largely responsible for its ineffectiveness today...and not a source of strength."[31] The call for comprehensiveness was, to them, the Trojan horse by which Anglo-Catholicism and Modernism would infiltrate the Evangelical citadel of Sydney.

In the light of events in England, the Conservative Evangelical antipathy to Liberal Evangelicalism was understandable. They felt that the Church's witness had been enervated by vainly trying to embrace a whole range of opinion, and that it would have done better to articulate only one viewpoint. But their response was too extreme. They threw the baby out with the bath-water: while justifiably rejecting Anglo-Catholic and Modernist positions which were clearly outside the comprehensive tenets of the Church of England, they also refused to countenance a legitimate plurality of opinion and belief:

"Men speak of the comprehensiveness of our Church", declared one long-time Conservative synodsman. "...Away with such sophistry. Little is done to check the sponsors of the Oxford Movement. It is only the innate Protestantism of the Anglican Church that will keep it from union with Rome. It is now that we need to be alert for the time seems to be coming when the Reformation battle will have to be refought. We must have justification by faith alone."[32]

There it was: A fear of Rome, a deep abiding anti-Papalism lay at the heart of this opposition to "comprehensiveness". In the eyes of Conservative Evangelicals, the Liberal Evangelicals were the naive catspaws of an Anglo-Catholicism which was a mere staging post on the downhill road to Rome.[33] Their influence in the Diocese would, therefore, have to be checked. The accord which Conservative and Liberal Evangelicals reached in 1928 over the Constitution was not a reconciliation but merely a truce. It was only a matter of time before another issue would produce an irreparable schism.

IV

The crisis came after the death of Archbishop Wright in February 1933. Wright had administered Sydney for twenty-three difficult years. His early action against vestments had precluded the spread of ritualism in the Diocese, and had therefore been crucial in the development of the strongly Evangelical character of the Diocese. His identification with his flock and his enduring sense of duty during the War were exemplified in his legendary early morning visits to farewell every troopship which left Sydney during World War One.[34] He wisely oversaw a period of diocesan expansionism in which the number of parishes had increased by half. And, although continual ill-health during the 1920s limited his administrative effectiveness, he nevertheless exhibited throughout his episcopate a great capacity for holding men of diverse views and interests together. Wright's desire for peaceful harmony between different schools of thought was not only clearly evident as Primate during the Constitution debates but also as Diocesan of Sydney where he excelled as a patient, temperate and conciliatory chairman of synods, conventions and committees and made episcopal appointments which revealed no suggestion of favouritism for any one group.[35]

Wright's moderating, temperate influence upon the Diocese was resented by Conservative Evangelicals who believed that he over-emphasised his administrative role and failed to give sufficient direction and leadership to his flock. They wanted an initiating Father-in-God, not a Moderator. They were disappointed with his deliberate policy of non—directive leadership, by which he sought to make churchmen individually — and the diocese as a whole — assume responsibility for their own situations. Conservative Evangelicals saw this as weak and indefinite.[36] They wanted to follow a leader who would formulate the policy, and take far more initiative in making the decisions and performing the tasks. They conveniently ignored the fact that Wright's non-intrusive style of leadership had allowed the A.C.L. the freedom to grow in power and influence. Above all, Conservative Evangelicals wanted Wright's successor to be a "definite Evangelical", who identified with their own Conservative Evangelical viewpoint, and in whose hands their Evangelical heritage would be secure. Liberal Evangelicals, on the other hand, believed that such a man would alienate other schools of thought which had a legitimate place within the Church, and party conflict would then be inevitable. To them, Archbishop Wright's leadership had been sound and constructive, if admittedly unspectacular, and the Liberal Evangelicals therefore sought a successor of similar temperament and disposition who would be the centre of unity in the Diocese, not the nominee of the strongest party.[37]

These conflicting ideals made a clash between Conservative and Liberal Evangelicals over the identity of Wright's successor inevitable, and political campaigning began in earnest soon after Wright's death. The Conservative Evangelicals were the first to swing into action. They quickly decided that they would only support "three definite Protestant Evangelicals, and only three," for the Final List to ensure that there was no possibility that a non-Conservative Evangelical would be elected.[38] In actual fact, they only had one genuine candidate: Howard West Kilvinton Mowll, the 43 year old missionary Bishop of West China who had already indicated to Conservative leaders that he would accept the post if elected.[39] It only remained for the Conservative Evangelicals to marshal the numbers for him.

Bishop Mowll was well known in Sydney. As Assistant Bishop (from 1922) and later Bishop (from 1926) his exciting experiences as a missionary in the turbulent and anarchic conditions of West China had won the admiration of Evangelicals throughout the world.[40] Then, in August 1931, Mowll had come to Australia on deputation work. He spent two weeks in Sydney and was immediately idolised for his evangelistic zeal, his heroic courage and his evangelical soundness.[41] Even his height (6'4") impressed: "He's gigantic; he's magnetic; he's courageous; and he's humble", one admirer exclaimed.[42] When the time came to choose Wright's successor, Conservative Evangelicals knew exactly whom they wanted.[43]

The Conservative Evangelicals' campaign for Mowll took two forms. First, four A.C.L.-sponsored meetings of selected synodsmen were held which were, in effect, private party caucus meetings.[44] Next, there was an energetic propaganda campaign. The *Australian Church Record*, whose directors were all Conservative Evangelical A.C.L. members, mounted an unabashed pro-Mowll campaign. Theirs was a strong candidate: a Cambridge graduate who had taught at Wycliffe College, Toronto, and then become a famous missionary. Who could ask for more?[45] The Conservative Evangelicals also chose to anticipate the Liberal Evangelical propaganda by warning Sydney churchmen against the specious pleas for "a man of broad sympathies", "a man of tolerance", and "no narrow partisan". There lay the danger, as far as Conservative Evangelicals were concerned.[46] They believed that an indefinite Liberal Evangelical prepared the way for the Anglo-Catholics: "Other dioceses in Australia were built on Evangelical foundations, but where do they stand to-day?" The *Record* asked. "Induced at critical stages in their history to compromise and select some 'via media' person as Bishop, they gave way."[47] The Conservative Evangelicals pleaded with Sydney synodsmen not to barter their birthright but to vote for a man who would uphold their "sacred trust."[48]

There were two serious campaigns mounted by non-Conservative Evangelicals. The first was by an organisation called the Sydney Diocesan Reform Association which had been formed in July 1932, after a bitter dispute over the appointment of a rector to St. Barnabas' Chatswood.[49] The S.D.R.A. aimed to reform the method of parochial appointments of clergy which it believed had unjustly foisted an unwanted rector onto the unhappy parish of Chatswood.[50] Conservative Evangelicals, however, claimed that the Association meant to disrupt "the settled traditions" of the Diocese and saw a hidden hand of Anglo-Catholic intrigue behind the S.D.R.A. activities.[51] But the Association was not an Anglo-Catholic front. Certainly none of its members were Conservative Evangelicals, and the Association clearly aimed to loosen the grip of the A.C.L. machine on the Diocese, but the sole reason its members involved themselves in the election of Wright's successor was because they knew that if a man were elected who did not identify with any one party, and displayed a disposition to work with sympathy and understanding with all schools of thought, their goal would be greatly advanced.[52] With that aim in mind, the Association proposed the name of John Moyes, the young Australian-born Bishop of Armidale, who had already made his mark by his efforts to "contextualise" Australian Christianity and who often spoke out boldly on social and economic issues.[53]

The S.D.R.A. campaign, led by Professor F.A. Bland and the Rev. H.N. Baker of St. Thomas' North Sydney, did not imitate the A.C.L.'s caucus methods and aggressively support one candidate. Instead, public meetings were held, and the public press was utilised to raise what the S.D.R.A. considered were the crucial issues. Moyes' name, however, never figured prominently in the Association's campaign, perhaps because the Association wanted to avoid the impression of counter-caucusing and electioneering. It was a voluntary restraint which greatly weakened the effectiveness of the S.D.R.A.'s campaign.[54]

The sponsors of the third serious contender in the election, Joseph Wellingon Hunkin, the Rector of Rugby and Archdeacon of Coventry, were Dean Talbot and Archdeacon D.J. Davies, the President and a Vice President of the A.C.L. Both men had argued within the A.C.L. for a man who would be "a centre of unity" in the Diocese, a scholar and intellectual who would consolidate the Evangelical influences in the Diocese, and prevent the bifurcation into Conservative and Liberal Evangelical groups. They had maintained that Hunkin, a conservative member of the A.E.G.M., was such a man: a definite Evangelical who was liberal in scholarship and strongly Protestant. Archbishop Wright had been a moderating influence upon extremists of every school. Hunkin, they argued, would pursue a similar policy.[55] But the Conservative Evangelical 'Old Brigade' of the League — men who had invariably received their training at Moore College under Nathaniel Jones more than thirty years before — were unconvinced. They suspected any Liberal Evangelical, no matter who supported him. In what amounted to a no-confidence vote in their League's President, they plumped for Mowll.[56]

This stinging rebuff left Talbot and Davies in an impossible situation. Senior members of the League were not only vigorously opposing the candidature of a man whom they believed eminently suited to fill the See, but were also openly suggesting that their nominee endangered Evangelical truth and encouraged Anglo-Catholic excesses.[57] More than this, the Conservative Evangelicals were using the organisational base of the A.C.L. and its lines of communication to lobby support for their candidate. Wounded, Talbot and Davies had no option but to withdraw from the A.C.L. Council.[58]

The Sydney Synod began its private deliberations to elect a new Archbishop on Tuesday, 4 April 1933, and it quickly became clear that the Conservative Evangelicals were determined to leave nothing to chance. Although twelve nominations were received, only four survived the first vote: Hunkin, Mowll, Canon Arthur Grant of Norwich, and Canon Laurence Grensted of Liverpool.[59] Significantly, the name of Bishop Moyes was eliminated after only perfunctory debate: the Conservative Evangelicals obviously refused *en bloc* to give his name further consideration. He received only 44 clerical votes out of a house of about 135, and 67 of the 225 lay votes.[60]

Not everything went the way of the Conservative Evangelicals. Canon Grensted of Liverpool, who was backed by the Liberal Evangelicals, surprisingly secured 88 clerical votes. Thus two Conservative Evangelicals, Mowll and Grant, and two Liberal Evangelicals, Hunkin and Grensted, were still in the contest and, although Mowll was clearly the favourite, the Liberal Evangelicals were still in with a chance. Yet the Conservative Evangelicals, confident of Mowll's own availability, had raised doubts about whether Hunkin would accept. Liberal Evangelicals knew that they would have to scotch these doubts before their nominee's prospects of election were damaged. They rang Hunkin in the middle of the English night, and bluntly asked him whether he would accept. The rather sleepy Rector of Rugby replied that he would consider the matter most seriously if elected, but that it was unlikely that he would be able to see his way to accept.[61] It was tantamount to a refusal, but his Liberal Evangelical backers were unshaken. They triumphantly informed the Synod that Hunkin had just indicated that he "would be prepared to consider acceptance" if elected. The Liberal Evangelicals had kept their nominee in the running.[62]

The Conservative Evangelicals knew that Joseph Hunkin was their main danger and attacked him with acerbity in the final debate. One Conservative Evangelical demonstrated from back issues of *The Modern Churchman*, to which Hunkin had contributed articles, that Hunkin did not believe that the Scriptures were *verbatim* the words of God.[63]

Another, John Bidwell, damned Hunkin by association when he introduced into the debate the book *Liberal Evangelicalism*, to which Hunkin had contributed an essay on "The Kingdom of God". The essay was in itself a conservative, amillenarian statement which stressed the eternal nature of God's Rule, and also focussed on the Christian's social responsibility. But it was extremely damaging for Hunkin's cause that this article was within the covers of a book which contained far more radical chapters by men such as Vernon Storr, R.T. Howard and the controversial E.W. Barnes. Despite a score of interjections from Dean Talbot, who objected to the use of the book in debate, Bidwell effectively condemned Hunkin as a "Modernist".[64]

It was an unfair attack. Hunkin rejected the verbal inspiration position but he certainly upheld the concept that the Bible was divinely inspired. Nor did his acceptance of the tools of language, psychology, archaeology and history in biblical criticism and research imply that he resiled from a basically Evangelical theological position. Nevertheless, that he had been found associating with "Modernist" sinners was enough to deliver a fatal blow to his nomination. The Rev. John Bidwell later recalled that Hunkin "was wiped out properly" when it came to the vote. "He only got a few votes. A lot of the laymen came to me (Bidwell) afterwards and said

'If you hadn't said what you did we were going to support the Dean and Davies, we thought we could, being Evangelicals you see. But when we heard what this chap was, we voted against him.'[65] Although the Final List contained three names — Grant, Grensted, and Mowll — the final vote was a mere formality: 115 clergy and 191 laymen overwhelmingly voted for the election of Howard West Kilvinton Mowll as Archbishop of Sydney. With Hunkin out of the race, only 23 clergy and 35 laymen dissented.[66]

Hunkin's premature elimination from contention is evidence of the "painfully obvious dread of 'Modernism'" in Sydney.[67] This fear was partly due to events in England, but was also caused by the controversy over the teachings of Dr. Samuel Angus, the Presbyterian Professor of New Testament exegesis and theology at the United Theological Faculty at St. Andrew's College in the University of Sydney. Since 1929 Angus had caused considerable disquiet amongst Conservative Evangelicals in all Protestant churches. His heterodoxy had caused the Methodists to remove their theological students from the United Theological Faculty, and in his own Presbyterian Church, Conservative Evangelicals declared that "an alsatian is attempting to destroy our sheep and lambs...The Church is being white-anted...Christian theology is being turned upside down by perverts...certain professors should be bundled out of the country... before our Church goes Unitarian."[68]

Conservative Evangelicals claimed that Angus was a Pagan philosopher, not a Christian theologian, because they believed he denied Christ's deity, rejected his Virgin Birth, and held views on the Atonement and Resurrection which were false. Although no formal heresy charges were ever laid, Angus came to personify for Conservative Evangelicals the Modernism which was eroding the foundation of the Christian faith.[69], Angus' Modernist influence deeply troubled Conservative Evangelicals in the Anglican Church. They were particularly concerned that Canon Arthur Garnsey, the Warden of St. Paul's College, openly supported Angus, and that Garnsey, Talbot and Davies apparently had social and professional associations with Angus.[70] Conservative Evangelicals were convinced that these Anglican associates of Angus were fellow-travellers, and warned synodsmen before the Election that the Diocese was being threatened not only by "sacerdotalism", but also by a Modernism which undermined

> ... the very foundation truths of our faith. It is common knowledge that this ...(Modernism) is at present time disrupting a sister Church, and in our opinion it has an increasing following in this Diocese. We are speaking here of things that are vital to our faith and to the Church's life and witness."[71]

The Liberal Evangelicals believed that 'Modernism' was merely "a grand bogey": "Get a hundred men of any Church together and shout 'Look out for Modernism!' and they will scuttle about for shelter."[72] But for Conservative Evangelicals, the Angus controversy had given the threat a potent immediacy. It reinforced their belief that they could not risk a Liberal Evangelical like Hunkin: "We must", they concluded, "have a man who is sound in the Faith." They had to have Mowll.[73]

V

Howard West Kilvinton Mowll was only 43 years of age when he was elected Archbishop of Sydney. He had graduated from King's College, Cambridge in 1912, where he had been President of the strongly Evangelical Cambridge Inter-Collegiate Christian Union (C.I.C.C.U.) in 1911.[74] He was ordained in 1913 by Bishop Knox at Manchester (for Canterbury) and sailed immediately for Canada where he taught for ten years at Wycliffe College, Toronto.[75] In Canada Mowll demonstrated that he was a simple proclaimer of the Gospel rather than a theologian.[76] In 1922 Mowll accepted the appointment as Assistant Bishop in the Diocese of West China, and was consecrated in Westminster Abbey in June of that year. In 1926, he succeeded William Cassels as Bishop of the Diocese and continued to administer that vast and troubled missionary diocese until his call to Sydney.[77]

Howard Mowll's career before he came to Sydney gave clear evidence that he was "an unhesitating Evangelical in theology and churchman-ship."[78] He had been prominent in the secession of C.I.C.C.U. from the Student Christian Movement in 1910, by which C.I.C.C.U. preserved its Conservative Evangelical character and S.C.M. became increasingly inclusivist.[79] His years in Canada had been spent both in teaching in a Conservative Evangelical college, and participating in evangelistic mis-sions throughout North America. His service in China had been in areas which were almost exclusively the domain of the; Evangelical missionary societies, the China Inland Mission and the Church Missionary Society. It had been a career of tremendous achievement, but it also had been limited in exposure to different schools of churchmanship. Before Mowll arrived in Australia, he had only worked and associated with Conservative Evangelicals. Although he remained "an Englishman to the finger-tips to the day of his death," he had never ministered in England and had no first-hand experience of the changes and trends of Anglicanism in the Mother Country.[80] He certainly had had little experience of the Anglican ideal of comprehensiveness. This unfamiliarity and inexperience was to be an important factor in his early years as Archbishop of Sydney.

Unlike his predecessors Howard Mowll came to Sydney with ten years' episcopal experience. As a missionary bishop, he had sought to develop a strong and independent Chinese Church, administered by the Chinese themselves, rather than paternally ruled by English missionaries. Mowll's episcopate in West China was crucial in facili-tating that transition.[82] But his China experience in no way tempered the authoritarianism which had been a notable feature of his character ever since his Cambridge days, when he had ruled C.I.C.C.U. "with an iron hand".[83] Rather, the exigencies of the mission field, where one had to be ruthless in the direction of people and funds, had cultivated it. Yet he spared no-one less than himself, and his inability to delegate, a characteristic which had also been reinforced by the loneliness of the mission field, meant that he placed an enormous physical burden on himself: throughout his twenty-five years in Sydney, he regularly worked eighteen to twenty hours a day.[84]

Nevertheless, the authoritarianism which had led C.I.C.C.U. friends to call him "the Pope", his simple, uncomplicated faith which rested upon the supreme authority of the Scriptures and the absolute necessity of Justification by Faith alone, and his "astonishing flair for detail", which expressed itself in a reluctance to delegate, were also the characteristics of a leader of men, whose physical stature and presence commanded the respect of his followers, and whose single-mindedness gave them confidence in their cause.[85] This was the bold leader that the Conservative Evangelical leaders had secured for Sydney so that Sydney Conservative Evangelicalism could itself be made secure.

VI

The differences between the Conservative and Liberal Evangelicals were not patched up after the Conservative victory in the Election Synod. Instead, the rift widened as accusations and counter-charges flew in wild exchanges of party propaganda. Hunkin supporters were disgusted that "so much deliberate misrepresentation and poisoning of the mind of synod" had occurred.[86] Others accused the Conservative Evangelicals of the "organised hypocrisy of, reciting Veni Creator Spiritus, after making as sure as possible that God should have no part in the election."[87] Even the dispassionate Sir Philip Game, the Governor of N.S.W., was shocked by "the methods employed by the extreme Evangelical faction" and wrote privately that they "...were, to put it mildly, a disgrace, and savoured of a Tammany ruled American election."[88] He was also alarmed by the victorious jubilation of the Conservative Evangelicals who "make no secret of the fact that they regard Archbishop Mowll as their man and will, I have no doubt at all, use every endeavour to commit him to their cause." The Governor feared that Mowll would become increasingly identified as the Bishop of a party, and not of the whole Church.[89]

The Conservative Evangelical leaders were unrepentant. They struck back at the "monstrous allegations" made against them, and charged their accusers with jaundiced humbug and cant. The *Church Record* proudly stood by its part in the election of Mowll: "...we make no apologies for our share in publicity! We know what we are about. It is our firm belief that Bishop Mowll will prove the man of God's choice..."[90]

Dean Talbot and 'Ben' Davies did not indulge in the acerbic press debate after the election synod. But the election synod had been a critical turning point for them. The short shrift they had been given by Conservative Evangelical party colleagues made political reconciliation impossible. "The nasty bumps" they had received from "the party bosses" in the Election Synod left them with no option but to part company with the Anglican Church League.[91] On 10 May 1933, Talbot resigned as President and as a member of the League, and Davies followed soon after.[92] Together, they resolved to establish a new movement, "The Anglican Fellowship". Talbot and Davies, reported Arthur Garnsey,

> say that for 20 years they have been trying hard to do con-
> structive work in the Diocese and having failed to shift the Old
> Brigade so now they are definitely breaking with them and will
> henceforth work on their own lines (sic). Their lines are...a
> la such men as Woods, Bp. of Croydon, Archd. V.S. Storr of
> Westminster, J.W. Hunkin, and I suppose Raven — and the
> Liverpool Cathedral type.[93]

The ideals of the Anglican Fellowship were practically identical with the Anglican Evangelical Group Movement in England, of which Davies and a number of other Sydney clergymen were already members:

> We stand for freedom of inquiry and study;" proclaimed Dean Talbot at the Fellowship's inaugural meeting. "We welcome new knowledge as a gift from God (and) we recognise the progressive nature of the revelation of God in the Bible, but our final thought of Him is based upon the Person and teaching of Jesus Christ.[94]

The Fellowship was also designed to strengthen the spiritual and intellectual life of the Church by teaching, missions, literature, and devotional gatherings and work for a Christian order of society, while never departing from the principles of the Church. Indeed, a significant departure by the Anglican Fellowship from the A.E.G.M. model was its strong articulation of its Evangelical tenets, including the supreme authority of the Scriptures.[95]

Canon Arthur Garnsey, the Warden of St. Paul's College, quickly joined the Fellowship. He knew that there had been deep divisions in the League for some time, and was excited that Davies and Talbot had finally taken this plunge:

> Some such move was badly needed here to shake the domination of the narrow obscurantist set who have lorded it over God's heritage for so long. The Dean and D.J.D. have come over from *them* to *us* and are putting *vim* into the move — but we are going on sound, true lines, which are open to no possible objections."
> He was particularly pleased that Talbot had made the move: "Always before, I felt that he was doing less than justice to his own powers by trying to walk with one foot in splints. He is capable of better things than he has yet done in Sydney.[96]

Arthur Garnsey frankly stated that the Fellowship had vital political significance and constituted a challenge to the Anglican Church League: "The idea is to work against the power of the machine in Church politics and to consolidate the influence of all those who love the light." Thus, ever-mindful of the danger that they would become "mechanical and light-fearing" themselves, the Liberal Evangelicals threw down the gage at the Conservatives' feet.[97]

The Conservative Evangelicals initially hesitated to pick up the challenge. The League's Council was stunned by the resignation of its President and deputed two senior laymen to ask him to reconsider. The delegates failed, however, to meet Talbot before the Anglican Fellowship was established. By then, it was too late. Events had overtaken them.[98] Nevertheless, a number of A.C.L. councillors made a last-ditch attempt for reconciliation. They realised that unless some accord was quickly reached, the Diocese would become embroiled in an unparalleled level of organised party strife, in which Evangelical opposed Evangelical. Thus, at an A.C.L. Council meeting on 9 June 1933, which was conspicuous for the absence of eight or nine of the League's senior members, these men made a move for peace in the following terms:

> That the members of this Council have heard with sincere regret that another Evangelical organisation has been formed in this Diocese. It unanimously agrees that the leaders thereof be invited to meet four of our members in a conference in the earnest hope that the whole body of evangelical churchmen of this Diocese may be united in one for the better promotion of the cause of Christ in this State."[99]

The motion was passed by the Council, but when the absent party bosses learnt of it, they were horrified:

I am strongly opposed to the resolution passed." Wrote Canon Langford Smith. "The League has done nothing for which it has any reason to apologise to any other organisation.

The Dean and Archdeacon Davies and their friends have a perfect right to unite together in an association they feel will be helpful to them, and I claim exactly the same right for myself. In my humble opinion", he concluded tartly, "it is the endeavour to be comprehensive that has led to most of our present troubles and not a little of the abuse to which some are being subjected.[100]

Langford Smith and four other senior party members urgently requested an extraordinary meeting of the Council at which they foreshadowed their intention to rescind the earlier resolution.

The meeting on Friday 23 June 1933 was crucial for the future of the A.C.L. The party elders who had been caught out by the motion which had been passed in their absence, were there in force to correct that aberration. W.J.G. Mann, the pugnacious 73 years old barrister who in recent years had become "only a passenger" as the League's Chairman and had wanted to resign only four months previously, presided.[101] Canon Langford Smith, who had just retired at 64 to the clerically popular Wentworth Falls, travelled down from the Blue Mountains for the meeting. Other senior members who were present that night after missing the previous meeting were the Rev. W.G. Hilliard, 46, the headmaster of Trinity Grammar School who was soon to take over as President of the A.C.L.; the Rev. William Greenwood, a former member of the P.C.E.U. and a founding member of the A.C.L. and now the 81 years old rector of Coogee; the Rev. D.J. Knox of Gladesville, 58, a Vice President of the League for twenty years; and two younger Conservatives, the Rev. R.A. Pollard, 49, of Bondi, the League's clerical secretary, and the Rev. R. B. Robinson, 45, of Chatswood.[102]

It was Robinson who moved that the resolution of the previous meeting be rescinded. He argued that it was beyond the power of the Council of the League "to make overtures to another organisation with the idea in mind of making the two organisations one." He was supported by other speakers who claimed that the irenical resolution had been unconstitutional and William Mann, in the Chair, declared it "undoubtedly out of order." The protests of two sponsors of the original resolution, who claimed that the resolution had merely sought to have leaders of both the League and the Anglican Fellowship explore matters in which they could agree and co-operate, were in vain. The motion to rescind the resolution of the previous Council meeting was carried overwhelmingly by nineteen votes to two.[103] The 'Old Brigade' had won the day.

The developments within the Anglican Church League in 1933 dramatically revealed both the power and the identity of the so-called 'Old Brigade', the Conservative Evangelical leaders. Their influence was not only evident in the Election Synod where they routed the Liberal Evangelicals, but also in subsequent events within the League. Their ability to overturn the conciliatory efforts of more moderate men within the League demonstrated the effectiveness for the Conservative Evangelical cause of the network of Vice Presidents in the League. But the rejection of reconciliation by the Conservative Evangelicals also served to emphasise the strongly clerical character of the Evangelical party's leadership. Power in the Diocese was still fundamentally held by the clergy. The 'Old Brigade' of the A.C.L. were, with the important exception of William Mann, all ordained men. In a period of crisis for the League, laymen quite clearly had little influence within the party. It was the clergy who ultimately determined the character and direction of the A.C.L. This confirms the earlier observation (in Chapter Five) that the distinctiveness of the Evangelical party in Sydney was its predominantly clerical membership and leaders. It also exposes the irony of the calls by the Evangelical party leaders for the laity to defend the Evangelical cause, when the clergy were always there as determined, resolute backstops to make sure that the *character* of that Evangelicalism remained pure, undefiled — and avowedly Conservative.[104]

The clear identification of the seven protagonists who were responsible for the overturning of the irenical resolution justified the label, 'Old Brigade', which some Liberals had attached to them. The average age of Mann, Langford Smith, Greenwood, Hilliard, Knox, Pollard and Robinson, was sixty. Moreover, the six clergymen had all been ordained for an average of 32 years, and even the youngest of them had already served 22 years. None of them had attended Moore College under the principalship of D.J. Davies but had, with the exception of William Greenwood who had attended St. Aidan's Birkenhead under Dr. Saumarez Smith, received their training from Davies' predecessor, Canon Nathaniel Jones. More than twenty-two years after his death, these party leaders still proudly bore the stamp of Jones' strong Conservative Evangelical teaching.[105]

The Anglican Church League's rejection of reconciliation with the Anglican Fellowship meant that the split between the two groups was irreparable: Talbot, Davies and their Anglican Fellowship were irretrievably separated from those loyal to the Anglican Church League. The die was cast, and the stage was set for five years of unprecedented faction fighting between Conservative and Liberal Evangelicals. It was a bitter struggle which vitally affected the future character of the Diocese and left the Liberal Evangelicals without influence in the Diocese, and the Conservative Evangelicals stronger than ever before.

VII

The Anglican Fellowship initially flourished. Its ranks soon included clergymen like Frederick Walton, the Director of Education for the Diocese, Ernest Cameron of Hornsby, William Siddens of Mortdale and Penshurst, A.J.A. Fraser of Haberfield, O.V.A. Abram of Epping, H.N. Baker of North Sydney, and laymen such as Professors F.A. Bland and Tasman Lovell of Sydney University, R.H. Swainson, the General Secretary of the Y.M.C.A. and synodsman for Vaucluse, F.C. Pretyman, the synodsman and Town Clerk of Marrickville, T.L. Warren, a solicitor from Northbridge, and R. Vine Hall, a Wollstonecraft engineer who represented St. Thomas', North Sydney in the Synod.[106]

As part of its aim to be a positive influence in the Diocese, the Fellowship deliberately cultivated a low political profile and refrained from public controversy: it even declined to react publicly to attacks on it by Conservative Evangelical opponents.[107] Instead, it chose to develop quietly, conducting small devotional gatherings, producing literature on various topical subjects, and organising public lecture meetings on matters of Christian social concern. In 1935, one Fellowship member organised a Christian Council comprising Anglicans, Presbyterians, Congregationalists, and Methodists with discussions on unemployment, dole payments, and even "Milk for the people".[108]

The quiet organisation by the new Movement did not go unchallenged. After its decisive rejection of a policy of detente on 23 June 1933, the A.C.L. moved swiftly to counter the drift away from the Conservative Evangelical party, and the concomitant growth of the Liberal Evangelical forces. First, there was a shake-out of the League's organisation. Decision-making in the League had become cumbersome with councillors, vice presidents and office-bearers entitled to vote at Council meetings. The reins of control of the League were therefore tightened by the immediate re-establishment of an Executive of seventeen members. This committee no doubt relieved the Council of much mundane work, but it also meant that the League's decision-making was effectively concentrated into the hands of a smaller coterie.[109]

The second step taken by the A.C.L. was to augment its. membership. While ever the League had been the only Evangelical party in Sydney, its leaders had been content with a membership of about 100, and had never actively recruited new members.[110] This had ensured that the League could effectively operate as a political caucus, rather than as a popular grass-roots party. But the changed political environment necessitated a change of policy. There was now the very real risk that the Anglican Fellowship would develop in an area which the A.C.L. had neglected, and develop as a strong, popular party with a large rank-and-file membership. The League's elders recognised the danger and began an earnest and concerted campaign for new members. They immediately warned all synodsmen of "determined efforts..(which)..are being made both directly and indirectly to alter the character of the Sydney diocese", and invited them to join the League as a positive contribution to the checking of these efforts.[111] "...we are anxious" said the A.C.L., "to secure the co-operation of all those who desire to maintain and extend the Evangelical teaching of our Church and Diocese."[112]

The recruitment drive produced spectacular results. In twelve months the membership of the League jumped by almost 40%, and continued to grow by about twelve per cent annually in the next five years. By early 1938 there were 78 clerical and 90 lay members.[113] The recruitment campaign was initially directed at synodsmen, but the A.C.L. also sought to marshal the support of two groups which had hitherto remained outside the party organisation: women, and the young men of the Diocese. The Conservative Evangelicals were particularly worried that young men, particularly Moore College students, would be attracted into the Anglican Fellowship, through the influence of Principal Davies. Davies' influence on young ordinands was already all too evident: whereas at least half of Nathaniel Jones' students had joined the P.C.E.U. and later the A.C.L., only one in five of Davies' students joined the League, and, worse, an increasing number showed a decided antagonism to the League.[114]

The Conservative Evangelicals acted quickly to counter the influence of Davies' Liberal Evangelicalism. In April 1934, twelve "definitely

Evangelical" Moore College students, many of whom were already financial members of the A.C.L., established the Young Evangelical Churchman's League, with the encouragement and blessing of the A.C.L. The two leagues were separate, but were nevertheless closely linked, and the Y.E.C.L. adopted the A.C.L. Constitution as its own; In the same year, a women's branch of the League was established, with members enjoying the privilege of associate membership of the A.C.L.[115]

Tightening control of the decision-making processes of the League and augmenting its membership were the A.C.L.'s two tactical responses to the emergence of the Anglican Fellowship. But the League also acted to match the Fellowship in the dissemination of propaganda. Before 1933, the annual general meeting had been the only meeting for the League's rank-and-file membership. In 1934, quarterly lectures and discussions on worthy Reformed subjects were introduced for the benefit of the whole membership of the League.[116] While these public meetings reinforced the convictions of the converted rank-and-file, the A.C.L. also moved to strengthen links with the most effective instrument of Conservative Evangelical propaganda in the diocese, the *Australian Church Record*. There were already close personal ties: the *Record's* editor, the Rev. S.H. Denman of Marrickville, was a Vice President of the League and most of its N.S.W. Directors were members of the A.C.L.[117] Further, the League and the *Record* had co-operated closely in the past.[118] But the League had not previously financially supported the *Record* which, with its limited circulation of 1,600, had always struggled to survive.[119] The changed political context and the emergence of Liberal Evangelical propaganda organs induced the A.C.L. to recognise its common interest in the *Record* and the paper's vital importance to the League's overall strategy to remain the pre-eminent political force in the Diocese. The party began to support the paper to the extent that its limited funds would allow, while a sharp increase in personal donations to the paper from individual League members indicated that the League's personal links with the paper were being immeasurably strengthened.[120]

The Conservative Evangelical party had responded decisively to the emergence of the Anglican Fellowship. They had stream-lined decision-making in the A.C.L.; they had strengthened their ties with their organ of propaganda, the *Record*; they had launched a vigorous recruiting drive; and their bold move in establishing a junior Conservative Evangelical league based at Moore College right under Davies' nose demonstrated their determination to carry the fight to the Liberal Evangelicals in every quarter. The ultimate success of their campaign against the Liberal Evangelicals would, however, be decided in the Diocese's legislature, the Synod.

The November 1933 Synod was the first occasion on which the strength of the respective parties could be tested. The vital importance of this assembly was greatly augmented by the fact that, because it was the first session of a new synod, crucial elections were to be held in which 107 new parochial representatives would vote: "Think of that!" One A.C.L. official exclaimed, "over 100 New men who will come into a New Synod when they have to vote on a big election."[121] The voting propensities of these men, who constituted 29% of the Synod, was crucial. A.C.L. officials went to great lengths to count heads and ascertain the new configuration of the parties in the Synod. Their conclusion was that the new men had not in fact upset the existing party strengths in the Synod, and there had been little organised electioneering against the A.C.L. hegemony. There still existed a core of 295 Conservative Evangelicals in Synod together with about 70 "swingers" who would probably side with them. This constituted a total of 365. By comparison, the strength of all other groups — the Anglican Fellowship, the Sydney Diocesan Reform Association, High Churchmen, churchmen from outlying parishes who were seeking representation for the "country", and mavericks — was only 155.[122]

Although their research revealed that the Conservative Evangelicals were still theoretically pre-dominant, the A.C.L.'s leaders knew that the League could still in fact suffer defeat in the Synod if all the non-A.C.L. forces were successfully marshalled so that they constituted a majority of a meeting of Synod which had less than 60% of members present. That prospect was by no means unlikely. Indeed, for fewer than 300 of the 500 members of Synod to attend each session was a practical certainty. The A.C.L. chiefs were, therefore, concerned that "their" men were well-marshalled and well aware of the issues and the candidates to be discussed at the Synod.[123] They therefore circulated, for the first time, a list of "recommended" candidates for each election to all sympathetic synodsmen, and, for the particular benefit of "their" new representatives, a special luncheon was held on 8 November 1933.[124] It was no mere coincidence that the Synod elections took place that same afternoon and evening.[125]

The concerted efforts of the A.C.L. officials in counting heads, organising private caucus luncheons, and issuing "how-to-vote" tickets to selected synodsmen were rewarded by a stunning victory for the Conservative Evangelicals in the 1933 Synod elections. A.C.L. candidates were elected to 106 of the 109 contested positions. There were only three lonely men who successfully defeated A.C.L. nominees. Harington B. Cowper, the lay secretary of Synod, was elected to the Council of the Home Missionary Society instead of A.L. Short; the Rev. O.V.A. Abram defeated the Rev. W.J. Roberts for the Barker College Council; and Canon Arthur Garnsey survived a challenge to his position on the Board of Education from the Rev. F.W. Tugwell.[126]

These few isolated cases did not detract from the magnitude of the A.C.L. success, and the Conservative Evangelicals were ecstatic at the result: "There were hosts of aspirants to office," the *Record* trumpeted, "but in spite of "Reform" and "Country" and "Fellowship" — the well-tried and trusted committeemen went back into office. Once again the laymen of the Synod stood true to strong Evangelical conviction. Faithful clerics were in their place. For the whole situation, as it emerged from Synod, we thank God and take courage."[127] The *Record* could well have appended its thanks to the Anglican Church League's organisers as well.

VIII

The "narrowly partisan" 1933 Synod elections were typical of all synodal elections throughout the 1930s.[128] The dominance of the Conservative Evangelicals increased from year to year as League-endorsed candidates white-washed their opposition. At each session of Synod from 1934 to 1937, only one Liberal Evangelical nominee to a synodical committee survived the A.C.L. onslaught as the Conservative Evangelicals waged a determined and sustained campaign to extinguish the influence of Liberal Evangelicalism in the Diocese.[129]

The success of this Conservative Evangelical campaign was no more clearly evidenced than in the elections to the Board of Education. The Board had been constituted in 1919 to co-ordinate and improve the work of the parish Sunday schools, and Religious Instruction in the Public Schools. It was, among other things, responsible for the publication of *The Trowel*, a quarterly resource magazine for Sunday School teachers. The Diocesan Director of Education since 1926 was the Rev. F.A. Walton, and he was responsible to the Board, which consisted of four members nominated by the Archbishop and twelve members elected by Synod.

The first public intimation that the Conservative Evangelicals were deeply concerned about the Board of Education was in 1932. Their dissatisfaction was not with the methods or the effectiveness of Walton but with his theology, his heterodox scholarship and, in particular, his historical viewpoints. In 1932, one Conservative Evangelical rector claimed that *The Trowel*, which Walton edited, was "Modernist".[130] Soon after, a group of Conservative Evangelicals, led by Canon Langford Smith, pushed for Walton's dismissal because, according to a friend of Walton, "he thinks that the Book of Daniel was written in the second century B.C."[131] Then in 1936, *The Trowel* became the subject of an intensive A.C.L. investigation which strongly criticised its editor and claimed that the magazine not only failed to give the Bible "its rightful place" and rarely mentioned the Atoning nature of Christ's death, but also published distinctly 'anti-Evangelical' material.[132] The Conservative Evangelicals' grave dissatisfaction with *The Trowel* and the Liberal Evangelicalism of the Director of Education caused them to start a campaign to win control of the Board of Education.[133]

Before 1933 the character of the Board was predominantly Liberal Evangelical with a number of High Churchmen also serving as Board members. The elected clerical members in 1932 — Dean Talbot, Archdeacon Davies, Canon Garnsey, and Revs. A.J.A. Fraser, O.V. Abram and F.A. Walton, the Director — all later joined the Anglican Fellowship while *none* of the laymen — Professor Tasman Lovell of the Sydney University Psychology Department, F.B. Wilkinson, a solicitor from Christ Church St. Laurence, and a former President of the 1910 Church Defence League, L.C. Hutchinson, a barrister, Harold Earlam, the superintendent of the N.S.W. Institute for Deaf and Dumb, W.J. Williams, the City Council's Superintendent of Markets and a synod representative for St. Hilda's Katoomba, and Alfred King, a commercial agent from St. Luke's Mosman — were members or even fellow travellers of the Anglican Church League.[134]

The predominantly Liberal Evangelical complexion of this Board before 1933 had, of course, only been possible because, as one of its members put it, "the dominant faction have left us alone — not contesting the seats."[135] But its character rapidly changed when the A.C.L. "decided to capture the Board", in the polarised atmosphere of 1933.[136] Four Board members were due for re-election — Walton, Garnsey, Earlam and

Williams — and the League nominated four candidates to oppose their re-election, including Bishop Kirkby, the Administrator of the Diocese. The result was decisive: Garnsey "alone survived the attack".[137] With four positions on the Board due for election each year, the Conservative Evangelical forces gained an overwhelming majority on the Board by 1936. Only three non-Conservative Evangelicals — Garnsey, A.J.A. Fraser and Lloyd Hutchinson — withstood the A.C.L. campaign which saw three of the four positions each year filled by A.C.L. members.

The Conservative Evangelicals' campaign against the Board of Education was "pre-concerted and carried out by means of preliminary caucus meetings and a carefully imposed 'ticket'."[138] The A.C.L. demonstrated political cunning in its use of the ticket: the nomination in 1933 of the Administrator of the Diocese, Bishop Kirkby, for example, ensured the defeat of a popular Liberal Evangelical, the Rev. F.A. Walton. The League's campaign also seemed to disregard a candidate's qualification, ability and effectiveness, and expressed an over-zealous interest in his churchmanship: in 1936, an A.C.L. accountant was preferred to Professor Tasman Lovell, a man of obvious "standing and distinction in the world of education."[139]

More importantly, this unashamedly partisan campaign demonstrated the sincerity and purpose of the Conservative Evangelicals in seeking to check what they believed was heterodox teaching. The whole motivation of the Conservative Evangelicals' campaign was not simply to win control of yet another committee, but to rein in *The Trowel* under Walton's editorship, and re-direct educational policy in the Diocese. It should have come as no surprise, therefore, that once the Conservative Evangelicals controlled the Board of Education, they quickly placed constraints on Walton's editorial freedom, and effectively stripped him of many of his responsibilities as Director, making him little more than a secretarial assistant without delegated power. The Conservative Evangelicals clearly intended that Walton toe their line — or resign.[140] Walton did not quickly accommodate them. He could not in all conscience change his viewpoints, nor would he happily oblige them with his resignation. The Conservative Evangelicals had to wait until 1938, when Walton accepted a similar position in Religious Education in the greener pastures of Melbourne, before their victory over Liberal Evangelicalism in the area of Diocesan Education was complete.[141]

IX

The struggle for control of the Board of Education was indicative of the respective fortunes of Conservative and, Liberal Evangelical parties in Sydney at that time. By 1936, when the Conservative Evangelicals secured control of the Board, the Anglican Fellowship was a spent political force. It had promised much in 1933 but three years later it was in no position to threaten the dominance of the Conservative Evangelicals.

The underlying cause behind the Fellowship's change in political fortunes was its electoral dependence upon its founders, Dean Talbot and Archdeacon D.J. Davies. Both men were identified with the reasonable moderation of the late Archbishop who had appointed them. While others around them laboured under "modernist" labels, Davies and Talbot were so unequivocally Evangelical men of God that they commanded strong popular support throughout Evangelical circles in the Diocese. Their defection from the party machine demanded the attention of ordinary synodsmen and demonstrated that the division in Sydney was determined far more by temperament, a division between conservative and liberal spirits, than by churchmanship.[142] It became equally clear that those who united under the banner of progressivism in the Fellowship had no unanimity of opinion at all: their unity was not based on agreement about theological, churchmanship, social or political issues, but by their mutual desire "to consolidate the influence of all those who love the light" against the power of the machine.[143]

That was the Fellowship's great weakness. It was not an institution-alised organisation; there was no party machine. And its great electoral dependence upon the personal popularity of Davies and Talbot meant that the sudden deaths of these two men in 1935 and 1936 was a fatal blow to the Fellowship's political prospects. Talbot and Davies had been the focus around which a discrete group of clergy and laymen had gathered, and provided the dynamic impetus which had energised them. They had had a reputation for earnest Protestantism in churchmanship, and a respected caution, rather than a radical Liberalism, in scholarship.[144] Their unexpected departure robbed the Anglican Fellowship of a leader-ship which was attractive to many independently-minded Evangelicals. Indeed, the Fellowship had lost the two members who had most given it respectability.[145]

Their loss was immediately felt in political terms: while the A.C.L. was active for months in preparing for the important election of new lay synod representatives in mid-1936, the Anglican Fellowship's political activities were disjointed, disorganised and ineffectual. Further, the reluctant successor to Talbot as President of the Anglican Fellowship, Canon Arthur Garnsey, knew "full well (that) I am not the man to lead it in a Diocesan campaign".[146] He lacked the political connections in the Diocese which Talbot and Davies had had, but he realised that there was no-one better equipped to assume leadership of the Fellowship. Despite his diffidence towards becoming a leading protagonist in a diocesan campaign and "right in the thick" of controversy, Garnsey realised that the dearth of leadership potential in the Fellowship necessitated it: "Woe is me," he wrote, "that I have to be a man of strife and contention!"[147]

The deaths of Talbot and Davies not only gravely affected the polit-ical prospects of the Anglican Fellowship but also dealt it a crippling psychological blow. It made the surviving Liberal Evangelicals feel more and more an isolated and embattled minority. In five short years they had lost virtually all their elder statesmen. Only Canon Arthur

Garnsey remained, as a lonely, unwilling leader of the young Liberal Evangelicals who remained in the flagging Fellowship.[148] This is a critical factor which underlies party conflict in Sydney in the 1930s. By 1936, the Liberal Evangelicals were not a strong and growing opposition threatening the dominance of the Conservative Evangelicals, but were cornered, outnumbered rivals, who had been soundly whipped at Synod elections, whose leadership had been decimated by illness, and whose forcefulness had been seriously eroded. They were keenly aware that they were a minority and that the Conservative Evangelical forces were triumphant.

X

The episcopate of Bishop Barker (1854-1882) is invariably considered as the foundation of the Conservative Evangelical character of the Diocese of Sydney. The years 1890 to 1909 has been considered by one commentator as a formative period "in which many chickens were hatched which later came home to roost."[149] But the 1926-1936 decade stands alongside these as a most important chapter in the history of the Diocese and one which determined that it would remain predominantly Conservative Evangelical for at least the next fifty years.

It was a decade from which Conservative Evangelicalism emerged victorious in the Diocese at a time when, elsewhere in the Anglican Communion, an aggressive Anglo-Catholicism and an articulate but irresolute Liberal Evangelicalism was in the ascendant. By 1936 in England, the Conservative Evangelicals had been virtually extinguished as a force in the Church of England. In other Australian Dioceses; Evangelicals were in the minority. In all Queensland dioceses they were an extinct species, and in most other Australian dioceses they were being steadily squeezed out. For example, under Bishop Hart of Wangaratta, Victoria, "definite 'low churchmen' tended to disappear until", his biographer admits, "by about 1939 there were none left in the diocese."[150] Despite denials that the extinction of Evangelicals in that country diocese was not a deliberate policy, there is no gainsaying the fact that Anglo-Catholics were distinctly encouraged and preferred to Evangelicals by Bishop Hart, and were gaining in numbers and influence.[151]

The tendency towards the monochrome was as great in Wangaratta as in Sydney. The difference was, however, that Wangaratta was more typical of other Australian dioceses in the direction it was heading. In most Australian dioceses, the militant Anglo-Catholics were becoming more intolerant and extreme. They plainly believed that they had time on their side and, within a generation, they would dominate the whole of the Australian Church.[152]

The gains of the Anglo-Catholics in the rest of Australia were matched in Sydney by the overwhelming victory of the Conservative Evangelicals. They had soundly defeated the Liberal Evangelical challenge by 1936 and were triumphantly proud of the fact that they were a unique bastion of Conservative Evangelicalism, without parallel in all Anglicanism. In 1926, the Liberal Evangelicals had been an important and influential group in the Diocese. They — together with a number of High Churchmen — had then held 73 of 169 (43.2%) important positions in the Diocese. But ten years later, in 1936, only 35 of 185 positions (or 18.9%) were held by Liberal Evangelicals (together with one "Broad" Churchman and no High Churchmen). Their representation in positions where they could influence Diocesan policy had been slashed by almost two-thirds, and they had become an isolated and largely unrepresented minority. Concomitantly, the Conservative Evangelicals had tightened their grip on the Diocese in these ten years and, by 1936, occupied more than 80% of all influential, decision-making positions at the Liberal Evangelicals' expense.[153]

Some reasons for this defeat of Liberal Evangelicalism in the Diocese of Sydney have been advanced in this chapter. First, the Constitutional issue had polarised opinion in the Church of England in Australia, and fostered a defensive extremism in Evangelical circles which was antagonistic to Liberalism. Second, the Angus affair had made Conservative Evangelicals of all denominations suspicious of anything which smacked of unorthodoxy — indeed anything which was new. Biblical scholarship which did not conform to the traditional shibboleths came to be regarded as the means by which the sacred fundamentals of the faith was being destroyed. Biblical scholars may have been great thinkers, but Conservative Evangelicals preferred to be in the company of great believers. Third, Sydney Conservative Evangelicals had witnessed events in England where Liberal Evangelicalism had enervated the influence and power of the Conservative Evangelicals. They were therefore determined not to be beguiled by a Liberal Evangelicalism which they perceived had already betrayed the Evangelical cause in the Mother Church.

The English experience induced the Conservative Evangelicals in Sydney to launch a pre-emptive attack upon Liberal Evangelicalism. This meant that they opposed what they thought Sydney Liberals believed and attacked what a they feared these men represented with scant regard for what they actually believed. That these Australian Liberal Evangelicals were identified with the Liberal Evangelicals in England was understandable. But it was unfair and inaccurate to assume a consonance of belief between men like Talbot and Davies and the Liberal Evangelical leaders in England, such as Canon Vernon Storr or the Rev. R.T. Howard. These men had a certain consonance of temperament and a similar liberal attitude towards biblical scholarship, but there were crucial differences in their theological standpoints. Talbot and Davies were in fact quite theologically conservative and their campaign for the maintenance of the Fundamentals of belief in the Constitution debates in the 1920s and their unswerving allegiance to the 39 Articles bore testimony to that conservatism.[154]

The fourth reason for the defeat of Liberal Evangelicalism in Sydney during this period was the quite evident lack of leadership. The Liberal Evangelicals in England enjoyed the leadership abilities of a young and highly talented group of individuals, while their Conservative Evangelical counterparts were forced to rely upon the services of a diminishing number of old warhorses. But the reverse was true in Sydney. In that diocese, the successive deaths of Liberal Evangelical leaders from 1931 to 1936 dealt a telling blow to the Liberal Evangelical cause. They were mortal blows from which the Liberal Evangelical movement never recovered. By contrast, the Conservative Evangelicals had solid, if unspectacular, leadership before 1933, which was strengthened immeasurably by the arrival of two dynamic, charismatic leaders in Archbishop Mowll in 1934 and the Rev. T.C. Hammond in 1936. It is significant that this Conservative Evangelical leadership was almost exclusively clerical. Since the laity's deep involvement in extra-parochial affairs in the 1880s and 1890s, the laity's participation in the political affairs of the Diocese declined markedly. The 1920s and 1930s were a 'trough' period for lay involvement in diocesan decision-making and this was reflected by the preponderance of clergymen in leadership positions in the A.C.L. during this turbulent period of its history. The laity's ostensible lack of interest allowed their clergy, amongst whom Conservative Evangelicals were dominant, to determine the future direction and character of the Anglican Church League and the Diocese as a whole.

Despite the fact that the Liberal Evangelicals were quite plainly a beleaguered, under-represented minority by 1936 they remained a significant section of the churchmen in the Diocese. They were certainly vanquished; they were indeed angrily wounded. Yet they were not extinguished. In fact, the next few years brought them into greater prominence than ever before as they struggled to articulate their viewpoints in a Diocese where they continued to be considered suspect by the Conservative Evangelicals in power.

NOTES - CHAPTER EIGHT

1. The *Record* England. 18/1/1909 p.22.
2. *ibid.* 29/11/1917 p.97.
3. Cross and Livingstone, *op. cit.*, p.648.
4. E.A. Knox, *op. cit.*, pp.327-329; Lloyd, *op. cit.*, p.39.
5. T. Guy Rogers, "Religious Authority" in *op. cit.*, pp.44-45.
6. V.F. Storr, *Freedom and Tradition* A.E.G.M./Hodder and Stoughton London 1940 p.172.
7. See "X", "Liberal Evangelicalism: What it is and What it stands for: The Essence of Evangelicalism", in The *Churchman* March 1915 p.195.
8. Walmsley, *op. cit.*, pp.127, 151-2. I cannot agree with Walmsley that the Liberal Evangelicals also moulded these tendencies into "a coherent philosophy and theology". The only coherence in the Liberal Evangelical movement was that they were anti-the negativists; Cf. E.C. Dewick, "Evangelicalism in England...", in *The Constructive Quarterly*, 1915, pp.801, 803 *passim*.
9. Eugene Stock, "The Recent Controversy in the C.M.S." in *Church Missionary Review*, 1923. pp.29, 33-34.
10. J.E. Watts-Ditchfield to "My Dear Brother" (Circular) 13/5/1922, for Summer Conference at Birmingham Diocesan House, Coleshill Park, in *Minute Book* of the Group Brotherhood (A.E.G.M.) 12/6/1922. DEM 1/15. A.E.G.M. Papers.
11. Stock, *op. cit.*, pp.33-34: Joan Bayldon, *Cyril Bardsley, Evangelist* S.#75.
12. Only three Vice-Presidents, four Life Governors and two missionaries resigned from the C.M.S. to join the B.C.M.S., and only a few

parishes switched support; Stock, *op. cit.*, pp.33-35; Walmsley, *op. cit.*, pp.197, 199.

13. Knox, *op. cit.*, p.329.

14. L. Hicken to Ronald Williams, Bishop of Leicester 18/1/1968 DEM 7/24, A.E.G.M. Papers.

15. *Minutes* of the Group Brotherhood 8/4/1923: 8/6/1923, A.E.G.M. *Minutes* 12/1/1926 DEM 1/15 A.E.G.M. Papers.

16. L. Hicken, "Liberal Evangelicals in the Church of England" in *Church Quarterly Review*, 1968. pp.43-54.

17. Memo, Vernon Storr et al. to Bishop Nickson of Bristol n.d. (Feb. 1927), "Prayer Book Revision" Special Subject Series 1927 Box 5, in Davidson Papers.

18. T. Guy Rogers ed. *Liberal Evangelicalism* Hodder and Stoughton London 1923 (3rd ed.)

19. The book's contributors included Bishops Guy Warman and Linton Smith of Hereford, two theological college principals, Howard of Birkenhead and Gooding of Wycliffe Hall, Oxford, and a number of other scholars including J.W. Hunkin of Cambridge (later Bishop of Truro) and Dean Burroughs of Bristol (later Bishop of Ripon).

20. J.W. Walmsley, *op. cit.*, p.214. The Fellowship of Evangelical Churchmen did reply to Liberal Evangelicalism in 1925 with a collection of essays entitled Evangelicalism, edited by J. Russell Howden. (Thynne and Jarvis London 1925)

21. See A.E.G.M. *Minutes* 11/10/1923 e.g...

22. A.H. Garnsey to D.A. Garnsey 19/4/1932; Bidwell Transcript p.10.. G.A. D'Arcy-Irvine to Davidson 7/4/1914, Davidson to D'Arcy-Irvine 21/5/1914 in "Prayer Book Revision" Box 1 in Davidson Papers;

23. Loane, *Moore College*, pp.137-138.

24. A.H.G to D.A.G. 9/6/1936; F.W. Head, Talbot's tutor at Emmanuel College, Cambridge, and Archbishop of Melbourne from 1929 was an active member of the A.E.G.M.

25. A similar study group affiliated to the A.E.G.M. met in in Melbourne. Membership Lists DEM 4/1 A.E.G.M. Papers; *A.C.R.* 31/10/1935 p.6, 14/11/1935 pp.11-12, 28/11/1935 p.10, 9/1/1936 p.3.

26. Bishop Knox, Prebendary H.W. Hinde, and Mr. Guy Johnson, secretary of National Church League kept the Conservative party in Sydney informed on the situation in England. See A.C.L. Minutes 28/3/1933.

27. A.H. Garnsey to D.A. Garnsey 2/4/1935, 22/10/1935, 24/3/1936, 14/7/1936

28. Church attendance may have increased slightly during the Depression but clergymen did not seem to notice the larger numbers. Instead, they were troubled by the larger indifference of their parishioners. See *A.C.R.* 6/12/1928 p.6; *S.D.M.* Jan 1930 p.29, March 1930 pp. 19,23, May 1930 pp.8-9; *S.M.H.* 30/6/1930 p.10, 1/9/1930 p.8, 5/10/1936 p.6, 4/5/1931 p.8.

29. *A.C.R.* 21/4/1932 p.11 (D.J. Knox).

30. *ibid.*, See also *ibid.* 14/2/1929 p.7, 17/8/1933 p.6, 21/4/1932 p.11, 4/10/1934 pp.1-2.

31. *A.C.R.* 5/1/1928 p.4.

32. 32. Henry Rogers, Synodsman for Bondi 1907-35, and St. Peter's, East Sydney 1936; *A.C.R.* 27/2/1930 p.6 (ed); *S.M.H.*; 11/11/1931 p.12.

33. *A.C.R.* 27/2/1930 p.6, 11/11/1937 p.20, 26/5/1938 p.7; See Chapter Seven.

34. *S.M.H.* 25/2/1933 p.14.

35. *S.D.M.* March 1933 p.5; J.A.I. Perry to Abp. Cosmo Lang 30/1/1932, Sir Philip Game to Lang 26/9/1933. 1932 S.7. Lang Papers.

36. J.A.I. Perry to Archbishop Cosmo Lang 30/1/1932, *loc.cit.*; *S.D.M.* April 1933 p.8 S.M. Johnstone.

37. Sir Philip Game to Lang 26/9/1933. *loc.cit. S.M.H.* 1/4/1933 p.14 (D.J. Davies).

38. A.C.L. *Minutes* 23/3/1933.

39. Loane, *Mowll*, p.125.

40. *A.C.R.* 26/11/1925 p.1, 17/3/1932 p.7.

41. Loane, *Mowll*, p.119.

42. *A.C.R.* 13/4/1933 p.1.

43. *S.M.H.* 7/2/1934 p.12.

44. A.C.L. *Minutes* 28/3/1933

45. *A.C.R.* 30/3/1933 p.8.
46. *A.C.R.* 16/3/1933 p.10.
47. *ibid.*
48. See *A.C.R.* 4/5/1933 p.6.
49. *S.M.H.* 18/7/1932 p.4; See Sydney, Diocese. St. Barnabas' Chatswood. 1932. S.7. Lang Papers.
50. *A.C.R.* 2/3/1933 p.11.
51. *A.C.R.* 30/3/1933 p.11.
52. *S.M.H.* 14/3/1933 p.8, 8/7/1933 p.14; A.H.G. to D.A.G. 28/2/1933, 21/3/1933.
53. A.H.G. to D.A.G. 28/2/1933.
54. *S.M.H.* 25/3/1933 p.13, 3/4/1933 p.10; A.H.G. to D.A.G. 28/2/1933, 21/3/1933.
55. *S.M.H.* 1/4/1933 p.14.
56. S.H. Denman and nine others to synodsmen 30/3/1933. Corish Papers. Of the ten men who signed the letter to synodsmen urging their support for Mowll, seven were students of Jones, and none had attended Moore College during Davies' principalship.
57. *A.C.R.* 13/4/1933 p.1; Bidwell Transcript p.2.
58. A.C.L. *minutes* 28/3/1933; Talbot to Corish 10/5/1933, Corish Papers.
59. The twelve nominations were three Sydney clergymen — Bishop Kirkby, Dean Talbot and Canon W.G. Hilliard — and two Australian Bishops, Moyes and de Witt Batty of Newcastle, and six Englishmen — the Rev. T.W. Gilbert, the Principal of St. John's Highbury, Canon Arthur, Grant of Norwich, Canon Laurence Grensted of Liverpool, Canon Charles Raven, Regius Professor at Cambridge, and Hunkin and Mowll; *S.M.H.* 3/4/1933 p.10.
60. Synod officially consisted of 166 clergy and 334 laymen. However it would appear that no more than 142 clergy and 234 laymen attended at any one time. See *A.C.R.* 1/6/1933 p.11, and annotated Business Paper for Wednesday 5/4/1933 in Corish Papers.
61. Bishop Mervyn Haigh (Coventry) to Alec Sargent 12/4/1933. 1933. S.7. Sydney, Archbishop of. Lang Papers. Haigh was Hunkin's bishop.

62. *S.M.H.* 7/4/1933 p.13.

63. See e.g. J.W. Hunkin, "The Reformation and the Scriptures" in *The Modern Churchman* 1932, pp.286-7.

64. Bidwell Transcript pp.2-3; pp.174-193. Guy Rogers, *op.cit.*,

65. Bidwell Transcript, p.3; The Conservatives may have preferred to have only Grant and Grensted on the Final List, but the Ordinance precluded this. If only two names had proceeded from the Select to the Final List, **all** the names on the Select List would have become the Final List. They therefore merely eliminated the major threat.

66. *D.T.* 7/4/1933 p.l: *S.M.H.* 7/4/1933 p.13, *A.C.R.* 1/6/1933 p.11.

67. A.H.G. to D.A.G. 12/4/1933.

68. Dili 14/5/1932 p.4; A. Dougan, "Samuel Angus" in Bede Nairn and G. Serle, *Australian Dictionary of Biography* v.7. M.U.P. 1979. pp.73-4.

69. I am indebted to Susan Emilsen for much of this information.

70. *D.T.* 4/1/1933 p.7; A.H.G. to D.A.G. 1/3/1932. Garnsey, Talbot and Davies were in fact associated with Angus in a discussion group called the Heretics Club. Whether this was known by Conservative Evangelical leaders is uncertain. I am indebted to Associate Professor K.J. Cable for information about the Heretics Club.

71. S.H. Denman and nine others to Evangelical Members of the Diocesan Synod of Sydney 30/3/1933. *loc.cit.*

72. A.H.G. to D.A.G. 12/4/1933.

73. A.H.G. to D.A.G. 25/4/1933.

74. Loane, *Mowll*, p.52.

75. Mowll was ordained priest in 1914 by the Archbishop of Canterbury.

76. Loane, *Mowll*, pp.198, 204-205.

77. *ibid.*, pp.81-82; 102-103.

78. *ibid.* p.204.

79. Douglas Johnson, *Contending for the Faith*, Inter-Varsity Press Leicester 1979 pp. 68-78; Loane, *Mowll*, pp.51-53.

80. Loane, *Mowll*, p.200.

81. *ibid.* pp.125-126.

82. *ibid.* pp.103-109.

83. *ibid.* pp.207-208.

84. *ibid.* pp.200-201.

85. *ibid.*

86. *A.C.R.* 18/5/1933 p.11 (Abram)

87. Veni Creator Spiritus (Hymn "Come Holy Ghost, Our Souls Inspire"); A.H.G.'to D.A.G. 25/4/1933; *A.C.R.* 4/5/1933 p.7; A.C.L. members hotly denied that 80 men at an A.C.L. luncheon just before the election had pledged themselves to support Mowll. See also *A.C.R.* 18/5/1933 p.11; 13/4/1933 p.9 (Hinsby): 18/5/1933 p.11 (Abram).

88. Sir Philip Game to Archbishop C.G. Lang 26/9/1933 1933.S.7. Sydney, Archbishop of. Lang Papers.

89. *ibid.*; see also A.H.G. to D.A.G. 25/4/1933.

90. *A.C.R.* 13/4/1933 p.1, and see also 4/5/1933 p.7; A.H.G. to D.A.G. 25/4/1933.

91. A.H.G. to D.A.G 30/5/1933.

92. A.H.G. to D.A.G. 27/6/1933; A.E. Talbot to Hugh Corish 10/5/1933. Corish Papers.

93. A.H.G. to D.A.G. 30/5/1933.'See also 27/6/1933.

94. *S.M.H.* 30/5/1933 p.8 — report on meeting of clergy and laymen on 29/5/1933.

95. *ibid.*; The principles of the Fellowship have an implicit tilt at the over-emphasis by Conservative Evangelicals of Reformation theology and theologians; See also *S.M.H.* 1/6/1933 p.10 and Aims of the A.E.G.M., DEM 1/13. A.E.G.M. Papers.

96. A.H.G. to D.A.G. 3o/5/1933. See also 27/6/1933.

97. A.H. Garnsey to D.A. Garnsey 30/3/1933.

98. A.C.L. *Minutes* 12/5/1933. J.A.I. Perry and C.P. Taubman were the two men deputed to see Talbot. Talbot declined to reconsider his resignation and this reply was recorded in the A.C.L. *Minutes* of Council 23/6/1933.

99. A.L. Short and the Rev. J.P. Dryland unsuccessfully attempted to defer the motion to the next meeting. The original motion was

moved by the Rev. A.R. Ebbs and seconded by Malcolm D'Arcy-Irvine: A.C.L. *Minutes* 9/6/1933.

100. Langford Smith to Corish 13/6/1933; secretaries of A.C.L. to Council members (n.d.) Corish Papers.

101. W.J.G. Mann to Corish 25/2/1933. *loc.cit.*

102. A.C.L. *Minutes* 9/6/1933 and 23/6/1933.

103. *ibid.*

104. See *A.C.R.* 11/1/1928 p.6 and 3/2/1939 p.4.

105. Two important former students of Jones who became more prominent in the A.C.L. later in the 1930s but who were not involved in the heady events within the party in 1933 were the Revs. H.S. Begbie (62) and Stephen Denman (51). Other A.C.L. members who trained under Jones but who were less influential included A.E. Rook, John Bidwell and Andrew Colvin.

106. A.H.G. to D.A.G. 27/6/1933; A.E. Talbot et al, "Open Letter to Synodsmen" 6/9/1934. Corish Papers.

107. *A.C.R.* 28/11/1935 p.3; A.H.G. to D.A.G. 10/12/1935 28/1/1936. A.H. Garnsey's Diary 6/12/1935.

108. H.N. Baker was the organiser of the social issues council. See A.H.G to D.A.G 10/12/1935.

109. The A.C.L. Executive Committee seems to have been disbanded sometime between late 1927 and August 1929. See A.C.L. *Minutes* 16/8/1929, and also Council and Exec. *Minutes* 20/11/1933, 13/10/1933. In 1933 the Executive was the Revs. W.G. Hilliard, R.A. Pollard, S.E. Langford Smith, D.J. Knox, S.H. Denman, R.B. Robinson, J.P. Dryland, Leo Gabbott and laymen W.J.G. Mann, M.P. Brownrigg, C.P.Taubman, H.A. Corish, A.L. Short, M.M.D'Arcy-Irvine, K.E. Barnett, and J.D. Walker.

110. In 1930-31 there were 54 clerical and 43 lay members. See Lists in Corish Papers.

111. W.G. Hilliard and nine others to synodsmen 27/10/1933. Corish Papers.

112. *ibid.*; see also A.C.L. *Minutes* 13/10/1933, 20/10/1933 and 24/10/1933.

113. See Membership Lists. Corish Papers.
114. See Loane, *Moore College*, pp.185-192; A.C.L. Membership Lists, Corish Papers.
115. A.C.L. Minutes 8/8/1930, 20/10/1933, 13/4/1934, 1934 AGM Annual Report, and 24/8/1934, and membership application forms. Corish Papers; M.L. Loane, e.g., joined the A.C.L. on 3/11/1933 but was instrumental in the establishment of the Y.E.C.L. in the next year.
116. 1934 Executive Report to A.G.M. of the A.C.L. Corish Papers; In 1934, e.g., two lectures were given on "Aspects of the 39 Articles in relation to the Holy Communion" by the Rev. J.P. Dryland, and "Confession and the Confessional" by the Rev. W.T. Price.
117. Six of the seven *Record* Directors and 11 of the 13 members of the Board of Management were A.C.L. members. A.C. *Record Minutes* 17/10/1933. There were five Victorian Directorships of which only three were filled — Dr. A. Law, Canon T. Langley and Dr. Barcham Clamp — all A.C.L. (Melbourne) members.
118. For evidence of earlier co-operation see *A.C.R.* 4/3/1926 p.1, 22/7/1926 p.5 and A.C.L. *Minutes* 6/9/1921, 12/6/1931. Corish Papers.
119. For circulation figures, see *A.C.R. Minutes* 30/4/1925 (Circulation of 1900); 15/10/1929, (1600) and still 1600 at 25/1/1938.
120. In May 1934 the A.C.L. as a body gave fifteen pounds, five shillings to the *Record*, but *A.C.R.* registers and cash ledgers reveal much greater personal support from individual A.C.L. members. See also 1934 A.C.L. Annual Report. Corish Papers.
121. H.C. Leplastrier to "My Dear Brother" (Corish) 19/10/1933.
122. Leplastrier to Corish 20/5/1933, Corish Papers. The only real anti-A.C.L activity was by the Anglo-Catholics who put up Messrs. F.C.G. Tremlett and R.B. Symington as representatives for Mulgoa, whereas they had previously represented Christ Church, St. Laurence, and of course their positions there were taken by like-minded people. See *Year Book* Of the Diocese of Sydney. 1934 pp.222, 227, 263.

123. 23. H.C. Leplastrier to Corish 20/5/1933, 19/10/1933. *loc.cit.*

124. *ibid.*, R.A. Pollard and Corish to selected synodsmen 30/10/1933.

125. *Year Book* of the Diocese, of Sydney 1934. pp.335,339.

126. *ibid.* Pollard and Corish to selected synodsmen 30/10/1933. Corish Papers.

127. *A.C.R.* 23/11/1933 p.1.

128. A.H.G. to D.A.G. 14/11/1933, in which Garnsey protests to Kirkby about allowing himself to be part of the attack on the Board of Education, an action Garnsey thought "highly improper" for the Administrator of the Diocese; A.H. Garnsey *Diary* 9/11/1933.

129. In 1934 D.J. Davies was elected instead of Rev K.W. Pain to the Board of Education; in 1935 the Rev. W.J. Cakebread defeated the Rev. H.N. Powys to fill a vacancy on the Standing Committee, while Canon H.N. Baker defeated the Rev. J.P. Dryland for a position on the council of Shore; in 1936 Cakebread was elected in favour of the Rev. E. Potter to the Council of H.M.S. See *Year Books* 1934 to 1937 and A.C.L. "Recommendation" (how-to-vote) letters dated 30/8/1934 (Corish and Pollard), 12/9/1935 (Begbie, Knox, A.E. Rook, Bidwell, Mann, Taubman, J.D. Walker, and J.W. Spain) to selected members of Synod, and annotated Nominations List 5/9/1936. Corish Papers.

130. A.H.G. to D.A.G. 13/4/1932

131. A.H.G. to D.A.G. 6/8/1934, 22/10/1935, 3/12/1935, 17/11/1936.

132. A.C.L. Council *Minutes* 6/3/1936.

133. *A.C.R.* 19/3/1936 p.1; A.H.G. to D.A.G. 17/11/1936.

134. Mr. F.B. Wilkinson died just six weeks before the 1933 session of Synod at the age of 72.

135. A.H.G. to D.A.G. 14/11/1933.

136. *ibid.*

137. W.J. Williams to Pollard and Corish 6/11/1933; Pollard and Corish to Evangelical members of Synod 30/11/1933. Corish Papers; The other A.C.L. nominees were the Rev. F.W. Tugwell, and Messrs. C.P. Taubman and M.P. Brownrigg. Only Tugwell was unsuccessful.

138. A.H.G. to D.A.G. 14/11/1933

139. A.H.G. to D.A.G. 29/9/1936. Mr. A.L. Short, an A.C.L. Councillor, was the successful candidate against Professor Lovell, 17/11/1936. Garnsey Papers.
140. A.H.G. to D.A.G. 17/11/1936. Garnsey Papers.
141. *ibid.*, and 30/3/1937; *C.S.* 7/10/1938 p.10.
142. *S.M.H.* 30/5/1933 p.8; A.H.G. to D.A.G. 30/5/1933, 27/6/1933.
143. Garnsey and Talbot, for example, clearly disagreed on some social and political issues. See A.H.G to D.A.G. 1/12/1931, 9/2/1932, 22/3/1932, 31/5/1932, 20/6/1932; *S.M.H.* 17/8/1917 p.5, 20/8/1917 p.8, *C.S.* 24/8/1917 p.3: and *A.C.R.* 31/8/1917 p.1.
144. Loane, *Moore College*, pp.137.
145. A.H.G. to D.A.G. 14/7/1936.
146. *ibid.*
147. A.H.G. to D.A.Garnsey 30/10/1941. See also 15/9/1931, 5/10/1931, 25/4/1933, 2/3/1935, 30/3/1937, 24/1/1942; *A.C.R.* 8/12/1938 pp.8-10, 9/2/1939 p.16, 23/2/1939 p.5, 9/3/1939 pp.12-13, and 6/4/1939 pp.7-8; A.H. Garnsey, *Diary* 7/9/1936.
148. A.H.G. to D.A.G. 14/7/1936
149. Robinson, *Origins*, p.9.
150. T.B McCall, *The Life and Letters of John Stephen Hart*, Church of England Information Trust Sydney 1963 p.97.
151. *ibid.*, pp.97-99
152. H.T. Langley to Langford Smith 28/3/1935. Langford Smith Papers.
153. The members of the Standing Committee, the Synod Nominators, the Moore College Committee, the Moore College Trustees, the representatives to the General and Provincial Synods, the members of the Board of Education and the Home Mission Council, were the positions of influence surveyed for 1926 and 1936. See *Year Books* 1927 pp.23-35, and 1937, pp.246-260.
154. See e.g. *A.C.R.* 4/3/1926 p.6 (Davies) and 16/9/1926 p.4 (Talbot).

CHAPTER NINE - THE MEMORIAL

I

The years 1936 to 1938 witnessed the last stand of Liberal Evangelicalism in the Diocese of Sydney. The crushing defeats they had suffered in the early 1930s had reduced them to an ostracised minority without influence in the Diocese. Liberal Evangelicals reacted to their plight in two ways. First, they brought their struggle out into the open by the publication of a number of controversial periodicals. This raised tensions within the Diocese to an explosive level but, having been defeated at the ballot box, Liberal Evangelicals were determined to become at least an articulate opposition to the ruling Conservative Evangelicals. The second response of the Liberal Evangelicals to their embattled position was to appeal to the Archbishop. This final protest — the Memorial of 1938 — came to be regarded as the most serious challenge to the Conservative Evangelical character of the Diocese of Sydney's history.

The first signs of Liberal Evangelical propaganda appeared in 1936. In that year, the Rev. W.G. Coughlan published *The Church Times*, a short-lived journal about which very little is known; and a second, anonymously published paper was produced called *Outlook*. Both publications were designed to link together those clergy "who for too long have had no means of effective expression, or opportunity of making a constructive contribution to the corporate life and work of the Church."[1] *Outlook*'s editor disclaimed a policy of narrow diocesan isolationism, in which there would be little interchange with other dioceses, but was convinced that Liberal Evangelicals were confronted by a situation in which "frequent (parish) changes (were) enjoyed by a small number (of 'sound' clergy)" while other able men were ignored because they were not considered "safe".[2] This was "justification for our out-spokenness...the whispering and the repressions of the past three years (since 1933) have made necessary our protest."[3]

Outlook was immediately provocative. In its first issue it criticised the appointment of the Rev. T.C. Hammond, the Secretary of the Irish Church Missions in Dublin, as the new Principal of Moore College on the grounds that Hammond's combative, hibernian temperament would exacerbate the existing divisions in the Diocese.[4] Its second number was equally controversial by attacking two clerical appointments. *Outlook* claimed that the appointment of "a middle-aged Assistant Curate from the Diocese of Melbourne" to an important industrial parish, and the further importation of "a very junior clergyman" to Moss Vale were harbingers of an expected flood of imported clergy at the expense of those already in the Diocese who could not "subscribe to certain outworn shibboleths".[5]

These anonymous Liberal Evangelical attacks on the Conservative Evangelical regime were swiftly rebutted by the Record which questioned the purpose of these "clergy who suppose themselves to be in the mainstream of Anglican life... Are they out to stab Sydney Diocese in the back or prepare it for that day when either 'a cold moderatism' or a full orbed sacerdotalism shall prevail?"[6] *Outlook's* editor was unperturbed by the Conservative Evangelical ripostes and continued to protest at what he believed were disturbing developments in Diocesan policy.[7]

The Church Times and *Outlook* were only fleeting expressions of Liberal Evangelical dissent in Sydney and both publications disappeared by 1937. Their place was more than adequately filled in August 1937 by the quarterly magazine *Challenge: An Organ of Central Churchmanship*. This journal was also the product of a group of Liberal Evangelicals who felt that their desire to contribute to the life of their church was being frustrated by the Conservative Evangelical regime in Sydney and the Anglo-Catholic majority elsewhere in Australia:

> "for a long time past, there has been a lot of unrest among some of the younger (and older) men in this Diocese." One of their number explained. "All the key positions are now in the hands of men who are satisfied with what they learned long ago -- men who incline towards Tennesseeism (sic) though they would not, of course, carry their inclinations to the point of absurdity. On the other side, outside Sydney, there are the dear good Anglo-Catholics who preach 'Church' and 'Sacraments' till they get things lop-sided."[8]

With the Rev. Robert Harley Jones of Liverpool as its editor and a literary committee headed by Arthur Garnsey, *Challenge* quickly became the best ecclesiastical journal in Australia. The six articles of about 1200 words each which appeared in every issue were expressions of a self-conscious Liberal Evangelicalism which would otherwise have been without propagation or voice. The magazine's publication was a deliberate attempt to marshal support for a position which eschewed "the shortsightedness of the enthusiasts" at both extremes of the ecclesiastical spectrum.[9]

The new journal's ethos was encapsulated in its first issue by an article, "Central Churchmanship", written by Canon Arthur Garnsey. Garnsey maintained that Central Churchmanship did not indicate a compromising middle path, but rather "a point within a circle, so essential that without it no circle can be described."[10] He asserted that a central churchman sought to interpret Christian truth and practice in the light of Christ who was in the Centre, and not from any section of the circle. He endeavoured to employ "the sharp tool of intellect, itself the gift of God, to pierce through the veils which popular theology has woven round the Christ as he is revealed to us in Scripture." Christians in every generation, Garnsey argued, needed to re-examine their theology, not their religion. The temptation of over-emphasis had led to accretion and, "when the legitimate interpretation of one generation becomes the authoritative orthodoxy of the next, the process of obscuration is likely to begin."[11] *Challenge's* motto reinforced this assertion: "Adaptability to new environment is the law of life, and any institution that tries to remain stationary in a moving world is doomed."[12]

Sydney Conservative Evangelicals quickly recognised that the new journal was directly "challenging" them.[13] The *Record* claimed that these "Central Churchmen" were "dizzy on their fundamentals" and were obviously intent on undermining Reformed theology, the sacred trust so dearly cherished by the *Record's* supporters.[14] Its readers were firmly reminded that, in the words of Bishop J.C. Ryle, "Let it be called illiberal and uncharitable…(there is) no resting place between downright Evangelical Christianity and downright infidelity…"[15] The Conservative Evangelicals believed that Liberal Evangelicals were willing to barter with Truth for the sake of peace. They were particularly scathing about Arthur Garnsey's claim that Christians must always re-examine their theology: "Eternal truths do not *have* to be restated in every age." One of the *Record's* correspondents thundered. "There is such a thing as minds being adjusted to the truth." The "breadth" which *Challenge* advocated was, this Conservative Evangelical believed, "merely the spread-out shallowness of a river which has no well-defined banks. This usually becomes …a stagnant swamp."[16]

The appearance of the *Church Times*, *Outlook*, and *Challenge* did nothing to facilitate harmony in the Sydney Diocese; instead the spirit of controversy and dispute, which had hitherto been contained in the Synod and its committees, was now publicly evident in print. As Conservative and Liberal Evangelicals openly traded blows in print, the atmosphere of the Diocese became heavier than ever before. A tension which fed on fear and suspicion developed. On the one hand there was fear that a concerted and sinister attempt was underway to alter the Evangelical character of the Diocese; on the other, there was suspicion that the Conservative Evangelical majority was seeking to strengthen its grip on the Diocese still further and, just as Evangelicals in other Australian dioceses were being 'squeezed' out by Anglo-Catholics, the Conservative Evangelical majority in Sydney was determined to 'squeeze' all dissenters, so that the unity of the Diocese would be based on a mere uniformity of churchmanship.[17] This Liberal Evangelical suspicion was strongest whenever the highly political question of clerical appointments was raised. There was a strong and growing conviction amongst Liberal Evangelicals that only Conservative Evangelicals would be permitted into the Diocese and that those who already served in Sydney, but were considered "unsound", would have little prospect of preferment. These suspicions were based on the treatment of several clergy, but were exemplified by the treatment of Geoffrey Franceys Cranswick.

Cranswick was the youngest son of a Sydney Evangelical clergyman, Canon Edward Glanville Cranswick, who had died in 1934 at the age of 80. He had attended both The King's and Shore Schools, before he had graduated in Arts from Sydney University in 1916. Geoffrey Cranswick had entered Moore College in that year, and had been a resident tutor there for two years. He had then served from 1917 to 1919 as travelling secretary for the Australian Student Christian Movement before reading at Ridley Hall, Cambridge. He was ordained by the Bishop of Chelmsford in 1920 and, after three years as curate at West Ham in London, he had gone to the Mission Field in India. The N.S.W. branch of the C.M.S. had intended to support Cranswick but, because it had had insufficient funds, the English Society had footed the bill. Then, after thirteen years in the Diocese of Calcutta, Cranswick returned to Sydney in 1937 with the intention of working there.[18]

Geoffrey Cranswick was very much a protege of Archbishop Wright. Wright had encouraged him to study at Cambridge, had secured for him the Marsden Scholarship for that purpose, and had also advised Cranswick to be ordained and serve a curacy in England under his Group Brotherhood friends Bishop Watts-Ditchfield of Chelmsford and the Rev. T. Guy Rogers at West Ham. Cranswick had then gone to India as a Sydney missionary and had continued to hold a licence from Wright to serve in Sydney throughout his years on missionary service. This was a standard practice of Archbishop Wright: he wanted to encourage missionary service, and by granting missionaries from Sydney a diocesan licence he hoped to make the Mission Field more attractive because it would mean that overseas service would not disadvantage them in terms of seniority in the Diocese when they returned. The practice continued after Wright's death, and in 1937 eighteen "Sydney clergy" were listed as serving overseas or with the Bush Church Aid Society.[19] Cranswick had used this licence while in Sydney on furlough in 1927, 1930, and in 1934. But, when he returned to Sydney in 1937, he discovered that his name had been removed from the List by the Archbishop himself.[20] Archbishop Mowll had already told Cranswick's mother in mid-1937 that "his policy is to keep this diocese predominantly Evangelical and that he does not think Geoffrey would fit!... because he is not sufficiently 'Evangelical'!"[21] The deletion of Cranswick's name from the Clergy List seemed to confirm that policy. Cranswick immediately sought an interview with Mowll to clarify his status, but Mowll gave him little comfort: the Archbishop informed Cranswick that he was unlikely to be nominated to any worthwhile parish and, therefore, his "best advice" to Cranswick was to work in England. The Archbishop also issued him with an authority to officiate which was renewable annually. Cranswick promptly returned this new licence to Mowll stating that he already "had authority to officiate in this diocese (from Wright). As your Grace has not cancelled that or declared it invalid, and as I am leaving for England next month I return herewith your new Authority."[22]

Cranswick felt betrayed. Together with other missionaries, he had been assured by Archbishop Wright that service rendered in the mission field would be treated as if it had been service in the Diocese of Sydney. This had now been disregarded by Wright's successor :"I am forced to the conclusion", wrote Cranswick, "that in my case, at any rate, security of tenure in Sydney diocese is a misnomer."[23] He took Mowll's "best advice" and left for England. Ironically, he returned to Australia only six years later as Bishop of Tasmania and undoubtedly met in the Australian House of Bishops the man who had not been able to find him parochial work in Sydney.[24]

The Cranswick episode deeply troubled Liberal Evangelicals. Nor was it an isolated case which may have been explained away as a clash of personalities rather than as the result of a policy decision. Arthur Garnsey's son, David, a Rhodes scholar who had just concluded his studies and a three year curacy in Oxford, was also rejected in 1937 for service in Sydney, and been advised by Mowll to serve in the Diocese of Goulburn.[25] Liberal Evangelicals did not deny the Archbishop's right to licence whomever he pleased, but these two cases clearly indicated to them a settled policy to favour only Conservative Evangelicals and to execute this policy with a disturbing, ruthless rigidity. The services of Geoffrey Cranswick and David Garnsey were rejected at the very time that Archbishop Mowll was launching an ambitious campaign to augment the number of clergymen in the diocese by 100 in five years. The number of clergy had not grown commensurately with the Anglican population of Sydney, which had rapidly increased with the influx of British, and predominantly Anglican, migrants in the immediate post-war period. Archbishop Mowll's scheme called for one million shillings (50,000 pounds) to be raised every year for the next five years to pay for both 100 additional curates in the Diocese and the planned extension of the Cathedral.[26]

The scheme attracted immediate public criticism. Its most vocal critics believed that 50,000 pounds a year was beyond the resources of parishes which were already reeling from the plethora of recent appeals for financial assistance from other diocesan institutions: these "appeals for funds", one rector cried, "are killing the life of the parishes."[27] The principal objection of Liberal Evangelicals to the Million Shillings' Fund was, however, that it would facilitate an importation of clergy from overseas who would be "of one particular type, and that thus the spirit of comprehensive toleration which until recently marked the diocese of Sydney would be destroyed."[28] In the light of the rejection of the services of Geoffrey Cranswick and David Garnsey, Liberal Evangelicals concluded that this financial appeal would provide the means whereby Sydney would be flooded with young, probably Irish, Conservative Evangelicals. That prospect filled them with foreboding.[29]

Conservative Evangelicals, led by the new Irish Principal of Moore College, the Rev. T.C. Hammond, quickly leapt to the defence of Archbishop Mowll's proposal, and the protracted controversy which ensued spilt over into the columns of the daily press.[30] There had been many previous occasions in which the conduct of the Conservative Evangelical party and its dominance of Sydney had been criticised, but this was the first occasion in which the Archbishop's policies and administration of the Diocese had been publicly attacked. It was a censure which signalled a new low in Conservative-Liberal Evangelical relations.

The acute tensions within the Sydney Anglican community were immeasurably exacerbated by another question which was quite extraneous to matters of churchmanship: the proposed design for the extensions to St. Andrew's Cathedral. In late 1937, it was announced that Messrs. Pinckney and Gott of London had won the international design competition for the enlargement of the comparatively small cathedral.[31] The announcement of the award and the publication of the proposed design met with immediate criticism in the public press. With one accord the design was denounced: the intended edifice was likened to a crematorium, a barracks, an entrance to a railway station, a glorified fire station, and even a Dachshund. No other church controversy had excited so much criticism and resentment both inside and outside Anglican circles. No proposal had ever been so roundly condemned by a public which usually looked upon the debates of churchmen with little more than bemused interest. Dozens of letters on the issue were printed by a daily press which, in the light of the near unanimous public dissent from the assessors' decision, urged the diocesan authorities to reconsider "before they commit themselves to an irretrievable mistake."[32]

Public opinion was reflected in the Synod, where the supporters of the design, who came from all schools of churchmanship, were hopelessly outnumbered by opponents of the design. Outright defeat in Synod of the proposed design was certain, and was only averted by burying the matter in a committee, whose deliberations were soon interrupted by the outbreak of war. The virtual rejection of the winning design was a slap in the face for Archbishop Mowll, who had been one of the three judges who had selected it, as well as its most ardent advocate. Although he took the winning design's defeat with "a stout heart and a stiff upper lip", Mowll could not help but take the widespread censure of the design personally.[33] It was a severe disappointment to a man who was already exhausted by four years of unceasing hard work.

Although the Cathedral controversy cut completely across party lines, with Mowll and his loyal lieutenants Archdeacons T.C. Hammond and S.M. Johnstone finding themselves in the company of Arthur Garnsey against Revs. S.E. Langford Smith, D.J. Knox, W.J. Siddens, and William Mann and Minton Taylor, it nevertheless aggravated the discord and bad feeling in the Diocese to the point that it affected the treatment and development of more partisan issues.[34] It cultivated an atmosphere in which belligerent confrontation was more likely to occur than peaceful conciliation and accommodation.

II

A second dispute arose at the same time as the Cathedral issue which also engendered great controversy. This row involved the issue of churchmanship: the changes in ritual introduced at St. James', King Street, by the new rector, the Rev. E.J. Davidson. Davidson succeeded the Rev. P.A. Micklem who had returned to England after twenty years at St. James'.[35] As soon as he arrived in February 1938, Davidson "simplified" the ritual at the church. He substituted the Service of Mattins for Solemn Eucharist at 11 a.m. on three out of every four Sundays; he abolished the "Children's Eucharist" and substituted a more regular Sunday School; he discontinued Anglo-Catholic practices during the service of Holy Communion; and the 1928 Prayer Book was replaced by the 1662 Book of Common Prayer.[36]

The changes stunned the congregation: "If the (parochial) nominators had had the slightest inkling of what Mr. Davidson intended", said one churchwarden, "he would never have been nominated:...They were misled by information about him which they had received from what they thought were reliable sources."[37] Davidson claimed that his principal motive in initiating the changes was to heighten the significance of Holy Communion by removing obscuring ceremonial. He maintained that although he possessed "a thorough-going sacramental outlook", the Sunday programme had been too crowded and the number of services had to be reduced.[38]

The controversy at St. James' could well have remained a domestic dispute between the members of the congregation who believed that they had been duped into accepting a man who had promptly sold them out, and a rector who was adamant that he had to obey the Prayer Book. But the dispute quickly attracted wider significance when the Rev. G. Stuart Watts, the editor of the Anglo-Catholic *Church Standard*, claimed that Davidson "simplification" of ritual and his decision to dispense with Watts' own services at St. James', where he had preached, heard confessions and said week-day Masses for the past four years, had all been at the direction of the Diocesan Registrar, Archdeacon S.M. Johnstone. Watts asserted that these latest developments were but two elements in a determined and well-orchestrated campaign against the "Catholicism" of St. James' by the Conservative Evangelicals who were in power in the Diocese.[39] These were allegations which not only raised the spectre of conspiratorial intrigue, but also seemed to confirm the long-held belief of some Sydney clergy that Archdeacon Johnstone was "the devil in the background", the back-room enforcer of Conservative Evangelical policy.[40]

Coming hard on the heels of the Cranswick case and the launching of the Million Shillings Fund campaign to import clergy, Stuart Watts' "long pent-up moan" that his proscription and the "simplification" reforms at St. James' were all of a piece, and had been ordered by the Diocesan Registrar, seemed to give conclusive proof that there was a general pre-meditated policy being implemented by the Diocesan authorities which was designed to create a totally Conservative Evangelical diocese.[41] In fact, although Watts' allegation that Davidson had dispensed with his services on orders from Johnstone (and it is certain that Davidson quite gladly sacked him) was never substantiated, later evidence made it quite clear that Johnstone did in fact give Davidson a list of changes to be implemented. The fears of the non-Conservative Evangelicals were, therefore, quite cogent.[42]

Despite sustained agitation by malcontents at St. James', who organised a petition of 1,400 people to Archbishop Mowll over the episode, Davidson sat "tight in the saddle" at St. James', and Archbishop Mowll remained aloof and refused to "fetter a parish priest in the lawful exercise of his discretion."[43] The petitioners' protests were rejected as the unjustified posturings of a "disappointed minority".[44] Davidson continued as rector in the parish for seventeen years. Ironically, the simplification reforms lasted only five years: in the middle of World War Two the ceremonial which had been dispensed with at the behest of Archdeacon

Johnstone was quietly re-introduced by Davidson, who presumably then felt secure enough to ignore the directives of the Registrar.[45]

III

The years 1933 to 1938 had been a period of party strife without precedent in the history of the Diocese. The Liberal Evangelicals had been defeated at the ballot box and on the floor of the Synod; Conservative and Liberal Evangelicals had openly skirmished in the press. Conservative Evangelicals had seized virtually all the key positions in the Diocese and continued to guard them jealously.[46] Liberal Evangelicals believed that the intention of diocesan policy was palpably clear: create a diocese whose clergy were practically all Conservative Evangelical, exclude all others from taking up positions in Sydney and isolate and minimise the influence of non-Conservative Evangelicals already within the Diocese. Liberal Evangelicals reckoned themselves an endangered species in a Diocese which was rapidly becoming a closed shop.

A large group of Liberal Evangelicals decided that they could no longer accept this developing trend towards the monochrome without some major protest. At a meeting at Mosman on 18 February, 1938, twenty-five Liberal Evangelical clergymen proposed to outline their grievances in a written statement to Archbishop Mowll.[47] Their 1,500 word letter became known as The Memorial. The letter, which was written by Canon Arthur Garnsey, made four assertions. First, its Liberal Evangelical signatories maintained that "in a living church there must always be considerable diversity of thought and feeling, together with their outward expression in worship...", because no two people were exactly alike in mind, temperament, and character. But, despite that diversity, a real unity should exist, based on a common adoration of the God and Faith and a common discipleship of Christ. Second, these Liberal Evangelicals claimed that

> we do not find this spirit of unity and strength in the Diocese of Sydney as it is at present. Recent events appear to us", they continued, "to indicate that a unity of a different kind is being sought by men who have influence in the Synod, the Standing Committee, and — as it seems to us and to others also — with Your Grace...[48]

They further charged that although Anglicanism was generally recognised to embrace several schools of thought which reacted upon each another with mutual benefit, they had concluded "that Diocesan life in Sydney has for some time been marred by the unhealthy dominance of one school, namely, that of a rather rigid, conservative evangelicalism."

The Memorialists professed loyalty to the principles of the English Reformation and denied that they were extremists. They also stated that they had striven earnestly "to cultivate a spirit of friendly co-operation between the different types of Sydney Anglicanism", but had been frustrated

> by a certain intolerance in members of the dominant party — an intolerance that has been exhibited notably in the elections to important committees, in the work of the Diocesan Nominators, in Synod discussions and in published writings, in which the honesty, sincerity and good faith of brother churchmen have been called in question, often by anonymous writers.[49]

They therefore concluded that the Conservative Evangelicals were seeking a unity which was only to be gained by suppressing freedom of thought and discussion and persecuting the unorthodox.

The third claim of the Memorial was that Conservative Evangelicals had been so favoured by diocesan action in the previous few years, to the detriment of other schools of thought, "that there is some ground for fearing that in less than a generation the whole diocese may be reduced to a monochrome." They cited the "packing" of important committees such as the Board of Education, the case of Geoffrey Cranswick, and the fact that most of the key diocesan positions were in the hands of Conservative Evangelicals, as substantiating examples of this proclivity.[50] The outstanding exception to the dominance of Conservative Evangelicals in official diocesan positions, which the Memorialists omitted to mention, was Bishop Co-adjutor Pilcher, who had been appointed by Mowll in 1936. The Liberal Evangeficals saw Pilcher as a light in the darkness, who spread "sweetness and light" throughout the parishes.[51] Pilcher himself was clearly perturbed about the Conservative Evangelicals' treatment of their Liberal Evangelical brethren and later organised irenical meetings between the two parties in the early 1940s. Yet although the Assistant Bishop had a senior diocesan position, he had very little real power. He was only the Archbishop's assistant, and under his direction. He could attempt to influence and persuade, but he could not direct.[52]

The fourth assertion of the Memorialists was an implicit criticism of Moore College. The intellectual influence of the Church in Sydney would suffer, the Memorialists said, if all Sydney's clergymen were "to be trained along narrow lines."[53] Finally, the Memorialists insisted that they were loyal churchmen, but they nevertheless believed that it was only honest to let their Father-in-God know what was on their minds. They therefore requested an opportunity of discussing these matters with him, either as a group or by deputation.[54]

Arthur Garnsey's draft letter won the approval of that February meeting of Liberal Evangelicals at Ernest Cameron's home, and the assembled company decided to invite other rectors to endorse the Memorial. Garnsey was privately sceptical whether more than thirty clergymen would actually sign it: he believed that although many were sympathetic, prudence would induce most to decline. He was to be pleasantly surprised: 50 of the 160 rectors in the Diocese signed the letter within the month. The document was kept confidential and only selected clergy were invited to sign. No copies of the document were circulated in an attempt to keep reports of it out of the papers.[55]

Despite their efforts to maintain confidentiality, this Memorial soon became the pinnacle of political protest in the history of the Diocese. Although the episode was initially played down by one Conservative Evangelical leader as "a little local disturbance by a few disgruntled people", the Memorialists were soon described by Conservative Evangelicals as "a small determined band of men who are out to destroy the Evangelical character of the diocese, and have begun by seeking to discredit its leader."[56] The Memorial itself, which appeared to the dispassionate observer to be respectful and unexceptionally moderate in tone, was soon perceived as "hostile and almost malevolent", and its plea for freedom was dismissed as little more than the liberty to use vestments, and have children's Eucharists, auricular confessions, the reserved sacrament, and the other trappings of Anglo-Catholicism.[57] The Memorialists came to be regarded by Conservative Evangelicals as "the catspaw of the Anglo-Catholics", whose much-vaunted spirit of toleration clearly ran "in the grooves of Anglo-Catholicism".[58]

IV

Who were these Memorialists? Were they really the shock troops for the forces of sacerdotalism? Was, indeed, the Memorial part of a well-engineered attack designed to discredit the leadership of the Archbishop and to undermine the character of the Diocese?[59]

This study discloses for the first time the names of the fifty signatories to the Memorial (See Appendix One). Their identity indicates that there was little substance to the Conservative Evangelical allegations later made against them. In fact a comparison of the Memorialists with the other 119 "senior clergy" in the Diocese finds that there was little difference in educational status, ordination background, theological training, or practical pastoral experience between the two groups. The Memorialists were more likely to have been to university. 28% (14) had university degrees, principally in the Faculty of Arts, in which six had Master's degrees. By contrast 23.5% (28) of the non-signatories had attended university. The Memorialists were also more likely to have been ordained in Sydney. Only 30% (15) of the signatories were ordained outside Sydney, whereas 34% (40) of the non-signatories had been ordained elsewhere. Similarly, most of the Memorialists had undertaken theological training at Moore College: 35 of the 50 (70%) had attended Moore College, while only 65% (78) of the other senior clergy had been locally trained.[60]

The Memorialists cannot be therefore labelled as uneducated agitators who had come from outside the Sydney diocese in order to challenge its Evangelical character; in education, they were the equals, if not the betters, of their fellow clergy in the Diocese; and in terms of ordination and training, they were more likely to have been trained and ordained in Sydney than those who did not sign the Memorial. In fact, the only characteristic which did distinguish the Memorialists from other Sydney clergymen was their age and experience. Their median age was 47 (the average age was 49) with the youngest aged 29 and the oldest aged 74. Their median period of service as clergymen was 21 years (the average was 22 years), while the 119 other senior clergymen in the Diocese had a median period of experience of 24 years. The Memorialists were slightly less experienced than other Sydney clerygmen, but they were hardly fresh, raw ordinands, just out of college.[61]

The salient characteristic of the Memorialists was their lack of statistical distinctiveness from their brother clergymen. They were very ordinary Sydney clergymen who differed from their fellow clergy more in matters of personal temperament and outlook than in background and experience. They were not "extreme men": John Hope, the rector of Christ Church St. Laurence, Edward Pattison Clarke, of St. Mary's Waverley, and Adam Maclean, of St. Saviour's Redfern, the three truly Anglo-Catholic rectors in Sydney, were not signatories. They had not been invited to sign.[62] Yet the Rev. E.J. Davidson of St. James', King Street, who was at that very time weathering the dispute at his church over his cut-back in ritual, was a Memorialist. Davidson's actions had certainly not made him a darling of the Anglo-Catholic movement: he could hardly be described as a "catspaw" of the Anglo-Catholics.[63] Moreover, none of the rectors who signed the Memorial conducted auricular confessions, wore the chasuble or cope, reserved the Sacrament, or conducted children's Eucharist, and only a minority of them would have permitted candles and crosses, let alone servers at Holy Communion in their churches. The majority would have conducted services which were virtually indistinguishable from those of their Conservative fellows.[64]

V

The most distinctive feature of the Memorialists was their open-mindedness. This standpoint may be best seen in the opinions and attitudes of Canon Arthur Garnsey, the leading light and principal organiser of the Memorialists. Garnsey supported the idea of Modernism. He believed that its ideal — to strip away by critical research the mountains of tradition in order to discover the simple truth — was salutary: "the true 'Modernist' is the truest 'Primitive'", Garnsey wrote, "being eager by critical research to find the simple truths by which Jesus (and the great saints of Old and New Testament times) lived, and content with those as the essentials of religious life, for churches as well as for individuals."[65]

When Conservative Evangelicals alleged that Biblical Criticism was helping "the intellectual attack on Christianity", Garnsey retorted that "criticism simply meant using your *judgment* on the questions that inevitably arose to confront the careful student and that the critical faculty had its place in the Dispensation of the Spirit."[66] This argument did nothing to persuade Conservative Evangelicals, who had been shaken by the advances of Modernism in the English Church and were keenly aware of the presence in Sydney of the Presbyterian Samuel Angus. It merely made them suspicious of these Liberal Evangelicals in their midst. Arthur Garnsey was, however, no blind disciple of modern research. He was keenly aware of its defects and severely critical of the scornful statements made by anti-Conservative critics:

> 'They are (stumbling blocks) put in the way of these little ones' about which the Lord was so severe. And that sort of saying has been Angus' outstanding folly. If these people only knew *the cost in blood* and tears when an earnest man has to fight his way out of a devout traditionalism into a devout modernism — they wd. bite their tongues into two before flying out their miserable quips and quiddities and sarcasms.[67]

Nor was Garnsey an Anglo-Catholic sympathiser as some Conservative Evangelicals suggested.[68] He believed that the growing ecclesiasticism outside Sydney was destined to alienate the Australian people from the message of the Gospel: he felt that the Church in Adelaide "was too Church-cramped .... by somewhat 'spikey' presuppositions about the Ministry, the Apostolic Succession and Sacramental Grace"; and he despairingly concluded that the worship at the "sadly sectarian" Christ Church St. Laurence in Sydney was based on "an unspiritual conception of our relationship to (God)."[69]

Arthur Garnsey's own emphasis was upon spirituality: that devotion of the whole personality which is so much greater than "the pursuit of truth". Discipleship was not dependent upon the critical and reasoning faculties alone: "'Christ is the Way and Life, not only the Truth'", wrote Garnsey. "The knewlegge of God through Jesus Christ involves the activity of the whole man."[70] Garnsey contended that this was the only basis on which unity within the Church of England could ever be attained. The attempts to reach accords on doctrinal definitions or statements of belief would always be frustrated: the only possible basis of agreement would be "along the line of personal discipleship in the One Lord."[71] Conservative Evangelicals, on the other hand, demanded a more emphatic proclamation of the Truth.

Garnsey's perception of his vocation most clearly differed from that of Conservative Evangelicals on the question of evangelism. Although he believed that his vocation was "to interpret and commend the Faith of Christ to the learned and the unlearned (not forgetting the half-learned)", he disagreed with the "aggressive" approaches adopted by revivalistic missioners.[72] He preferred a more personal form of evangelism whereby people would "be helped by us to see and know God in and through the fields where their conscience is working already."[73] He did not see his job as trying "to bring in the Kingdom" but rather "to proclaim it as a present fact." Nor was it his job to adopt or advocate a certain theological position, but to seek out "more and more of the unsearchable riches of Christ."[74]

Arthur Garnsey's theological viewpoint was not shared by every Memorialist. Some were more Conservative, others were more Liberal.

But his position was emblematic of their temperament and outlook, and demonstrated that the similar backgrounds of the Memorialists and their more Conservative brethren belied very marked differences. The Memorialists critically welcomed new scholarship and new knowledge as a gift from God; the Conservative Evangelicals, however, rejected liberal scholarship outright or viewed it with suspicion. Conservative Evangelicals believed the Bible was the Word of God; the Memorialists believed the Bible was authoritative, but not inerrant. Finally, the Memorialists believed that Conservative Evangelicals erred in not recognising the valuable contributions of others in enhancing Man's understanding of God and his relationship to Him. There were, of course, differences of opinion on other matters. But the fundamental belief which set the Memorialists apart from the Conservative Evangelicals was their conviction that there must of necessity be diversity, not uniformity, in the unified Body of Christ. They were alarmed by the dogmatic authoritarianism at both ends of the ecclesiastical spectrum. They were not attempting to undermine the Evangelical character of the Diocese: they were as troubled by Anglo-Catholic advances outside Sydney as their Conservative brothers. Their goal was simply to work for "a return to the old policy (under Archbishop Wright) of live and let live, with a friendly understanding between the different schools of thought and impartial treatment from those in authority and power."[75] In an environment which was becoming more and more polarised, these Liberal Evangelicals were determined to make a stand for a

> charity that is based upon knowledge of the Truth — distinct on the one hand from the false charity based upon the notion that we can't be certain of anything, and on the other from the narrowness based upon knowledge of the eeme Truth, and the failure to perceive that other men know other portions of the Truth.[76]

VI

The Memorial was submitted to Archbishop Mowll on 10 March 1938. Its signatories were under no illusions that it would be warmly welcomed: "it will certainly be seen by two or three others, such as Archdeacon Johnstone, T.C. Hammond and perhaps another. So I am preparing for a salvo..." Garnsey wrote. "We are up against something very hard and tough. The triumvirate, or duoviri (Johnstone, T.C. Hammond with or without D.J. Knox) that pull or seems to pull the strings, will not give back without a struggle, beginning probably with a big effort at bluff."[77]

Although Archbishop Mowll did no more than acknowledge receipt of the document for ten weeks, other developments soon escalated the Memorial into a matter of public debate. One Memorialist lost his part-time job lecturing at Moore College; within a fortnight a counter-Memorial was circulated to all clergy (not just rectors) in the Diocese, and attracted over 200 signatories; and the *Church Record* revealed a comprehensive knowledge of the document's contents in two attacks (on 13 and 28 April 1938) against these "unworthy, discontented clergy" who, it believed, sought a libertarian freedom to open the floodgates to vestments, children's eucharists, confessions and other accessories of Anglo-Catholicism.[78] What had been written as a private memorandum had quickly become the centre of a public dispute.

Although the Memorialists had not been publicly identified, the adverse publicity which their "confidential" letter had attracted made them very nervous. They renewed their request to the Archbishop for a personal interview in which they "could scatter to the winds those aspersions on our loyalty and good faith that have been made in certain quarters." They assured the Archbishop that they had been determined to keep the matter "a private affair" and could only surmise that the document had been leaked after Mowll had received it.[79] But Archbishop

Mowll was still not prepared to respond in detail to the Memorialists. Nor would he permit them an interview. He claimed that "the agitation over the Cathedral question and the demands that that matter has made on my time and thought" had obviated giving the Memorial "the attention which it requires."[80] The delay may indeed have been unavoidable. Or it may have been a deliberate bluff; but whatever the cause for the delay it certainly had a decided psychological effect upon the Memorialists. The cold shoulder treatment made them extremely edgy.[81]

At last, ten weeks after the Memorial had been presented, Archbishop Mowll replied. But his reply took an unexpected form. Whereas the signatories had written collectively, the Archbishop replied to each Memorialist personally in a letter which had been drafted by the Principal of Moore College, Thomas Hammond. It was both uncompromising and intimidatory. First, Mowll asked the Memorialists if they "fully realised the grave criticism of myself and others for which you have made yourself responsible", and unfairly accused them of leaking the document to the secular press and "giving publicity to these imputations on my good faith and fair dealing." He then demanded to know the grounds for their criticisms: he asked each of the signatories to answer a questionnaire — if indeed they wanted to "pursue the matter" at all. He requested that they confine their answers to matters within their own personal knowledge and experience. The Archbishop of Sydney was clearly determined to divide and rule.[82]

The fourteen questions were aggressively worded. The Archbishop demanded, for example, that the Memorialists name the men who were "guilty" of "unfairly handicapping any school of legitimate thought" and those who had suffered as a result. He questioned the Memorialists' "challenge" to the Bishop's right of discretion in admitting clergy into the Diocese and asked each signatory whether he was in fact personally acquainted with the reason behind Geoffrey Cranswick's "choice of a sphere of ministry" and on what grounds his "exclusion" could be attributed to Mowll himself. Indeed the Archbishop requested substantiating evidence for every statement made in the Memorial, from the grounds for criticism of the Moore College Principal to their meaning in claiming that committees were being "packed."[83]

The majority of the Memorialists declined to be divided by the Archbishop. Only three signatories — all young men — withdrew their endorsement of the Memorial after this stiff response from Mowll and the unexpected publicity which the Memorial had received.[84] The remaining forty-six (Cecil King had died on 18 April 1938) stood determinedly together and replied to the Archbishop as a collective. They were astounded by the legalistic tone with which Mowll had responded to their request "to discuss our distresses with our Father in God." In addition, they expressed astonishment "to find running through the questionnaire an implication that we have no right to offer criticism or raise questions in respect of matters which deeply concern us as your clergy, and that in so doing we invade domains which belong exclusively to Your Grace."[85]

The Memorialists' joint reply did not, in the main, supply the specific details which Mowll's questionnaire had demanded of them. They declined to be drawn into committing to paper the names of men and of caucuses, but stood firm in their request for "a conference between yourself and our representatives." They did, however, deny that they were challenging the Archbishop's "obvious right" to determine which clergy should be admitted to the Diocese, but submitted that they were not uninterested parties in the matter. They also denied, on the matter of caucuses and "stacking", that they were suggesting that parties could or should be abolished in the Diocese: "It is what a certain party has done, and continues to do, that constitutes the ground of our complaint." Finally, they bitterly rejected the Archbishop's imputation on *their* good faith, in suggesting that they had leaked the Memorial. They were adamant that they had not publicised the document, and retorted that the *Record's* tirades against them contained "unmistakable proof" that the publicity which now surrounded their private protest had been generated by sources close to the Archbishop himself.[86] The Memorialists were implicitly pointing the finger at the Principal of Moore College, T.C. Hammond, who was both an important member of the *Record's* editorial committee and the draftsman for Archbishop Mowll's replies to the Memorialists.

A stalemate was soon reached. The Archbishop refused to meet the Memorialists without detailed answers to the questions T.C. Hammond had drafted for him; the Memorialists had a healthy suspicion that their reply would be read by the Archbishop's advisors, and therefore declined to submit such details to paper. They would only substantiate their "distresses" in a private conference.[87]

The stalemate was never resolved and, as garbled reports of the matter began to appear in the secular press, any slim prospect of reconciliation disappeared. The published reports heightened the feelings of suspicion and bad faith on both sides.[88] Archbishop Mowll continued to believe that the Memorialists were responsible for these leaks and were attempting to pressure him by agitating in the secular press; the majority of the Memorialists, however, having been advised by the *Daily Telegraph* that it had not received its information from a signatory, believed that the leaks were part of a determined campaign to "discredit our representations by stigmatising them as the work of a factious, disgruntled and negligible minority of clergy, who are in rebellion against legitimate authority."[89] The seven man committee which acted on behalf all the Memorialists therefore decided that the inaccurate and sometimes malicious press reports had to be countered, and determined to set the record straight by publishing all of the relevant documents.[90]

This announcement by the Memorialists prompted Archbishop Mowll, who had previously refrained from public comment on the matter, to state his position. He informed the Diocese in a published letter that "a section of clergy, acting in a body *without any constitutional status* invited me to discuss with them, amongst other things, my general administration of the affairs of the Diocese."[91] Mowll stated that he had declined to grant the Memorialists an interview because they had refused to give him "precise and definite information" to substantiate their allegations and he could not "appear by the slightest action to countenance vague and indefinite charges against men in our midst who, so far as my knowledge carries me, are loyally seeking to carry out the highest principles of the Church of England, and indeed of our common Christianity."[92] The Archbishop also wrote at the same time in similar terms to each of the Memorialists.[93]

The correspondence which had passed between the Archbishop and the Memorialists was published by the Memorialists as a booklet, *A Plea for Liberty*, in August 1938. Its appearance served as a corrective to the earlier erroneous press reports, but also invited public judgment of the controversy. The editor of the *Sydney Morning Herald*, for example, was strongly critical of Archbishop Mowll's handling of the incident. He believed that the correspondence showed that a "more sympathetic consideration of the grievances of the dissentient clergy (by Mowll) might have prevented the present open breach." Instead, Mowll had sent "a brusque and searching questionnaire" which astounded this dispassionate observer: "Any course less calculated to allay discontent it would be difficult to imagine. Dr. Mowll took a purely legalistic stand where a sympathetic hearing might have arrested the mischief which was being wrought."[94] Indeed, Mowll's insistence that the Memorialists had no "direct constitutional status", was to the mind of the *Herald's* editor, incredible: "...as if a sense of grievance shared by more than one-fourth of the rectors of the diocese was not sufficient to constitute a right of approach to its head!".[95]

This assessment of the controversy provided little comfort for the Memorialists. Archbishop Mowll had no intention of changing his mind. He departed for India and England on 1 September 1938, without granting an interview to the Memorialists or to any delegation from them. With his departure, the Memorialists could not see what else they could do: they remained discontented and without recourse. Their only remaining hope was not that any positive benefits would result from their protest but that, eventually, "that history will approve the stand which we are now making for conscience sake."[96] It was an anti-climactic and unsatisfying end to what had been the last stand of defeated Liberal Evangelicalism in Sydney.

VII

The Memorial of 1938 was the culmination of ten years of internecine hostilities between Conservative and Liberal Evangelicals. It was an act of frustration on the part of the fifty signatories, who had vainly fought the oppressive rule of the Conservative Evangelicals in the decade up to 1938. It came at the end of three years which had been marked by successive controversies. The debates over the Million Shillings Fund and the Cranswick case were directly related to the Memorial and were vital precursors to it; the two disputes involving the extension of the Cathedral and the "simplification" of ceremonial at St. James' heightened the excitement of the Diocesan political scene at the time and made it less possible for the Memorial to be treated dispassionately by the Archbishop. The cause of the Memorialists was most damaged by the nexus drawn between their letter and the protest at St. James' over Davidson's changes in ritual.[97] It must be stressed that while disputes at St. James' have historically been harbingers of wider unrest, the Memorial and the 1938 controversy at the church were unrelated. Conservative Evangelical propaganda deftly associated the two with good effect, but the Memorialists were themselves always keen to steer clear of the St. James' issue; indeed, the fact that Davidson, the leading antagonist of the protestors at St. James', was one of the fifty signatories indicated that the notion that there was a conspiratorial relationship between the two was pure Conservative Evangelical fiction.

The Memorial was poorly handled by Archbishop Mowll. He gave short shrift to one-third of the incumbents of the Diocese who had let their Father-in-God know their distresses. They deserved better treatment: a mollifying morning tea with their representatives could well have defused the situation, without even the merest suggestion of policy changes. The Archbishop's reaction to the Memorialists was that a young missionary bishop whose style of leadership had not adapted to the more complex milieu of a metropolitical see, and who had been wearied by four years of ceaseless activity in which there had been a succession of difficult disputes. Archbishop Mowll had "the weakness of his own greatness, and when he made mistakes they were to scale".[98] His unbending, heavy-handed treatment of the Memorialists was the other side of the coin to a leadership which was directive, authoritative and selflessly demanding.[99]

Nor was Archbishop Mowll well served by his lieutenant, T.C. Hammond. First, Hammond drafted all of Mowll's responses to the Memorialists with the result that all Mowll's responses to the Memorialists bore a typically hibernian spirit of aggressive confrontation.[100] The drafts were hardly documents designed to cultivate good relations between the Diocesan and one-third of his clergy. One must speculate whether the Memorial issue would have proved less "sad and distasteful" if the irenical Bishop Co-adjutor, C.V. Pilcher, had been charged with the responsibility of drafting Mowll's response to the Memorialists instead of Hammond.[101] Second, it seems most credible that the principal source of the *Record*'s exclusive reports on the Memorial on 13 and 27 April 1938 was T.C. Hammond, a member of the *Record*'s editorial committee.[102] The reports in the Record escalated the Memorial from a private letter to a public controversy which was soon taken up by the secular press.

Yet both Mowll and T.C. Hammond were sincerely convinced that the cause of Conservative Evangelical truth was at stake. Both men were used to situations in which they believed they had to stand their ground and refuse to compromise or conciliate: Mowll had led the Cambridge Inter-Collegiate Christian Union out of the Student Christian Movement because of theological differences. He had been uncompromising in 1910 and was no different in 1938. Similarly, T.C. Hammond was obliged as General Secretary for the Irish Church Missions in Dublin to be unswerving in his articulation of the Protestant position to a hostile Roman Catholic audience. In the late 1930s, both Mowll and Hammond were keenly aware of the successful intellectual and political challenges to Conservative Evangelicalism in England and the gradual isolation of Sydney from the rest of the Anglican Church in Australia. The notion of conciliation with the Memorialists went against their instincts, their past experiences and the realisation of their worst fears elsewhere in Australia and in England.

Above all, the Memorial symbolised the final destruction of the Evangelical consensus which had been forged nearly thirty years before. In 1909 there had been a consolidation of all Evangelicals to form a united political force; in the five years to 1938 that coalition disintegrated; and the 1938 Memorial was an index for the fortunes of the Conservative and Liberal Evangelical groups in the decades to come. At the end of Archbishop Mowll's episcopate twenty years later, only fourteen Memorialists (28%) remained actively engaged in parish work in the Diocese. Some had died, some had gone to greener earthly pastures, and the rest had retired. Concomitantly, the proportion of Conservative Evangelicals in the Diocese had increased: the Memorialists' prophecy "that in less than a generation, the whole diocese may be reduced to a monochrome" was never completely realised but, nevertheless, the Conservative Evangelical character of the Diocese had been secured.[103]

NOTES - CHAPTER NINE

1. A.H.G. to D.A.G. 24/3/1936; see *Outlook* January 1936 p.1.
2. *Outlook* March 1936 pp.1-3. The Rev. W.M. Corden to Erskineville, and the Rev. R.C. Firebrace to Moss Vale.
3. *ibid.*, ps3:
4. *ibid.*, January 1936 p.1.
5. *ibid.*, March 1936 pp.2-3.
6. *A.C.R.* 23/1/1936 p.1 (ed).
7. *Outlook* March 1936 p.1.
8. A.H.G. to D.A.G. 2/3/1937. See also A.H.G. Diary 5/3/1937 and 19/3/1947.
9. *Challenge* August 1937 p.1; see also A.H.G. to D.A.G. 14/4/1937, 20/4/1937, 22/6/1937, 20/7/1937; A.H.G. *Diary* 5/3/1937, 19/3/1937, 18/6/1937, 9/7/1937 and 24/9/1937.
10. *Challenge* August 1937 p.1; The first number of *Challenge* also included articles on "the Church and the Social Gospel" by the Rev. O.V. Abram, on "Youth's Claim upon the Church" by the Rev. W.G. Coughlan, on "Dictatorship in the Church" by the Rev. W.J. Siddens, and on "Worship: An Interview with Cranmer" by the Rev. H.N. Baker.
11. *ibid.*, pp.1-3.
12. *ibid.*, p.1.
13. A.H.G to D.A.G. 24/3/1937.
14. *A.C.R.* 2/9/1937 p. 22.
15. *ibid.*, p.19.

16. *ibid.* 22/12/1937 pp.6-7 (his emphasis); for later criticisms of *Challenge* see *A.C.R.* 9/12/1937 p.1, 17/2/1933 p.8, 17/3/1938 pp.1 and 8.

17. *A.C.R.* 24/11/1933 p.3; A.H.G. to D.A.G. 10/12/1937.

18. The Rev. M.G. Hinsby confirmed in 1938 that the *only* reason Cranswick was not sent to India by the N.S.W. Branch of the C.M.S. was the indebtedness of the branch. See *A.C.R.* 23/6/1938 p.13.

19. Wright's "Licence and Authority to Officiate as a clergyman on the roll of clergy of this Diocese sent forth on Foreign Service in the Mission Field" was perpetual, not annually renewable. See 1931 *Year Book* of the Diocese of Sydney. The Revs. C.E.W. Bellingham, R.C. Blumer, Keith Brodie, G.G. Brown, G.A. Conolly, E.R. Elder, W. Wynn Jones, R.H. Noble, and F.C. Philip were listed as "on missionary service".

20. *C.S.* 14/1/1938 p.13; Cranswick's name appears in the 1936 *Year Book* but not in 1937 one.

21. A.H.G. to D.A.G. 8/6/1937.

22. G.F. Cranswick to H.W.K. Mowll 29/10/1937 reported in letter by G.F. Cranswick to editor of *C.S.* 14/1/1938 p.13.

23. G.F. Cranswick to editor of *C.S.* 14/1/1938 p.13; see also A.H.G. to D.A.G. 6/7/1937., 28/9/1937.

24. *ibid.*; Cranswick worked for C.M.S. in England as its organising secretary in the dioceses of Canterbury, Chichester and Rochester, and then as its Indian Secretary until 1943, when he was elected to Tasmania.

25. A.H.G. to D.A.G. 8/6/1937, 5/10/1937, 21/12/1937. David Garnsey's letter and Mowll's reply to it were dated 7/9/1937 and 30/11/1937 respectively. Garnsey served at Goulburn and Young from 1938 to 1945, became General Secretary of the Australian Student Christian Movement, and was then appointed Headmaster of Canberra Grammar School. After ten years in Canberra he was elected Bishop of Gippsland and served in that see until his retirement in 1974.

26. *S.D.M.* December 1937 p.170.

27. *S.M.H.* 3/9/1937 p.18 (Barder). See also The Home Mission Society, Moore College, the Broughton Centenary (in 1936) and the Cathedral Centenary Celebrations had all recently appealed for funds; the 1937 Synod had rejected an increase in parochial assessments from 3 to 4 per cent because many parishes could not afford it. The increase was limited to 0.5 per cent. See *S.M.H.* 2/9/1939 p.10; *C.S.* 10/12/1937 p.13.
28. *C.S.* 10/12/1937 p.13.
29. *ibid.*
30. *S.M.H.* 13/12/1937 p.12. See also 3/2/1938 p.6, 5/2/1938 p.5, 8/2/1938 p.6, 10/2/1938 p.5, 12/2/1938 p.5, and 14/2/1938 p.6; *A.C.R.* 22/12/1937 p.1; A.H.G. to D.A.G. 13/1/1938.
31. The three judges of the competition were Sir Giles Gilbert Scott, the designer and architect of Liverpool Cathedral, Mr. Bertram Waterhouse, President of the N.S.W. Board of Architects, and Archbishop Mowll. *A.C.R.* 25/6/1936 p.8.
32. *S.M.H.* 5/2/1938 p.10. See also 17/1/1938 p.6, 9/1/1938 p.10, 20/1/1938 p.5, 21/1/1938 p.4, 22/1/1938 p.5, 25/1/1938 p.8, 27/1/1938 p.4, 28/1/1938 p.5, 29/1/1938 p.5, 31/1/1938 p.8, 1/2/1938 p.8. 2/2/1938 p.10, 4/2/1938 p.9, 5/2/1938 pp.5, 7/2/1938 p.6, 11/2/1938 p.8.
33. A.H.G. to D.A.G. 8/2/1938; Loane, *Mowll.* pp.150, 211. See also *S.M.H.* 21/4/1933 p.12: 26/1/1938 p.9, 6/4/1938 p.17 and 7/4/1938 p.16.
34. A.H.G. to D.A.G. 19/4/1938.
35. *S.M.H.* 30/1/1937 p.18, 3/11/1937 p.12.
36. *ibid.* 27/8/1938 p.13; 18/2/1938 p.14; A.H.G. to D.A.G. 8/2/1938; *C.S.* 11/2/1938 pp.5, 9, 10.
37. *S.M.H.* 7/2/1938 p.12, 8/2/1938 p.10.
38. *ibid.*, 7/2/1938 p.12.
39. *C.S.* 11/2/1938 pp.5, 9, 10; *S.M.H.* 7/2/1938 p.12 and 11/2/1938 p.10.
40. A.H.G to D.A.G. 8/2/1938.
41. *ibid.*

42. I am indebted to Professor K.J. Cable for this information re: the extant list of "simplification" reforms which Johnstone requested Davidson make.

43. A.H.G. to D.A.G. 15/2/1938; *C.S.* 9/9/1938 p.10.

44. *C.S.* 9/9/1938 p.10.

45. This reversal by Davidson indicates that the changes were of no great importance to him, and that the initiative for them did not come from him. I am indebted to Prof. K.J. Cable for this information; *A.C.R.* 17/2/1938 p.1 claimed the matter was merely a domestic dispute. See also 3/3/1938 pp.1, 8, 9; *C.S.* (G.S. Watts) cited in *S.M.H.* 5/3/1938 p.18; A full text of the petition can be found in *C.S.* 25/2/1938 p.9. See also *S.M.H.* 8/9/1938 p.12, 9/9/1938 p.10.

46. But with one important exception. See A.H.G. to D.A.G. 28/12/1937; A.H.G. *Diary* 20/7/1937.

47. A.H.G. to D.A.G. 15/2/1938, 23/2/1938, 29/3/1938.

48. See p.1 of original Memorial in Box 479. Sydney Diocesan Archives.

49. *ibid.* p.2.

50. *ibid.*

51. A.H.G. to D.A.G. 28/12/1937.

52. A.H.G. *Diary* 20/7/1937; A.H.G. to D.A.G. 28/12/1937, 23/3/1943, 30/10/1941.

53. p.3 of Memorial, *loc. cit.*

54. See Original "Memorial" in Sydney Diocesan Archives. Box 479; Copy in Arthur Garnsey *et.al.*, *A Plea For Liberty* Worker's Trustees Sydney 1938.

55. A.H.G to D.A.G. 29/3/1938. Neither those in charge of parochial districts, which were not full parishes, nor curates, were invited to sign. In addition, Conservative Evangelicals who were obviously out of sympathy with the aim of the Memorial, and Anglo-Catholics whose support would have been a political liability, were not invited to sign.

56. *S.M.H.* 19/7/1938 p.10; *A.C.R.* 13/4/1938 p.9.

57. *A.C.R.* 13/4/1938 pp.8-9, 24/11/1938 p.3; A.H.G. to D.A.G. 29/3/1938;

58. *A.C.R.* 13/4/1938 pp.8-9; 24/11/1938 p.15.

59. "...there was an agreement that no names be made public, and this from A.H.G(arnsey)." E. Cameron to D.A. Garnsey 22/8/1979, kindly shown to me by Bishop D.A. Garnsey; *A.C.R.* 24/8/1939 p.9; M.L. Loane, *Mowll*, p.145.

60. See Archdeacon Johnstone's original tabulations, which indicate that he too was interested in any significant, perhaps stigmatising, characteristic in the background of the Memorialists. Sydney Diocesan Archives. Box 479. No retired clergy, curates or men in Parochial Districts are included in the calculations of the non-signatories, because "junior" clergy were not invited to sign the Memorial.

61. The youngest Memorialists were Clive Goodwin and Ronald Johnson (both 29), and the eldest was Cecil King, who died soon after in April 1938. The biographical information for this survey was obtained from the as yet unpublished biographical register compiled by Assoc. Prof. and Mrs. K.J. Cable, and the Rev. Noel Pollard.

62. See Memorial, paragraph three; A.H.G to D.A.G 8/2/1938.

63. *S.M.H.* 18/2/1938 p.14; *A.C.R.* 13/4/1938 pp.8-9. 24/11/1938 p.15.

64. For an example of the orthodoxy of one Memorialist, A.J.A. Fraser, see *S.M.H.* 29/6/1926 p.6, 22/6/1926 p.14, where he upholds the 39 Articles and the Ornaments Rubric.

65. A.H.G. to D.A.G. 1/3/1932; see also 17/10/1933 and *A.C.R.* 9/2/1939 p.16, 23/2/1939 p.5, 9/3/1939 p.12, 6/4/1939 pp.7-8.

66. A.H.G. to D.A.G. 30/5/1936. See also 24/3/1936.

67. A.H.G. to D.A.G. 17/10/1933 (his emphasis). See also 14/11/1933. For examples of where Garnsey disagreed with Angus see A.H.G. to D.A.G. 5/10/1931, 27/12/1932, 3/1/1933, 7/2/1933.

68. *A.C.R.* 24/8/1939 p.6.

69. A.H.G to D.A.G. 2/4/1935, 1/6/1937.

70. A.H.G to D.A.G. 3/7/1934.

71. A.H.G. to D.A.G. 18/1/1938.

72. A.H.G. to D.A.G. 1/3/1932, 27/6/1933. See also 4/7/1933, 3/7/1934.

73. A.H.G. to D.A.G. 1/3/1938.

74. A.H.G. to D.A.G. 14/11/1943. See also 6/8/1935, 8/3/1938.

75. A.H.G. to D.A.G. 1/3/1938.

76. A.H.G. to D.A.G: 17/11/1940.

77. A.H.G to D.A.G. 1/3/1938 and 8/3/1938.

78. Rev. F.A. Walton lost his lecturing job at Moore College in late
    February 1938, see A.H.G. to D.A.G. 1/3/1938; *D.T.* 13/7/1938
    p.1; The Rev. R.B.S. Hammond was responsible for the coun-
    ter-Memorial; H.W.K. Mowll to A.H. Garnsey 17/3/1938, in
    Garnsey, *op.cit.* p.6; the drafted reply is in the handwriting
    of T.C. Hammond, who was also a member of the Editorial
    Board of the Record, while the Memorial itself is annotated by
    "S.M.J(ohnstone)." and the appended table giving details of ordi-
    nation and education etc. is in the same hand. Box 479 Sydney
    Diocesan Archives; see also *A.C.R.* 13/4/1938 pp.8-9, 28/4/1938
    p.7, 1/9/1938 pp;8-9; *C.S.* 22/4/1938 p.7. The *Standard* did not
    report on the Memorial from the 22nd April until after the publica-
    tion of *A Plea for Liberty*, on the 26th August, 1938 p.6.

79. A.H. Garnsey to Mowll 18/4/1938 in Garnsey, *op.cit.* pp.6-7.

80. H.W.K. Mowll to A.H. Garnsey 23/4/1938. *loc.cit.*

81. A.H. Garnsey to Mowll 14/5/1938. *loc.cit.*

82. Circular from Archbishop Mowll to each Memorialist 16/5/1938,
    Draft and Final Reply in Box 479, Sydney Diocesan Archives. See
    also Garnsey, *op.cit.*, p.8.

83. *ibid.*

84. The three men who withdrew were the Revs. Clive Goodwin, H.
    Eric Felton, and Ronald Johnson; Garnsey *et. al.* state in *A Plea for
    Liberty* that a fourth man had intimated to Garnsey of his intention
    to withdraw also, but there is no evidence that this man, the Rev.

E.J. Davidson, actually did so. Davidson was upset at the "obnoxious press propaganda" of the Daily Telegraph and personally assured Mowll that he deplored the fact that there had been a leak. E.J. Davidson to Archbishop Mowll 14/7/1938. Box 479. Sydney Diocesan Archives.

85. Joint Reply by Memorialists to the Archbishop's Questionnaire 24/6/1938 in Garnsey: *op.cit.* pp.11-14.

86. *ibid.* pp.11,13.

87. Joint reply of Memorialists. See Garnsey, *op.cit.*, p.13, and Box 479. Sydney Diocesan Archives.

88. *D.T.* 13/7/1938 p.1, 19/7/1938 p.2; *S.M.H.* 19/7/1938 p.10. *S.M.H.* 20/7/1938 p.17; E.J. Davidson to Mowll 14/7/1938, *loc.cit.*

89. A.H. Garnsey to Mowll 15/7/1938. Box 479 Sydney Diocesan Archives; see also Garnsey, *op.cit.* p.13.

90. Garnsey *et. al.* to editor *S.M.H.* 19/7/1938, in Garnsey, *op.cit.*, pp.16-17.

91. *S.M.H.* August 1938 p.3 (my emphasis); also in Garnsey, *op.cit.*, p.17.

92. *ibid.*

93. Mowll to each of the Memorialists 2/8/1938. Box 479 S.D.A. T.C. Hammond had also prepared a treatise of some 3,500 words which was a point-by-point rebuttal of the Memorialists' collective answer to the questionnaire, but this was not sent. *loc.cit.*

94. *S.M.H.* 23/8/1938 p.10; Committee for Memorialists to Mowll 6/8/1938, in Garnsey, *op.cit.*, pp.19-20.

95. *ibid.* The Memorialists constitute closer to one-third of the incumbents of the Diocese.

96. *S.M.H.* 22/8/1938 p.11 (A.H. Garnsey). See also *A.C.R.* 1/9/1938 pp.8-9; Ls. 26/8/1938 pp.6-7.

97. See Loane, *Mowll*, p.145; *D.T.* 13/7/1938 p.1; *A.C.R.* 13/4/1938 p.9.

98. A.H.G. to D.A.G. 8/2/1938, 15/2/1938, 1/3/1938.

99. Loane, *Mowll*, pp.207-209.

100. See handwritten draft responses to Memorialists, Box 479, S.D.A.

101. Loane, *Mowll*, p.144.

102. *A.C.R.* 13/4/1938 pp.8-9, 27/4/1938 p.7; *C.S.* 22/4/1938 p.7.
103. The Memorial, p.2. Box 479 S.D.A. The fourteen survivors were Ernest Cameron, R.S. Chapple, William Kingston, W.E. Maltby, Hugh Marshall, Noel Rook, F.A.S. Shaw, William Siddens, C.A. Sumner, S.A. Turner, C.E.B.H. Burgess, and the three men who withdrew, Felton, Goodwin and Johnson.

CONCLUSION

The diversity of opinions which were held by Anglicans in the late nineteenth and early twentieth centuries was, ideally, the ingredients of a unifying comprehensiveness. In fact, it was invariably the cause of unhappy and tense divisions, which gradually became institutionalised in respectable political organisations: the circumspection of churchmen towards "party" was replaced by a conviction that while factiousness was un-Christian, political societies were natural and, indeed, essential expressions of Anglicanism's richness.

In England ecclesiastical political groupings could never completely control the decision-making processes. There was no autonomous church legislature and the Crown, not churchmen, made ecclesiastical appointments. Within the constraints of Establishment, church parties were only able to lobby and influence. The direct exercise of power was never possible. In the unestablished context of the colonies, however, power was always directly exercised by churchmen. For most of the nineteenth century the bishops dominated the colonial power structure. They had over-arching authority, the clergy had parochial responsibility and the laity co-operated. This power structure changed as synodical government matured. Towards the end of the century clergy and laity began to share with the bishops in the decision-making process. This development resulted in a political context in which parties flourished, and eventually dominated the administration of power, as the inherently divisive legislative function of synod highlighted the divisions within the polity rather than its essential unity.

This pattern of political development was most advanced in the Diocese of Sydney where the change from an episcopally-oriented power structure to a synod-oriented one began to take place in the 1880s and 1890s. In those two decades, five church parties emerged as institutional expressions of different schools of thought. Yet with the exception of the extreme Church Association, these political groups were little more than propaganda and pressure cells and it was not until the establishment of the Anglican Church League in 1909 that the politics of the Diocese acquired greater sophistication. The emergence of the A.C.L. and the election of Archbishop Wright signalled an important shift in direction for Sydney's Evangelicals. The election of Wright was in part an acknowledgement by them of the need to avoid extremism and present themselves as a united and constructive force in the Church if they were to influence the future character of their Church. The founding of the A.C.L. was both the institutional expression of that unity, and the means by which their influence could be maximised.

The Anglican Church League quickly became the dominant party in the Diocese. Its rise to power was facilitated by four factors. First, Archbishop Wright's action in banning vestments de-polarised the politics of the Diocese in the long-term: his determination to act constitutionally meant that Anglo-Catholicism was never able to develop as a force in Sydney and, with the ritualist adversaries of the Conservative Evangelicals vanquished, the swing away from the Protestant Church of England Union to the new Evangelical centre-unity party accelerated. Archbishop Wright did, in fact, create an ideal political milieu for a party which stood for Evangelical consensus. The second factor in the A.C.L.'s success was its political machinery. The effective use of its caucus, its pre-selection of candidates and other electioneering methods were on a level which had until then been unknown in the Diocese. These political tools were employed at a time when the concentration of power in the hands of several synodal committees made electoral organisation of this kind axiomatic for control of the Diocese's decision-making processes. The third factor was the clerical nature of the League's leadership. While other Evangelical parties in Australia were almost exclusively lay in character, the predominance of clergy in the A.C.L. provided the League with the stability and depth of leadership necessary for its political success.

Yet the League's rise to power was also facilitated by a vital fourth factor: the Archbishop himself. Wright's perception of his role as an administrator and Chief Pastor meant that he did not seek to concentrate power at the top, nor did he seek to obstruct the activities of huddled coteries in the Diocese. Wright's detachment — caused as much by disposition as poor health — allowed a powerful political base — the A.C.L. — to develop below him.

The ostensibly happy coalition of Conservative and Liberal Evangelicals within an umbrella party did not last. From the late 1920s the coalition began to be racked by dissension, as the Anglican Church League steadily shifted away from a self-conscious "consensus" position to a rejection of the ideal of comprehensiveness and Evangelical con-solidation. The A.C.L. became a narrow, monochrome and exclusively Conservative Evangelical party. It is a contention of this dissertation that there were two underlying causes of this metamorphosis, each being essentially external to developments within the Diocese.

First, the push for a new Constitution for an autonomous Australian Church was strongest from 1923 to 1933. The debate which surrounded this issue thrust all Australian dioceses into negotiation to a greater extent than ever before, as Sydney's Evangelical distinctiveness became more clearly pronounced. It was an isolation which cultivated a defiant defen-siveness on the part of Conservative Evangelicals who were determined to preserve in Sydney, at all cost, what they believed was their sacred trust of a Reformed tradition. This ghetto mentality had a deleterious effect upon the Liberal Evangelical influences within the Diocese.

The second cause was the perceived threat of an enemy within the Diocese of Sydney. The Prayer Book Revision debates of the 1920s in England had seen English Liberal Evangelicals concede ground on a number of issues which Conservative Evangelicals believed were absolutely fundamental. English Conservative Evangelicals came to regard Liberal Evangelicals as a fifth column which had undermined the Evangelical cause. Conservative Evangelicals in Sydney noted this schism in England with alarm. With heightened determination, they wished to ensure that Liberal Evangelicals were given no opportunity to have the same influences in the Diocese of Sydney, even though their views were, in fact, by no means consonant with those of English Liberal Evangelicals. The breach between the two schools within what had once been an Evangelical coalition became quite evident after 1928, when Liberal Evangelicals supported the proposed new Constitution and the Conservative Evangelicals vehemently opposed it. A.C.L. members publicly opposed each other as relations between the two groups rapidly deteriorated.

The watershed for the Conservative-Liberal schism was the election of a successor to Archbishop Wright in 1933. Political reconciliation was impossible after the Conservative Evangelicals skilfully turned the party machine of the A.C.L. against the Liberal Evangelicals in their successful campaign for Howard Mowll. The consequent defection of key Liberal Evangelicals from the League in 1933 and the emergence of the Anglican Fellowship signalled the disintegration of the coalition which had been fundamental to the League's establishment and a major factor in its rise to political dominance of the Diocese. Ironically, the party machine which Conservative and Liberal Evangelicals had built together proved too strong for the Liberal Evangelicals in the ensuing struggle. The Conservative Evangelicals tightened their grip on the party, actively courting grass roots support in the Diocese, strengthening the party's links with its organ of propaganda, the *Church Record*, and white-washing the opposition at successive synodal elections. By 1936 the Conservative Evangelical victory was complete and the Liberal Evangelicals, who had ten years previously occupied about 40% of the important positions in the Diocese, were an isolated minority. Their response to their defeat culminated in the Memorial. That letter came to be regarded by Conservative Evangelicals later as a most serious challenge to Conservative Evangelicalism but, in fact, it should be more properly regarded as the final death throe of an exhausted and frustrated Liberal Evangelicalism.

The violent and unrelenting campaign of Conservative Evangelicals against their Liberal Evangelical brothers was, however, an understandable reaction. Elsewhere in the Anglican Communion an aggressive Anglo-Catholicism and an articulate but irresolute Liberal Evangelicalism were in the ascendant. By 1936 Conservative Evangelicalism had been virtually extinguished as a force in the Church in England while in Australia, Evangelicals of any complexion were rare in Queensland and Western Australia and were being steadily squeezed out of other dioceses. Conservative Evangelicals in Sydney had no guarantee that similar campaigns would not undermine Evangelicalism in their Diocese: they therefore ruthlessly attacked that spectre by refusing to countenance a plurality of opinion and belief within Anglicanism in Sydney.

Yet the trend towards the monochrome in Sydney in the period 1909 to 1938 was not abnormal for Anglicanism in Australia. Establishment in England encouraged the comprehension and cultivation of a via media; the absence of that centrifugal impulse allowed the natural development of extremes in the colonies. Concomitantly, the huge distances between population centres and the uncertain stability of the parishes meant that the diocese, not the province or the parish, became the dominant ecclesiastical institution in Australia. The independent development and self-determination of these diocesan units encouraged the perpetuation of distinctive diocesan traditions, traditions which invariably reflected the predilectiqns in churchmanship of the long-serving Australian bishops. An Australian Anglicanism which was characterised by extremes was the result. The Diocese of Sydney was,;however, unique in that national context for, as other diocese became more and more Anglo-Catholic, Sydney went the other way and developed a distinctively Conservative Evangelical tradition. It was a tradition which was rooted in the episcopate of Bishop Barker but one which was developed and secured between 1909 and 1938 by the political struggles between men who were sincerely intent upon the defence of their faith.

APPENDIX ONE

The Fifty Memorialists of 1938

- Abram, O.V.A.
- Adams, C.E.
- Armitage, Isaac D.
- Burgess, Colin
- Cameron, Ernest
- Cameron, R.J.
- Chapple, J.F.
- Chapple, Raymond
- Charlton, Leo
- Coughlan, William George
- Davidson, E.J.
- Dudley, L.S.
- Elder, F.R.
- Felton, H.E.(Withdrew)
- Fraser, A.J.A.
- Fielding, M.G.
- Firebrace, R.C.
- Garnsey, Arthur Henry
- Gee, Thomas
- Goodwin, Clive A. (Withdrew)

- Johnson, Ronald A. (Withdrew)
- Jones, R. Harley
- King, C.J. (Died 18/4/1938)
- King, C.R.
- Kingston, W.O.
- Lea, E.H.
- Lofts, H.J.H.
- Lucas, C.A.
- Maltby, W.E.
- Manning, G.J.
- Marshall, H.J.
- Meyer, F.B.
- Nisbet, W.G.
- Paul, T.G.
- Pitt Owen, R.H.
- Reeves, Arthur
- Rix, A.G.
- Robinson, R.K.
- Robison, E.C.
- Rofe, J.F.
- Rook, W. Noel
- Sanders, G.A.
- Shaw, F.A.S.
- Siddens, William John
- Stanger, W.H.
- Sumner, C.J.L.
- Turner, S.A.
- Walker, Edward
- Walton, Frederick A.
- Ware, G.P.M.

BIBLIOGRAPHY

I - Manuscript Material

Anglican Church League. *Minute Books*. 1916-1927; 1929-39. The 1916-27 Minutes are in Moore College Library, and those from 1929 are in the custody of the present Secretary of the League, the Rev. R.E. Lamb, of Caringbah.

The Archbishops and Bishops of the Dioceses in Australia and Tasmania, "The Anglican Church and the War" n.d. (1914) Box 194. Sydney Diocesan Archives (hereafter S.D.A.).

Anglican Evangelical Group Movement. Collection of the A.E.G.M., incorporating the Group Brotherhood and the "Liverpool Six". The University Archives. The Brynmor Jones Library. The University of Hull. England.

Archbishop's Overseas Advisory Committee. Papers. Lambeth Palace Library (hereafter L.P.L.).

Australian Church Record. Minute Books 1912-1939. Moore College Library (hereafter M.C.L.)

Benson, Edward White. Archbishop of Canterbury. The Papers of. L.P.L.

Bickersteth, The Rev. Samuel. The Papers of. L.P.L.

Carter, The Rev. Dr. James J. The Papers of. Boxes 481, 790. S.D.A.

Chronicles of Convocation of the Provinces of Canterbury and York. Selected Dates.

Corish, Hugh A. The Papers of. M.C.L.

Council of Churches in N.S.W. — Diocesan Registry File. Box 38. S.D.A.

D'Arcy-Irvine, Bishop Gerard Addington. The Papers of. Boxes 607, 1051. S.D.A.

Davidson, Randall Thomas. Archbishop of Canterbury. The Papers of. L.P.L.

Diocese of Sydney. Standing Committee of the Synod. *Minute Books* IV and V. 1909-38. S.D.A.

_____ *Minute Book* of the Synod of. 1906-1920. S.D.A.

Douglas, John Albert. The Papers of. L.P.L.

Ecclesiastical Statistics from Parochial Returns for the Diocese of Sydney. Box 46. S.D.A.

Garnsey, Arthur H. The Papers of. In the possession of Bishop D.A. Garnsey.

_____ *Diary* 1924-1943. In the possession of Bishop D.A. Garnsey.

Headlam, Arthur Cayley. The Papers of. L.P.L.

Irish Church Missions. Miscellaneous Papers of Secretary. (T.C. Hammond). I.C.M. 28 Bachelors Walk, Dublin 1. Irish Republic.

Johnstone, S.M. Correspondence as Registrar. Boxes 77, 611, 656, 670, 671, 673. S.D.A.

Kirkby, Bishop S.J. Papers of. Box 54. S.D.A.

Lambeth Conference. Central Consultative Council. Papers. L.P.L.

Lambeth Palace Library. Miscellaneous Manuscripts. (not catalogued — Mowll, Wright, etc.) L.P.L.

Lambeth Conference. Miscellaneous Papers and Correspondence. L.P.L.

_____ Verbatim Minutes of 1897, 1908, 1920 and 1930 Conferences. L.P.L.

Lang, Cosmo Gordon. Archbishop of Canterbury. The Papers of. L.P.L.

BIBLIOGRAPHY

"The Liverpool Six" and Group Brotherhood. *Minute Book* and Papers. In A.E.G.M. Papers (see above).

Memorial, The. Original Memorial, correspondence and related papers. Box 479. S.D.A.

Montgomery, Bishop H.H. Letters and Papers of. U.S.P.G. Library.

Moule, Handley Carr Glyn. *Diaries* and Letters of. Cambridge University Library.

Mowll, Archbishop Howard West Kilvinton. Papers. Boxes 109, 257, 370, 371, 372, 396, 418, 935. S.D.A.

Nexus — Legal *Opinion* Box 954. S.D.A.

Palmer, Bishop E.J. The Papers of. L.P.L.

Pan Anglican Congress. 1908. Collection, *Minutes*. L.P.L.

Parish Returns — Diocese of Sydney. Boxes 294, 455. S.D.A.

Pilcher, Bishop Charles Venn. Boxes 363, 364, 1048. S.D.A.

Riley, John Athelstan. The Papers of. L.P.L.

Rules of the Church of England Association of New South Wales (Sydney 1886). In the possession of Archbishop D.W.B. Robinson.

Smith, Sydney Edgar Langford. The Papers of. In the possession of the Langford Smith family.

Smith, William Saumarez. *Memorandum ad Clerum*. 1907-1909. Box 787. S.D.A.

Society for the Propagation of the Gospel. Letters, *Correspondence Books* of the Secretary. (H.H. Montgomery and Stacy Waddy). U.S.P.G. Library.

Temple, Frederic. Archbishop of Canterbury. The Papers of. L.P.L.

Temple, William. Archbishop of Canterbury. The Papers of. L.P.L.

Wright, Archbishop John Charles. Correspondence. Boxes 94, 369, 397, 1050. S.D.A.

II - Contemporary books

A Group of Clergy. *A New Prayer Book (The Grey Book).* 2 Vols. Humphrey Milford. London 1925.

Alcuin Club. *A Survey of the Proposals for the Alternative Prayer Book.* (The Orange Book) Mowbray London 1924.

Anon. *Shall the vestments of the Roman Mass be used in the National Church?* Book Room. London n.d. (1911-12)

_____ *The Proposed Constitution: Extracts from the columns of the "Church Standard"* Christian World Print. Sydney n.d. (1927).

Anglican Church League. *The Evangelical Position on the Proposed Constitution.* Edgar Bragg. Sydney 1926

Archbishop of Canterbury (Frederic Temple). *The Reservation of the Sacrament.* London 1900.

Archdall, Mervyn. *The Church and the Churches.* G.B. Philip and Son. Sydney 1912.

_____ *Liturgical Right and National Wrong: A Vindication of the Rights of the Church*; Church Association. London 1900.

Barnes, E.W. *Freedom and Authority.* A.E.G.M. Series/Hodder and Stoughton. London n.d. (1924)

The Book of Common Prayer with the Additions and Deviations Proposed in 1928 Oxford Univ. Press. London 1928.

Boyce, Francis Bertie. *Fourscore Years and Seven, The Memoirs of Archedeacon Boyce.* Angus and Robertson.

Carter, C. Sydney. *The English Reformation.* C.J. Thynne. London n.d. (1927).

Chavasse, C.M. *The Meaning of the Cross* S.P.C.K. London 1956.

Clarke, Edward. *Prayer Book Revision,* Book Room London. 1914.

Clarke, W.K. Lowther. *The Prayer Book of 1928 Reeuneidered.* S.P.C.K. London 1943.

Cowper, W.M. *Episcopate of the Right Reverend Frederic Barker*. Hatchards London 1888.

Creighton, Louise. *Life and Letters of Mandell Creighton*. Longman, Green and Co. London 1913.

Crotty, Horace. *The Church Victorious*. Longmans, Green and Co. London. 1938.

Colson, Percy. *Life of the Bishop of London*. Jarrolds. London 1935.

Dale, H. Montague. *Evangelicals and the Green Book* A.E.G.M. Series No.26./Hodder and Stoughton. London n.d. (1923)

Dark, Sidney. *Archbishop Davidson and the English Church*. Philip Allan and Co. London 1929.

Davidson, Randall T. *The Five Lambeth Conferences*. S.P.C.K. London 1920.

Davies, David John. *The Church and the Plain Man*. Angus and Robertson. Sydney 1919.

_____ *The Pastoral Ideal and the Personal Touch* Pepperday. Sydney 1915.

Downer, A.G. *The Alternative Communion Offices compared with the service of Holy Communion in the Book of Common Prayer*. Church Book Room Press London 1924.

Elliott, Spencer H. *Do This in Remembrance*. Richard Jackson. Leeds n.d.

Ferguson, Fisher. *The 39 Articles: Why the Attack Must Be Repulsed*. Protestant Truth Society London n.d. (1931)

Garnsey, Arthur Henry et al. *A Plea For Liberty*. The Worker Trustees. Sydney 1938.

Gore, Charles. *The Incarnation of the Son of God: Bampton Lectures 1891*. John Murray. London 1893.

_____ (ed.) Luz_Mundi. John Murray. London 1890.

Gowing, E.N. *John Edwin Watts-Ditchfield*. Hodder and Stoughton. London 1926.

Hammond, T.C. *Age-Long Questions* Marshall, Morgan and Scott. London n.d. (1942)

_____ *The Bathurst Bible Case.* George M. Dash. Sydney n.d.

_____ *The Church of Christ.* Thynne and Jarvis London 1924.

_____ *Comments on the Discussion. Hand v. Hammond.* Thynne and Jarvis. London 1924.

_____ *Did Protestants Rob Churches.* J.T. Drought. Dublin n.d.

_____ *Doubts of the Sons.* Connellan Mission. Dublin n.d.

_____ *Fading Light* Marshall, Morgan and Scott. London n.d.

_____ *In Understanding Be Men* I.V.P. London 1976 edition (first published in 1936).

_____ *The New Creation.* Marshall, Morgan and Scott. London 1953.

_____ *Priesthood, Ministry and Apostolic Succession.* Connellan Mission. Dublin n.d.

_____ *Reformation and Modern Ideals. Being the Substance of Lectures Delivered in Australia.* Connellan Mission. Dublin 1927.

_____ *What is an Evangelical?* Evangelical Tracts and Publications. Beecroft (Sydney) n.d. (1956).

Hart, John Stephen. *A Commentary on the Draft Constitution for the Church of England in Australia.* William Andrews. Sydney 1933.

Harvey, G.L.H. (ed.) *The Church and the Twentieth Century* Macmillan. London 1936.

Head, F.W. *The Church of England.* A.E.G.M. Series No. 17./Hodder and Stoughton. London n.d. (1923)

Headlam, Arthur Cayley. *The Church of England.* John Murray. London 1925 (2nd edition).

_____ *The Doctrine of the Church and Reunion.* John Murray. London 1920.

Henson, Herbert Hensley. *Bishoprick Papers*. Cumberledge/ Oxford
    University Press. London 1946.

Hinde, H.W. et al. *The Holy Communion*. (Islington 1924) Record
    Newspaper Office London 1924.

Howden, J. Russell (ed.) *Evangelicalism*. By Members of the
    Fellowship of Evangelical Churchmen. Charles J. Thynne and
    Jarvis London 1925.

Hunkin, Joseph Wellington. *Episcopal Ordination and Confirmation
    in Relation to Inter-Communion and Reunion* A.E.G.M./Heffer.
    Cambridge 1929.

_____ *The Resurrection*. A.E.G.M. Series No. 9./Hodder
    and Stoughton. London n.d. (1923)

Johnson. Humphrey J.T. *Anglicanism in Transition* Longmans. London
    1938.

Johnson, W.H. *George Merrick Long* St. John's College Press. Morpeth
    1930.

Johnstone, Samuel Martin. *A History of the Church Missionary Society in
    Australia and Tasmania*. C.M.S. Sydney 1928.

Joynson-Hicks, William. *The Prayer Book Crisis*. Putnam. London 1928.

Kirkpatrick, A.F. *Old Testament Prophecy* A.E.G.M. Series/Hodder and
    Stoughton. London n.d. (1924)

Knox, Edmund Arbuthnott. *On What Authority? A Review of the
    Foundations of Christian Faith*. Longmans, Green and Co. London
    1922.

_____ *Reminiscences of an Octogenarian. 1847-1934.*
    Hutchinson and Co. London 1934.

Lambeth Conference of Anglican Bishops. *1930 Encyclical Letter from
    the Bishops with the Resolutions and Reports* S.P.C.K. London 1930.

La Touche, Everard Digges. *Christian Certitude*. J. Clarke and Co.
    London 1910.

Matthews, C.H.S. (ed.) *Faith or Fear? An Appeal to the Church of England*. Macmillan. London 1916.

Millard, E.C. The Same Lord: an account of the Mission Tour of the Rev. George C. Grubb in Australia, Tasmania and New Zealand from April 3, 1891 to July 7th, 1892. Marlborough London 1893.

Mitchell, Albert. *The Holy Communion: a study in history and doctrine*. Church Book Room London n.d. (1925)

_____ *Reservation*. Church Book Room. London n.d. (1923)

Probyn, H.E.H. *The Dawn of the Reformation*. Church Book Room London 1920.

Rogers, T. Guy (ed.). *The Inner Life*. Essays in Liberal Evangelicalism. Hodder and Stoughton. London n.d.(1925)

_____ *Liberal Evangelicalism. An Interpretation*. Hodder and Stoughton. London 3rd edition n.d. (first published 1924).

Ryle, J.C. *Knots Untied*. Hunt. London 1877.

Smith, Sydney Edgar Langford. *The Case for a New Site. St. Andrew's Cathedral, Sydney*. Edgar Bragg. Sydney 1926.

_____ *The Sydney Diocese and Proposed New Constitution of the Church of England in Australia*. A.C.L. Sydney 1927.

Storr, Vernon *Freedom and Tradition* A.E.G.M./ Hodder and Stoughton. London 1940.

_____ *Inspiration*. A.E.G.M. No. 11/Hodder and Stoughton. London n.d. (1923)

_____ *My Faith*. A.E.G.M./S.P.C.K. London 1928.

_____ *Reservation*. A.E.G.M. Series/Hodder and Stoughton. London n.d. (1923)

Tait, Arthur J. *What is the Gospel?* A.E.G.M. Series No. 6/Hodder and Stoughton. London n.d. (1923)

Talbot, Arthur Edward. *Church of England Divines and the Anglican Tradition* (Moorhouse Lectures 1933). Endeavour Press. Sydney 1934.

Thomas, W.H. Griffith. *An Examination of Bishop Gore's Open Letter on "The Basis of Anglican Fellowship."* Robert Scott. London 1914.

_____ *The Principles of Theology.* Longmans. London 1930.

Wace, Henry. *Invocation of Saints.* Church Book Room. London n.d.

_____ *Prayer Book Revision: Proposals of the Canterbury Convocation.* London 1915.

Walsh, Walter. *The Secret History of the Oxford Movement.* Swan, Sonnenschen and Co. London 1899.

Wilson, H.A. (ed.) *The Anglican Communion. Past, Present and Future.* (Cheltenham Congress 1928). John Murray. London 1928.

_____ *Church Divisions and Reunion.* A.E.G.M./ Hodder and Stoughton. London n.d. (1924)

Woodlock, Francis. *The Reformation and the Eucharist.* Sheed and Ward. London 1928.

Wright, John Charles. *Confirmation.* Church Book Room Press. London 1928.

_____ *Thoughts on Modern Church Life and Work.* Longmans. London 1909.

III - Contemporary Articles

Beeching, H.C."The Permissive Use of the Vestments", in *Churchman* 1911, pp.169-173.

Carpenter, S.C. "The Necessity of Dogma", in *Churchman* September 1916, pp.582-587.

Cobb, W.F. "The Problem of the Church of England", in *The Hibbert Journal* v.9 1910-11, pp.584-597.

Dewick, E.C. "Evangelicals and the Problem of Ritualism", in *Churchman* January 1913, pp.8-16.

_____ "Evangelicalism in the Church of England. Its Present Position and Future Prospects", in *The Constructive Quarterly* 1915 pp.800-813.

Fox, H.E. "The Need of Definiteness in Faith and Action", in *Churchman*, September 1916 pp.566-574.

Henson, Hensley. "The Issue of Kikuyu" in *The Modern Churchman* March 1915 pp.611-625.

Herklots, B. "Evangelicals and the Problem of Ritualism", in *Churchman* 1913 pp.352-359.

_____ "The Permissive Use of Vestments", in *Churchman*, 1911 pp. 225-235.

Hunkin, Joseph Wellington. "Vision and Authority" in *The Modern Churchman* November 1929 pp.501-504.

_____ "The Reformation and the Scriptures" in *The Modern Churchman* 1932 pp.274-290.

Irwin, George F. "The Evangelical Interpretation of Anglicanism" in *Churchman* 1926 pp.101-108.

Johnson, W. Guy. "The Church Pastoral Aid Society" in *Churchman* 1935 pp.108-117.

_____ "The Doctrinal Basis of N.A. 84." in *Churchman* 1923 pp.204-208.

Knox, E.A. "Catholicity or Compromise; or 'Why Cannot Evangelicals Be More Tolerant?'" in *Churchman* April 1925 pp.111-118.

Pulvertaft, Thomas J. "The Lausanne Conference" in *Churchman* 1928 pp.7-14.

Sinclair, William. "Party Spirit" in *Churchman* February 1901 pp.263-271.

Smith, Harold. "Authority" in *Churchman* September 1920 pp.478-482.

Stock, Eugene. "Kikuyu Rediviva" in *The Constructive Quarterly* 1919 pp.259-275.

_____ "The Recent Controversy in the C.M.S." in *Church Missionary Review* 1923 pp.29-37.

Symonds, H. "The Kikuyu Statement and After" in Modern *Churchman* 1915 pp.172-175.

Wace, Henry. "The Fundamentals of Evangelical Protestantism" in *Churchman* January 1918 pp.11-20.

"X" "Liberal Evangelicalism: What it is and What it stands for." A Series.

1. "The Essence of Evangelicalism" in *Churchman* March 1915 pp.193-200;

2. "What Evangelicalism Implies" in *Churchman* April 1915 pp.277-285.

3. "The Bible", in *Churchman* May 1915 pp.371-379.

4. "The Problem of the Creeds" in *Churchman* June 1915 pp.439-448.

5. "The Sacraments and the Ministry" in *Churchman* July 1915 pp.513-521.

IV - Interviews

Bidwell, Archdeacon John. Tape and Transcript of Interview between Bidwell, D.W.B. Robinson and Bruce Ballantine-Jones. 7th August, 1972.

Farrell, Monica. Former secretary of T.C. Hammond. Interview 17/12/1979.

Faulkner, The Rev. Cecil William John.

Fox, The Rev. Norman.

Gough, Bishop Hugh Rowlands. Interview 2/12/1981. London.

Loane, Archbishop Marcus L. Interview 22/6/1981.

Martin, Mrs. A.V. Former Secretary (in Ireland) of T.C. Hammond. London 1981.

Sargent, The Rev. Canon Alec. Interview Canterbury 1981.

Sykes, Professor Stephen. Interview Durham 1981.

V - Theses

Aubrey, Keith Harold. "The Church of England in Northern New
   South Wales 1847-1867 and in the Diocese of Grafton and
   Armidale 1867-1892." Unpub. M.A. Thesis. Univ. of New
   England. 1964.

Broome, Richard Laurence. "Protestantism in New South Wales
   Society 1900-1914." Unpub. Ph.D Thesis. Univ. of Sydney.
   1974.

Chandler, Philip Walker. "Charles Walker Chandler" Unpub.
   Biographical Essay (non-degree New Zealand) n.d.

Coward, Dan. "The Impact of War on N.S.W.: Some Aspects of Social
   and Political History 1914-1917." Unpub. PhCDI AINIUI

Davis, Bernard Rex. "The Church of England in N.S.W.: The
   Beginning and Development of Training Men for its Ministry ...
   1825-1925." Unpub. M.A. Thesis. Univ. Newcastle. 1966.

Gilbert, A.D. "The Churches and the Conscription Referenda 1916-
   1917." Unpub. M.A. Thesis. A.N.U. 1967.

Hansen, Donald Edgar." "The Churches and Society in N.S.W. 1919-
   1939. A Study of Church Activities, socio-religious issues,
   community-Church and inter-Church relations." Unpub. Ph.D.
   Thesis. Macquarie Univ. 1978.

Howe, Renate. "The Response of Protestant Churches to Urbanization
   in Melbourne and Chicago 1875-1914." Unpub. Ph.D. Thesis.
   Univ. Melbourne 1971.

Martell, J.D. "The Prayer Book Controversy 1927-28." Unpub. M.A.
   Thesis. Univ. of Durham. 1974.

Parker, David. "Fundamentalism and Conservative Protestantism in Australia 1920-1980." Unpub. Ph.D. Thesis. Univ. Qld. 1982.

Raynor, Keith. "The History of the Church of England in Queensland." Unpub. Ph.D. Thesis. Univ. Qld. 1962.

Ryan, John. "The Australian Career of John Charles Wright. Archbishop of Sydney 1909-1933. The First Ten Years." Unpub. B.A.(Hons.) Thesis. Univ. Sydney. 1979.

Teale, Ruth. "By Hook or By Crook: The Anglican Diocese of Bathurst. 1870-1911." Unpub. M.A. Thesis. Univ. Sydney. 1967.

Westwood, Susan. "A Study of the Attitudes and Activities of the Church of England in the Illawarra during the First World War." Unpub. B.A. Thesis. Univ. Wollongong. 1980.

Walmsley, J.W. "The Evangelical Party in the Church of England 1905-1928." Unpub. Ph.D Thesis. Univ. of Hull, England. 1978.

VI -Lectures

Cable, Kenneth J. "Bishop Barker and his clergy." First Moore College Library Lecture. 17 April 1975 Transcript.

_____ "Good Government in the Church": The Inaugural Bishop Perry Memorial Lecture. April 1983. Transcript.

_____ "The Liturgy at St. James'". A Lecture delivered at St. James' Church, King Street, Sydney, on Sunday 28/6/1981. Transcript.

Hubbard, Nigel. "Strive to be Faithful": The Life of Adam Robert Maclean 1869-1943. Read before the Church of England Historical Society 1 April 1982. Transcript.

Robinson, D.W.B. "The Origins of the Anglican Church League." Second Moore College Library Lecture. 9th April 1976. Transcript.

Withycombe, Robert. "Francis Bertie Boyce: Clergyman and Reformer." Third Moore College Library Lecture 1980. Transcript.

VII - Later Works: Articles

Banks, Robert. "Fifty Years of Theology in Australia 1915-1965 Part One", in *Colloquium* v.9. no.1. October 1976.

_____ "Fifty Years of Theology in Australia 1915-1965 Part Two", in *Colloquium* v.9. no.2. May 1977.

Batt, Neil and Roe, Michael, "Conflict within the Church of England in Tasmania 1856-1858." *J.R.H.* v.4, no.1. June 1966 pp.39-62.

Bollen, J.D et. al. "Australian Religious History, 1960-1980", in *J.R.H.* 13,1, 1980 pp.8-44.

Bridston, Keith. "It Ain't the Heat: It's the Humility. Piety, Power in the Church", in *Lutheran Quarterly* v.21 May 1969 pp.106-115.

Cable, K.J. "Francis Bertie Boyce", in Nairn, Bede and Serle, Geoffrey (eds.) *Australian Dictionary of Biography* v.7. Melbourne Univ. Press. 1979.

_____ "Mrs. Barker and her Diary." *R.A.H.S.J.* v.54. part 1. March 1968 pp.67-105.

_____ "Protestant Problems in New South Wales in the Mid-Nineteenth Century", in *J.R.H.* III, 2, PP.119-135.

_____ "Religious Controversies in New South Wales in the Mid-Nineteenth Century. Part II. The Dissenting Sects and Education", in *R.A.H.S.J.* v.49. pt.2 July 1963. pp.136-147.

_____ "St. James' Church, King Street, Sydney 1819-1894 Part Two", in *R.A.H.S.J.* v.50 part 5, Nov. 1964, pp.346-374.

_____ "St. James' Church...Part Three", in *R.A.H.S.J.* v.50 part 6, Dec. 1964. pp.433-452.

BIBLIOGRAPHY

Carnell, E.J. "Fundamentalism", in Halverson, Marvin and Cohen, Arthur (eds.) *A Handbook of Christian Theology* Collins Fontana Glasgow 1960. pp.146-147.

Davis, R.P. "Christian Socialism in Tasmania", in *J.R.H.* v.7 no.1 June 1972 pp.51-68.

Daw, E.D. "Electing a Primate: Alfred Barry and the . Diocese of Sydney 1882-1883", in *J.R.A.H.S.* v.66, 4, pp.237-257.

_____ "Synodical Government for the Church of England in N.S.W. The First Attempt", in *J.R.H.* v.6 no.2 Dec. 1970 pp.151-176.

Dougan, Alan. "Samuel Angus", in Nairn and Serle, *op.cit.* v.7. 1979.

French, Maurice. "The Church Extension in South Australia: The Impact of Depression and Demographic Changes on Church Organization in the Late Nineteenth Century", in *J.R.H.* v.8 no.4, Dec.1977 pp.390-405.

Gilbert, A.D. "The Conscription Referenda 1916-17: The Impact of the Irish Crisis", in *Historical Studies* v.14 no.53 Oct. 1969.

Hilliard, David. Review of Michael McKernan's *Australia Churches at War* in *Flinders Journal of History and Politics* v.7, 1981 pp.104-105.

Lewis, C.S. "The Inner Ring", in *Screwtape Proposes a Toast and Other Pieces* Fontana Glasgow 1978-

Mansfield, Joan and Bruce. "Australian Religious History: 21-23 August 1975", in *J.R.H.* v.8,4, December 1975 pp. 413-420.

Marsden, George M. "Fundamentalism as an American Phenomenon, A Comparison with English Evangelicalism", in *Church History* 1977 pp.215-232

O'Farrell, Patrick. "Writing the General History of Australian Religion", in *J.R.H.* v.9,1, 1976 pp.64-73.

Paul, Leslie. "Power within the Church", in *Modern Churchman* v.12 Oct. 1968 pp.19-31.

Phillips, Walter. "The Defence of Christian Belief in Australia 1875-1914: The Responses to Evolution and Higher Criticism", in *J.R.H.* v.9, no.4 Dec. 1977 pp.402-423.

Robinson, D.W.B. "Thomas Moore and the Early Life of Sydney", in *R.A.H.S.J.* v.56-part 3. Sept.1970. pp.165-192.

Rodgers, Margaret. "The Reredos Controversy" in *The Australian Church Record* 15 Dec. 1980 pp.1,5 and 6.

Roe, Jill. "Challenge and Response: Religious Life in Melbourne 1876-1886", in *J.R.H.* v.5, no.2 Dec. 1968. pp.149-166.

_____ "A Tale of Religion in Two Cities", *Meanjin* 1/81

Smith, F.B. "Spiritualism in Victoria in the Nineteenth Century" in *J.R.H.* 3,3, 1965 pp.246-260.

Taylor, David M. "Bishop Gilbert White and the Council of Churches: A Chapter of Inter-Church Relations in Australia", in *J.R.H.* v.2, no.3 June 1963 pp. 234-248.

Teale, Ruth. "A Brave New World in the Australian Bush: The Anglican Diocese of Bathurst and its first Bishop, Samuel Edward Marsden", in *R.A.H.S.J.* v.53 part 2, June 1967. pp.139-157.

_____ "Party or Principle? The Election to the Anglican See of Sydney in 1889-1890", in *R.A.H.S.J.* v.55 pt.2 June 1969. pp.141-155.

Weinrich, E. Werner. "A Consideration of Some of the Underlying Assumptions and Consequences of the Ecclesiastical Ballot", in *Lutheran Quarterly* v.21 May 1969 pp.139-147.

VIII - Later Works: Books

Bachrach, Peter (ed.) *Political Elites in a Democracy* Atherton Press New York 1971.

BIBLIOGRAPHY

Balleine, G.R. *A History of the Evangelical Party in the Church of England* Church Book Room Press London 1951 edition (Appendix by G.W. Bromiley)

Barrett, John. *That Better Country: The Religious Aspect of Life in Eastern Australia 1835-1850* Melbourne Univ. Press 1966.

Bayldon, Joan. *Cyril Bardsley, Evangelist.* S.P.C.K. London 1942.

Bell, G.K.A. *Randall Davidson* (Two vols.) Oxford Univ. Press London 1935.

Bentley, James. *Ritualism and Politics in Victorian Britain. The Attempt to Legislate Belief.* Oxford U.P. 1978.

Blaikie, Norman W.H. *The Plight of the Australian Clergy.* Univ. Qld. Press. St. Lucia Qld. 1979.

Blondel, J. *Voters, Parties and Leaders.* Penguin London 1966.

Bollen, J.D. *Protestantism and Social Reform in New South Wales 1899-1910.* Melb. U.P. 1972.

_____ *Religion in Australian Society: An Historians View.* Leigh College Enfield 1973. (The Leigh College Open Lectures. Winter Series 1973.)

Border, Ross. *Church and State in Australia 1788-1872. A Constitutional Study of the Church of England in Australia.* S.P.C.K. London 1962.

Broome, Richard. *Treasure in Earthen Vessels: Protestant Christianity in N.S.W. Society 1900-1914.* Univ. Qld Press. St. Lucia. Qld 1980.

Cable. Kenneth J. *St James' Church, Sydney. An Illustrated History.* The Churchwardens of St. James', King Street, Sydney 1982.

Chadwick, Owen (ed.) *The Mind of the Oxford Movement.* Adam and Charles Black. London 1960.

_____ *The Victorian Church* (2 vols.) Adam and Charles Black London 1970/1971.

Church, R.W. *The Oxford Movement.* Univ. Chicago Press edition Chicago 1970. (First published 1891.)

Clarke, H. Lowther. *Constitutional Church Government*; S.P.C.K. London 1924.

Crowley, Frank (ed.) *A New History of Australia*. Heinemann Melbourne 1976.

Dougan, Alan. *A Backward Glance at the Angus Affair*. Wentworth Press Sydney 1971.

Dunstan, Alan and Peart-Binns, John S. *Cornish Bishop: Joseph Wellington Hunkin*. Epworth. London 1977.

Elkin, A.P. *The Diocese of Newcastle: A History*. Australasian Medical Publishing Co. Sydney 1955.

Fraser, A.J.A. *I Remember. I Remember* Dolphin. Sydney 1977.

Giles, R.A. *A Constitutional History of the Australian Church*. Skeffington London 1929.

Grocott, Allan M. *Convicts, Clergymen and Churches*. Univ. Sydney Press. Sydney 1980.

Gummer, Selwyn. *The Chavasse Twins*. Hodder and Stoughton. London 1963.

Hague, Dyson. *The Story of the English Prayer Book*. Longmans. London 1930.

Harris, Dorothy *et al. The Shape of Belief: Christianity in Australia Today*. Lancer Books. Homebush West. 1982.

Hinchliff, Peter. *The One-Sided Reciprocity: A Study in the Modification of the Establishment*. Darton, Longman and Todd. London 1966.

Johnstone, S.M. *The Book of St. Andrew's Cathedral, Sydney*. Edgar Bragg Sydney 1937.

Judd, Bernard G. *He That Doeth: The Life Story of Archdeacon R.B.S. Hammond*. Marshall, Morgan and Scott. London 1951.

Lancelot, J.B. *Francis James Chavasse*. Blackwell Oxford 1929.

Lloyd, Roger. *The Church of England 1900-1965*. S.C.M. Press London 1966.

BIBLIOGRAPHY

_____ *The Church of England in the Twentieth Century* (Two vols.) Longmans Green and Co. London 1946/50.

Loane, Marcus L. *A Centenary History of Moore Theological College.* Angus and Robertson Sydney 1955.

_____ *Archbishop Mowll.* Header and stoughton London 1960.

_____ *Hewn from the Rock* Anglican Information Office. Sydney 1976.

_____ *Makers of our Heritage* Hodder and Stoughton London 1967.

Lockhart, J.G. *Cosmo Gordon Lang* Hodder and Stoughton. London 1949.

McCall, T.B. *The Life and Letters of John Stephen Hart.* Church of England Information Trust. Sydney 1963.

Macintosh. Neil K. *The Reverend Richard Johnson, Chaplain to the Colony of New South Wales.* Library of Australian History. Sydney 1978.

McKernan, Michael. *Australian Churches at War. Attitudes and Activities of the Major Churches 1914-1918.* Catholic Theological Faculty/ Australian War Memorial. Sydney 1980.

Marsden. George M. *Fundamentalism and American Culture: The Shaping of Twentieth Century Evangelicalism 1870-1925.* Oxford U.P. New York 1980.

Mol, Hans. *Christianity in Chains — A Sociologist's Interpretation of the Churches' Dilemma in a Secular World.* Nelson Sydney 1969.

_____ *Religion in Australia — A Sociological Interpretation* Melbourne 1971.

Neill, Stephen. *Anglicanism.* Penguin London 1965.

Oliver, J. *The Church and Social Order. Social Thought in the Church of England 1918-1939*Mowbray London 1968.

Phillips, Walter. *Defending "A Christian Country". Churchmen and Society in New South Wales in the 1880s and after.* University of Queensland Press. St. Lucia Queensland 1981.

Prestige. G.L. *The Life of Charles Gore.* Heinemann. London 1935.

Ramsey, A.M. *From Gore to Temple: The Development of Anglican Theology between* Lux Mundi *and the Second World War.* Longman. London 1960.

Reed, Bruce D. *The Dynamics of Religion.* Darton, Longman and Todd. London 1978.

Robin, A. deQ. *Charles Berry: Bishop of Melbourne. The Challenges of a Colonial Episcopate 1847-1876.* University of Western Australia Press. Nedlands W.A. 1967.

Robinson, D.W.B. *The Church of God; Its Form and its Unity.* Jordan Books. Sydney 1965.

Rodd, L.C. *John Hope of Christ Church.* Alpha Books. Sydney 1972.

Rowland, E.C. *A Century of the English Church in New South Wales.* Angus and Robertson. Sydney 1948.

Rudge, Peter F. *Ministry and Management. The Study of Ecclesiastical Administration.* Tavistock/Hicks Smith London 1968.

Scarfe, Janet. *Diocese of Adelaide in the Nineteenth Century. Controversies over Churchmanship under Bishop Short.* Anglican Board of Christian Education. Adelaide 1982.

Shaw, G.P. *Patriot and Patriarch: William Grant Boughton 1788-1853 Colonial Statesman and Ecclesiastic.* Melbourne U.P. 1978.

Suttor, T.L. *Hierarchy and Democracy in Australia 1788- 1870. The Formation of Australian Catholicism.* Melb. U.P. 1965.

Sykes. Stephen et. al. *Authority in the Anglican Communion. Four Papers prepared for the Anglican Primates' Meeting.* Washington D.C. Anglican Consultative Council April 1981.

_____ *The Integrity of Anglicanism.* Mowbrays London 1978.

Wand, J.W.C. *The Anglican Communion: A Survey.* Oxford U.P. London 1948.

Wetherell, David. *Reluctant Mission: The Anglican Church in Papua New Guinea 1891-1942.* University of Queensland Press. St. Lucia 1977.

Wilkinson, Alan. *The Church of England and the First World War.* S.P.C.K. London 1978.

Wilson, Bryan R. *Religion in Secular Society: A Sociological Comment.* Watts. London 1966.

Wright, N.T. *Evangelical Anglican Identity: the connection between Bible, Gospel and Church.* Latimer Studies No. 8. Latimer House Oxford n.d.

Wyatt, Ransome T. *The History of the Diocese of Goulburn.* Bragg and Sons. Sydney 1937.

Yarwood, A.T. *Samuel Marsden: the great survivor.* Melbourne University Press 1977.

IX - Official Publications

Atkins, Robert (ed.) *Ordinances of the Synod of the Diocese of Sydney 1866-1908.* Madgwick. Sydney 1908.

Census of the Commonwealth of Australia for 3 April. 1911

Census of the Commonwealth of Australia for 4 April. 1921

Church Assembly. *Report* of the Ecclesiastical Courts Commission. S.P.C.K. London 1923.

Church of England in Australia Constitution Act. 1961.

Church of England Constitutions Act Amendment Act of 1902.

The Church of England in Australia Constitution Assenting Ordinance 1928

Church of England Trust Property Act, 1917.

Commission on Christian Doctrine. Appointed by the Arch- bishops of Canterbury and York in 1922. *Doctrine in the Church of England.* S.P.C.K. London 1938.

Commonwealth of Australia. *Quarterly summary of Australian Statistics.* March 1920.

Constitutional Convention. *Official Report of the Constitutional Convention of the Dioceses in Australia and Tasmania.* 12-25 October 1926. William Andrews. Sydney 1927.

Constitutional Convention. *Official Report of the Constitutional Convention of the Dioceses in Australia and Tasmania.* 11-24 October 1932. William Andrews. Sydney 1933.

The Constitution of the Church of England in Australia. Draft Bill for Consideration. 1926.

The Constitution of the Church of England in Australia. Alternative Bill for Consideration. 1926.

The Constitution of the Church of England in Australia. Draft Bill for Consideration. 1932.

English Church Union. *Report* of the Committee on Prayer Book Revision. E.C.U. London. 1922.

National Assembly of the Church of England. *Debates on the Prayer Book and the Psalter. 1923.* S.P.C.K. London 1923.

Proceedings of the Synod of the Diocese of Sydney. 1898-1922. (Thereafter in Year Books of the Diocese.)

Proceedings of the Special Session of the Twenty-First Synod of the Diocese of Sydney. 1928. Verbatim Report. (S.D.A.)

General Synod. *Official Report of Proceedings* of General Synod in Australia and Tasmania. 1921/1926/1932/1937.

Gotley, W.G.S. (ed.) *The Inside Story!* Sydney Diocesan Secretariat. Sydney 1983.

_____ *Sydney Anglican Handbook.* Sydney Diocesan Secretariat. Sydney 1976.

Provincial Synod. *Proceedings* of the Provincial Synod of New South Wales. 1900-1939.

Royal Commission on Ecclesiastical Discipline. *Report.* Wyman and Sons. London 1906.

BIBLIOGRAPHY

Year Books of the Diocese of Sydney 1884-1940.

Walsh, Charles Richard (ed.) *Ordinances of the Synod of the Diocese of Sydney 1908-1923*. Madgwick Sydney 1923.

IX - Newspapers

Australian Church Record. (also *Church Record*.) From 1914. M.C.L.

Australian Churchman. To 1910. M.L.

Challenge. An Organ of Central Churchmanship. v.1 no.1 (Aug 1937); no.3 (March 1938); no.4. (June 1938). Garnsey Papers.

Church Commonwealth. 1907-1912. M.L.

Church Missionary Review. 1922-23. C.U.L.

Church Standard. 1912-39. M.L.

The Church Times. (England) Selected Numbers. C.U.L.

The Churchman (England) 1898-1928. C.U.L.; 1924-35 M.C.L. Selected Numbers only.

Daily Telegraph. Selected years.

The Gazette (National Church League.) 1909-1930. B.L. Colindale.

The Intelligencer. (Church Association.) 1909-1930. B.L. Colindale.

Outlook. A Bulletin for the Clergy. Jan.1936, March 1936 St. Mark's Library, Canberra/Garnsey Papers.

The Record. (England) Selected Numbers. C.U.L.

St. Paul's, Burwood *Parish Paper*, 1905-1921. M.L.

Sydney Diocesan Magazine. 1910-1940. M.L./M.C.L.

Sydney Morning Herald. 1909-1939, and selected earlier numbers. M.L./Fisher.

The Times. (London) Selected Numbers. Fisher.

X - Reference

Australian Dictionary of Biography. Research School of social Sciences, Australian National University, Canberra. Biographical Card Indices.

Cross, F.L. and Livingstone, E.A. (eds.) *The Oxford Dictionary of the Christian Church*. Oxford U.P. Oxford 1978 (2nd edition)

Douglas, J.D. (ed.) *The New Bible Dictionary*. Inter-Varsity Press London 1978.

The Commonwealth of Australia. Electoral Rolls 1900-1940. (For Addresses and Occupations of Laymen)

Johnstone, J.R.L. *A Handbook of Church Law in the Diocese of Sydney*. Jordan Books. Punchbowl 1962.

Radi, Heather et al. *Biographical Register of the N.S.W. Parliament 1901-1929*. A.N.U. Press Canberra 1979.

Rydon, Joan. *A Biographical Register of the Commonwealth Parliament 1901-1912*. A.N.U. Press Canberra 1975.

Sand's Sydney *Directories*. 1900-1931. State Library of N.S.W.

www.ingramcontent.com/pod-product-compliance
Lightning Source LLC
Chambersburg PA
CBHW071845090426
42811CB00035B/2330/J